ARGENTINA

ARGENTINA

ILLUSIONS
and
REALITIES

SECOND EDITION

Gary W. Wynia

HM Holmes & Meier   New York • London

Second edition published in the United States of America 1992 by
Holmes & Meier Publishers, Inc.
30 Irving Place
New York, N.Y. 10003

First edition published 1986
by Holmes & Meier

Copyright © 1986, 1992 by Gary W. Wynia
All rights reserved

Library of Congress Cataloging-in-Publication Data

Wynia, Gary W., 1942–
  Argentina: illusions and realities.

  1. Argentina—Politics and government—1983–
I. Title.
F2849.2.W95 1992   982'.064   86-9839
ISBN 0-8419-1296-3 (pbk.)

Book design by Gloria Tso

Manufactured in the United States of America

F
2849.2
W 95
1992

U

JUN 10 1993

TALLAHASSEE, FLORIDA

To: *Daniel*
Gladys
David
Martin
and Johnny

FLORIDA STATE
UNIVERSITY LIBRARIES

FLORIDA STATE
UNIVERSITY LIBRARIES

Contents

Preface to the Second Edition

In an era when democratic government and free-market economics are in vogue in nations as different as Poland and Brazil, the Argentines recently decided to add their name to the list. Although many of them still have doubts about their chances, they are trying to find out if a more competitive economy can deliver the bounty that its proponents promise, as well as learn if political democracy will function effectively for very long within their conflict-ridden society.

Nothing has come easily to most Argentines during a decade that began with the military's blunder in the Malvinas Islands and finished with an elected president having to leave office five months ahead of schedule while suffering enormous unpopularity in the midst of the nation's struggle with hyperinflation. Yet, his successor was chosen by the people in free elections and not by the armed forces, no small feat in this nation of frequent political disruptions by a military that has often received substantial civilian backing.

In this revised volume we take a closer look at President Raul Alfonsín (1983–1989) in order to understand why this intensely partisan but sincerely democratic politician and his Radical party colleagues became so unpopular among people who had enthusiastically celebrated Alfonsín's defeat of the Peronists in 1983. If the constitution had not limited his tenure to one term, he would have suffered a devastating setback in a reelection bid. The Argentine economy plagued him as it had his predecessors, but exactly how much responsibility it bears for his demise is not obvious at first glance. That is why we must examine the way he managed the economy and how people inside and outside the country responded to it.

His successor, Peronist Carlos Saul Menem, came as a surprise to almost everyone when he won his party's national primary election in mid-1988. Even more startling was his sudden attempt to create something he calls free-market capitalism after he became president. We would be unwise to predict a Nobel Prize for his version of classical economics, but basic changes in Argentine political economy were attempted in 1990 and they merit scrutiny.

Finally, I have written an entirely new chapter to begin the book that deserves a little explanation. Argentines have always been eager to explain themselves, yet we often equate objectivity with relying upon our own observations to account for their conduct rather than reporting much of what they have to say. However, they obviously know more about their own thinking and behavior than any visitor does. No grand theory tells us much about how they have coped with their troubles during the last few years when they went through three rounds of hyperinflation that provoked a deep reexamination of their national condition and the reasons for it.

With this in mind I have devoted Chapter 1 to communicating a little of what they said to me when I lived among them during the first half of 1990. My sample is not a random one, but repeats the words of journalists, university students, lawyers, business people, taxi drivers, and apartment caretakers, some of whose conversations I recorded. I hope that the chapter conveys what a few Argentines were thinking and saying about their most recent political and economic travails. I also hope that it encourages others to ask their own questions and listen attentively to answers that will no doubt be even more informative and provocative than what is reported here.

Preface to the First Edition

A decade that began with Juan Perón's death ended with Raul Alfonsín's election in 1983. The burial of one president and the selection of another are not unusual events in most places, but seldom are they separated by seven years of military repression and soldiers killing nearly 9,000 citizens as they were in Argentina. Nor have many countries lost a war with Great Britain recently as Argentina did in 1982. No matter how one looks at it, it was an unhappy time for this troubled nation.

Political volatility is not new to Argentina, of course. As far back as 1930 the military was deposing democratic governments. In the 1940s an officer named Juan Perón was elected president, but ten years later he too was evicted by military colleagues. No one managed to govern the country successfully during the next eighteen years, and Perón's return in 1973 ended with another coup three years later.

Economic life has not been much more comforting. Three decades of rapid growth and prosperity ended with the 1929 depression, and ever since Argentines have been riding an economic roller coaster that descended into deep recession and hyperinflation in the 1980s. Self-sufficiency in petroleum, fertile prairies, hundreds of large industries, and a literate population are supposed to generate prosperity in this day and age, but they have not been enough in Argentina.

What went wrong? Many things, actually, nearly all of them related to one another. The nation's colonial origins and its disorganization after independence along with the narrow base of its economic development played a part. So has the way power was distributed in society and used for partisan advantage by those with the largest shares of it. Together they produced a politics known for its seemingly irresolvable conflicts. Modes of confrontation that most societies find dangerous and self-destructive became the way of life in Argentina. But while certain sectors in society thrived on it, the nation as a whole paid a high price for its political *modus vivendi*. That is why intense efforts to change old habits were begun in the 1980s despite dim prospects for success.

Interpreting Argentine behavior is challenging but never dull or disappointing. In preparing this volume I have learned a great deal from many prominent scholars, among them Guido Di Tella, Javier Villanueva, Roberto Alemann, Juan Carlos de Pablo, Guillermo O'Donnell, Felix Luna, Robert Potash, James Scobie, and Alain Roquie. I have also benefited immensely from the scholarship of a new generation of Argentine historians, economists, and political scientists whose writings began to appear in 1983 after press freedom was restored. Marcelo Cavarozzi, Carlos Escude, Jorge Schvarzer, Marcelo Luis Acuña, and Ruben Perina are just a few. And finally, I am indebted to the William Kenan Foundation for financing my recent visit to Argentina, to Holmes and Meier editors for inviting me to write the book, and to colleagues and students at Carleton College for tolerating my obsession with the completion of this project.

My education in Argentina started in 1963 as an exchange student in provincial Corrientes. Nine months later I returned to spend a year in Córdoba and Buenos Aires, and I have been going back ever since. The past twenty years have been exciting as well as depressing times, but being in Argentina was never more refreshing than it was in 1983 and 1984 when I witnessed a long-repressed people resurrect themselves and try harder than ever to deal with the real rather than the illusory world confronting them. I hope that I have communicated something of their experience in this book.

ARGENTINA

1

A Conversation in Buenos Aires

Q. Carlos, I find it hard to believe what I have been reading about Argentina lately, especially about inflation. Maybe I am mistaken, but I recently learned that between April 1989 and May 1990 your prices rose 10,000 percent. That's incredible; we are upset if prices in the United States rise more than 5 percent in twelve months, and there you are soaring off into space. Is this really true?

A. The numbers were somewhere up there. In six months we suffered more inflation than you have experienced since you were born. But you need to understand that we have been living with inflation of around 100 percent annually for more than fifteen years. I won't lie and claim that it has been easy, but we have developed some ways to cope with it. I don't mean big-time finance, though a few people play that game too, but simply doing whatever we can to keep from running out of money.

If you don't take the right steps at the right time, you can lose everything very fast. Inflation does that. One year from now 1 million australes may buy only 20 percent of what they buy today. Foreign journalists call us microeconomic virtuosos, but that goes a little far. Let's just say that some of us learn how to survive some of the time.

Q. How do you cope with inflation day by day?

A. By devoting most of our time to it. Naturally you try to get your employer to keep your wages in line with prices. If that doesn't work, you do all you can to get the government to compel employers to use

---

This conversation is fictional, but the words spoken by the Argentine are taken from what several Argentines told me in conversations in Buenos Aires during 1990. I have tried to report, as accurately as possible in just a few pages, what some people said. This is not a sample randomly selected but the words of scholars, university students, journalists, and people in business and politics.

a "cost-of-living" schedule that does the same thing. But even that is not always possible.

We also rely on credit as much as we can because it lets you buy something at today's prices and then pay for it a month later when your income is higher. Of course retailers know this, so they often refuse to supply credit. Or when they do let us use credit cards, they add 15 or 20 percent to the price to cover their costs between the time of purchase and when the credit-card company pays them. Understandably merchants want cash so that they can pay their own bills. Most of the time I stored my cards in my top drawer until they let us use them again.

High inflation also compels you to spend money fast, often buying more goods than you really want to buy. That may sound strange to you but look at it this way: if 100,000 australes will buy me a stereo today, but only half of one in six months because its price will double, I am going to buy it now. You can't hold on to money that will be worth so much less a few months from now after you've worked so hard to earn it.

Q. I understand what you're saying, but I also know that it became much worse midway through 1989. Instead of increasing 10 or 20 percent a month, prices were rising by nearly 200 percent in one month! I couldn't believe it. Suddenly you were infected with something everyone was calling "hyperinflation." How in the world did you survive it?

A. To begin with, when it occurred in June 1989 we really didn't know how bad it was going to be. You see, we always focus on current conditions, on prices today and where they might be next week. Only after a couple of weeks did we realize how fast prices were really moving.

Hyperinflation develops in two phases: first, as prices start to take off, rising 10 to 15 percent a week, you buy like crazy and hoard anything that you think you might need over the next month or so; then, when prices soar at 25 percent or more a week everything changes because you discover that you don't have enough money to buy much of anything but the most absolute essentials. You don't stop shopping entirely, but you don't even consider purchasing a new appliance or new clothes. We also stopped eating in restaurants and going to movies. I even switched from taxis to buses that took twice as long to take me to my office.

Q. What was it like shopping for groceries when you were in the midst of hyperinflation?

A. It was strange. Once, when we were standing in line waiting to pay, a voice came over the supermarket's public address system and announced: "At this moment we are increasing the prices of everything in the store by 15 percent." Since we only had enough money to pay for what we had put in our cart, we had to return several things before making our purchase.

Of course, as my cousin always reminds me, the store manager has problems of his own. His suppliers stop giving him credit to purchase goods so he has to stock less. And during hyperinflation his sales drop at least 30 percent or even more for things like wine, Coca-Cola, and cosmetics. People really do change their eating habits; believe it or not, we ate very little meat and more rice and pasta.

Q. This may sound a bit trivial, but were you able to pay your telephone and electricity bills?

A. That was never as simple as you might think, actually. Many of the bills we pay for our utilities lagged behind the rise in other prices since those bills don't reach us until a month or two after the service is rendered; for example, we pay in June for electricity used in April. If our income kept up with inflation, we actually paid very little for services. In other words, what had cost 20,000 australes in April we paid in June when our income was double what it had been in April.

Nevertheless, utilities still cost money. For instance, we own an apartment that is much like a condo in the United States. Some people in our building called a meeting in the middle of the hyperinflation and asked that we no longer buy heat for the building during the winter (fortunately it doesn't freeze here in Buenos Aires). We wanted to heat our place but we agreed to go along with them anyway. As it turned out, we saved a little on heating and spent it on more food.

Q. What you say makes sense, but I still don't understand how you could survive when inflation was over 100 percent. Doesn't that virtually wipe out your income? It seems terrifying.

A. I know this appears strange to a foreigner, but you should remember that we have been playing the inflation game a long time. Experience never guarantees success, or even survival, but we do have a few options to play with.

Remember dollars? They are often as important to our survival as they are to yours. When I received my check at the end of the month, I immediately spent 40 percent of it to stock up on food. Then I used what was left to buy dollars as quickly as possible. You see, during our hyperinflation the value of the dollar in australes was increasing as fast as prices were, and sometimes faster. So I bought $200 for 500,000 australes and held them for a while. Then I sold the dollars for 750,000 australes two weeks later. In other words, I managed to keep the value of some of my income up with the rate of inflation. Of course, if I hadn't bought and sold dollars I really would have suffered an enormous loss in income. But, fortunately, I had an emergency way out. None of this is ever automatic or guaranteed, but it sometimes works. Lest you think that only we middle-class people pull off such deals, you should know that when I visited my mother her servant always gave me australes to purchase dollars for her so that she too could survive. It was usually only enough to buy $10, but for her that was protection. She knew the rules of the game and why she had to play it.

You might wonder how we managed to change so much money in a city of over nine million people but only a few dozen exchange houses. There should have been lines a block long outside each exchange house, but there were none. You see, when there is money to make in the marketplace, a black market always develops. You didn't even have to go to the center of town where all the exchange houses are located. Suddenly people were appearing in our neighborhood to buy and sell dollars.

Reliance on dollars has its costs, of course. When our economy was becoming informally "dollarized," prices were sometimes given only in dollars, and eventually they too began to rise at the same rate as prices in australes. And when that happened even buying dollars didn't keep you ahead.

Q. Does the government know that you're playing around with dollars to survive?

A. Of course it does. Officials even know how we send our dollars out of the country when we want to save them for more than a week or two despite its being illegal to export dollars secretly. You only need to know someone in the exchange business. You give him your dollars and he calls New York and asks his banker there to transfer that amount from his account to yours. No doubt he does it for government officials too, and that is why they tolerate his exporting dollars all the time to New York to replenish his bank account.

We don't talk about it openly for obvious reasons, but there really are two parts to our economic lives: one we call the "official" part and the other the "unofficial." The first is regulated by the government and doesn't work very well. But we also rely on the unofficial one to survive, doing everything from buying money on the black market to making and selling goods that are never recorded by the government and taxed. You would be surprised how proficient we are at operating our unofficial economy and how enormous it is. Some economists claim that it is almost as large as the economy represented in national statistics.

Q. But I am sure that there are many people who don't make the kinds of deals that you make. What about the poorer people?

A. You're right, many people really do suffer. Persons living on their pensions were devastated since few pensions contained cost-of-living guarantees. Virtually all of my friends' retired parents moved in with them. And, as before, their children lived at home until they were in their late twenties or older. The unemployed also suffered brutally since we have no unemployment compensation like you do. Imagine paying twice as much for milk when you're out of work. The poor had to rely as much as they could on working relatives to help them out, but we can now see that their living conditions have declined dramatically during the past year. A colleague of mine who is a pediatrician in a public hospital reports that he is seeing more undernourished children than he ever saw before. It's depressing.

What scares me about inflation is not just what it can do to me, but also how it creates a social disaster. Even though some people are able to buy dollars, many can't afford to buy much of anything when prices rise so fast. Moreover, it makes it almost impossible for our government to sustain any of its social programs. As a result, poverty grows and crime along with it.

Q. How does the middle class suffer?

A. Though we never suffered as much as the poor, we had problems of our own. For example, health care became very hard to get. Under "normal" conditions government health programs and our insurance companies pay our hospitals and physicians within 30 to 90 days of treatment. But when we suffered hyperinflation our hospitals and physicians couldn't wait that long, so they refused to see patients who couldn't pay immediately. You had to pay up front, which most people could not afford to do, so we did without medical services until hyperinflation ended. You couldn't afford to get sick. Really.

Q. Doing business in Argentina seems incredibly unconventional, but how different is it, really?

A. Quite different in some ways, but it didn't begin with hyperinflation. Argentine investors have long been dominated by what you call a "risk-aversion" mentality and the government has nourished it. In Argentina the government produced nearly half of our national product, regulated the money supply, and bought billions of dollars in goods from private firms. It also protected our industries from foreign competition and helped finance their debts. Many of our people are not independent entrepreneurs but *jefes de empresas contratistas,* much like the defense industry in the United States. They wanted the government to ensure that they would not go broke by promising to buy goods from them, and it did.

We always instantly take advantage of opportunities created by our government. For example, a few years ago our president financed plenty of new housing for the middle class. And when he did, several thousand people immediately became contractors. It was a good deal since the government paid for the house and then sold mortgages to the people who wanted to live in them. You sold everything you built to the government immediately on completion. There was no market.

Speculation more than production dominates our approach to business. The old-fashioned private capitalist mentality frequently gives way to making money fast by trading money and other valuables. Inflation makes you do it to survive and then it becomes a way of life. It usually is riskier than we would like. Vicious circles envelop us; when people anticipate a change, they take measures to protect themselves from it; yet when they do, they often undermine government policy which creates new uncertainties for us.

Q. Do you think entrepreneurs will begin to change their conduct as soon as inflation ends?

A. I'm reluctant to call them entrepreneurs since that conjures up an image of free-market capitalists. Actually, accountants are the most valuable members of any corporation here, and often they wield almost as much power as the corporation presidents. Every day the best of them are examining where to put corporate funds to keep or improve their value. The kind of quarterly corporate analyses done in the United States are done almost weekly here in order to keep up with price changes. There are even stories of corporations that made so much profit in the financial market that they gave up on manufacturing.

Q. I know that Argentina faces some incredible economic problems these days, but that never prevents people from insisting that there is a simple solution to everything. Do they really know what they are talking about?

A. You must realize that people everywhere prefer a simple solution to a complex one. We're not really unique. But we do need to admit to ourselves that there is no easy solution anymore; if we don't, we will continue to suffer bitter disappointments.

You have to understand that proposing simple solutions is inherent in our politics. Nearly every sector in our society wants our economic problems solved without their having to pay much for the solution; that is why they always offer their own "perfect solution." Businesses that will benefit from less regulation claim that a free market is all we need to prosper, while those who are threatened by competition keep saying that protection is the answer. Union leaders claim that higher wages will generate more consumption and prosperity for the entire nation, while industrialists say lower wages will give them more profits to invest in new enterprises that offer more jobs. On and on it goes. Complex problems require a combination of solutions, obviously, and we need to stop looking for simple, magical ones that are so partisan.

Unfortunately, enterprising small firms are often casualties in this country. You may come up with a product that people want, but it's hard to get the financing you need to build your company since our banks lend very little to businesses anymore. You also get trapped between the prices you pay for the materials that you need in your product and what you charge consumers or retailers. In hyper-inflation you may run out of money for a very short time, but that can be enough to destroy your little firm. More and more people are becoming exhausted by repeated failures and are leaving the country.

Q. Will it be impossible to recover and become more like the prosperous capitalist countries in Asia and Europe?

A. That is the hardest question of all to answer. It is written nowhere that we must continue to suffer the conditions we have faced for the past half-century. We have the resources needed to prosper, but currently we produce little more than we did forty years ago when our population was half its current size.

But let's face it. Everyone is looking out for himself and cares little about the consequences of what he does for anyone else. We want to pretend that the government can work miracles for us, but we know it can't. Demagoguery is very entrenched in our politics, and honesty, as you define it, is rare.

Q. Your assessment is rather blunt. Do you think you're beginning to see yourselves more objectively than you did before?

A. For many years we have complained a great deal about the frustrations we suffer, albeit minor ones compared with most South American nations, but I think some of us are more realistic today. We know that we're not erecting the great Arcadia we once pretended to construct, you know, the kind of place where we would all prosper doing whatever we liked without dealing very much with the rest of the world.

I also think we're beginning to admit, privately at least, that we haven't built a very cohesive national community in this nation. We were a small country whose population was nearly doubled by immigrants immediately after the turn of the century. Many considered their new nation primarily a residential one, a place to work, gain wealth, and then return with it to Europe. Even those who stayed were kept outside the mainstream of politics and cultural life for more than a generation by our ruling class. There were no big political machines in our cities that integrated immigrants quickly into the political process. Even today citizens feel less a part of their nation than the Chileans and Brazilians do in theirs.

Q. This may be because Argentines are still more European than Latin American? Does that make any sense?

A. Not as much as you may think, actually. Our national culture draws its character not only from our Hispanic heritage and the culture that a few million Italian immigrants added to it, but also from the unusual circumstances in which immigrants found themselves in this new nation. Everything was supervised by a small economic elite and its British trading partners. Personal economic conquests came from property, trade, and finance, which together rewarded the cleverest and most ambitious immigrants as well as those already in power. You looked out for yourself, and with no wars to worry about, people didn't get too involved in defining their new nationality.

Our small ruling class became rather defensive when immigrants and members of our middle class asked them to share political power with them. This caused serious political divisions in our society that became even more intense in 1930 when, after sharing the government for a time with new political parties, the elite took it back using force. Some people began to believe that force was the only way to take and run the government in this country.

Q. But such words still leave me in a quandary. Argentines are generally well-educated compared with most of their neighbors and, in urban areas like Buenos Aires, quite sophisticated. They were even among the world's most affluent countries after World War I. Nevertheless, neither democracy nor orderly politics has come easily for them. What is it about their character or political preferences that make it so difficult?

A. I wish I had a simple answer for you but there is none. I sometimes feel that we're a strange collection of authoritarian anarchists. I know that sounds bizarre, but I'm not joking. Individually, we crave to do as we wish without interference by anyone else. We want to set our own rules and advance ourselves in any manner that we can. But as you might expect, such attitudes often generate unregulated conflicts among us, so we expect authorities to make sure that it does not get out of hand.

That is where our authoritarianism comes in. We expect our political authorities to look out for us and ensure that the opportunities we once had are still available to us. In other words, individually we want to do whatever we wish, but we also want our authorities to make sure that no one else gets in our way.

Q. Is that why it was so hard for your leaders to abide by the rules of democracy?

A. Perhaps, but we have also never been comfortable with "checks and balances" among the branches of government or our social classes. Presidents prefer to deal directly with our nation's problems rather than rely on a legislature to debate their policies or a court to determine their validity. For them democracy means electing an executive and then letting him rule the nation for a time. Presidents respond more to people with economic clout than to those espousing elaborate ideologies. And that is what our wealthiest people, and even the labor movement, want them to do.

Q. Lately people are complaining about something they call "excessive political theater" in your politics. What exactly are they talking about?

A. Our political leaders, both civilian and military, thrive on words and public performances even though they know that it has little to do with what is really going on. There's a huge gap between words and deeds in Argentine public affairs. Most politicians and bureaucrats know how to play the public role, though increasingly their rhetoric seems archaic, but they worry little about enormous differences between what they say in public and what they do with their power.

They are notorious for making deals behind the scenes, some of them legal but politically unpopular, and others illegal. The line is deliberately kept fuzzy. Meanwhile they perform publicly as if they were unaware that such things were going on. They love to portray themselves as deeply concerned about the welfare of the nation when in fact they seldom are.

We were once fascinated by the theatrics of politics and loved to talk about simple causes and solutions to all of our problems. We became addicted to spectacular events where crowds acted like they were attending a World Cup *futbol* [soccer] game. Instead of goals, we heard grand speeches that said little about what we are actually experiencing. But gradually most of us became cynical about the whole process and lost our enthusiasm for those who made the speeches.

If you listen to political speeches you will discover how repetitive and tiresome most still are. Only recently have politicians begun to talk frankly with us about the problems we face, but most of them are uncomfortable doing so. They prefer to use nice words and say nothing. Recently a Spanish friend who was visiting Argentina observed that many of our politicians sounded like secondary-school students who were reading speeches that were written a century ago. The sad part of it is that they seem to think that people really enjoy their theatrics when in fact we've grown very tired of them.

Q. How combative are they, then, if all of this is really theatrics?

A. Argentine politicians and military officers have always preferred to vilify their opponents rather than confront them directly or sincerely debate their ideas; the status quo prevails and most incumbents defend it when they are in charge no matter how much they talk of radical change. It's as if they are afraid of losing too much by addressing realities.

Hypocrisy, mediocrity, egoism, and laxity are much too common in our politics. We rely on rhetoric and martial rituals more than on facts and cautious analysis. We like to exaggerate our importance to the rest of the world and only now are beginning to realize that few beyond our borders pay us any attention.

Q. I hate to bring this up since it'll make me sound like a typical North American who doesn't really understand your country, but I must because I hear about it so often. Often Argentines complain of "corruption" within their political system and between government and business. What exactly do they mean by it?

A. I don't mind the question since I too complain about it. Civilians and military officers of all political persuasions have managed to come up with reasons why it was all right to break laws and enrich themselves. We also know that our underfinanced and antiquated judicial system does little to stop it.

Each political party has its own explanation for accepting bribes or other payments aimed at influencing its conduct. Some will tell you privately that they occasionally do it in order to finance their party so that it can build and defend democratic government. Others are less pretentious about it: they call bribes tips that are included in the price of the service rendered. It is a way of doing business to them.

But don't put all of the blame on the political parties. We've been doing business that way for a long time in Argentina. It is estimated that our people pay less than 50 percent of the income taxes that they owe the government. We have become experts at deceiving tax collectors. Lawyers, architects, and others in private practices are very successful at avoiding taxes, as are many businesses with accountants who have found hundreds of ways to hide their company's income. Only those who are paid salaries by an employer are trapped into paying income taxes.

Q. Didn't all of this "cheating" start long ago during colonial times?

A. We certainly learned something about deceiving authorities as far back as the colonial era when we resisted efforts by the Spanish crown to control us, but one shouldn't get carried away with such determinism. People break laws systematically to enrich themselves in all cultures including the North American one, more now than ever before. It occurs where it is profitable and where authorities are unable to find and punish the transgressors. It also happens when people find it useful to deal with a cumbersome and powerful bureaucracy. It's far easier to pay a bureaucrat a few thousand australes to speed up processing your requests than to wait hours, or never get it done at all. Even our legal system contributes to it since it is filled with far too many minuscule regulations that encourage people to find ways around them. None of this absolves cheating morally, but it does help explain it.

Q. Speaking of culture, we all know that Argentina is notorious for the conflict that occurs between its military officers and its civilians as well as among various civilians, conflicts that are intense and frequently uncompromising. What is it about your culture that motivates and allows this?

A. I wish I knew. A psychiatrist friend of mine recently said that people usually react in two different ways when they confront conditions that prevent their doing what they want: they either become frustrated, mad, and emotional, that is, irrational, or they look for an alternative way to do things and become innovative. There are many of the former among us. Their frustrations do not come from ethnic or religious discrimination as is common in many other societies; actually we are one of the most ethnically and religiously homogeneous societies in the Western world. Nor, until recently, did it come primarily from poverty. Rather it came from frustration with political elites who denied people the power and the goods they wanted, and from a government bureaucracy that was too huge and rigid to permit much innovation anywhere.

One of the reasons we used to go along with an authoritarian leader was our hope that he would break down a few bureaucratic doors and force people to become more reliable and productive. Now we know how naïve we were about such things.

Q. Why are the Argentine people not rising up and changing all of this? You talk as if everyone knew it and hated it.

A. We ask ourselves the same question all the time. A journalist loves to argue that the men in this country are still no more than little *machos* brought up by their mothers to crave a powerful patriarch who would wield a big stick against anyone who said that we were responsible for our individual failures.

That may be an exaggeration, but our society really is quite defensive and afraid to change. We prefer the status quo to reforms that might turn loose things that threaten us in ways that we don't understand. People find places in the bureaucracy and elsewhere to reside and want to be left alone. Doing the job is not as important as staying in place. We also want to restore the kind of affluence that we are told the country enjoyed nearly a century ago because we think that we deserve it and should not have to work too hard to get it.

And remember: we were devastated by the violence that terrorists used against us and the military against them and anyone else they selected for punishment in the 1970s. We're afraid to provoke such violence again and somehow think that by ignoring suggestions of change we can avoid it.

Finally, you know that changing this mentality is very difficult because changes in a culture always come slowly. We're beginning to try, though so far we haven't accomplished very much. Bit by bit we're learning that we can't do everything the same way as before, nor can we remain so independent of other nations and their cultures as we once were. We're less isolated from the rest of the world culturally than we were previously: the popular media—including cable television networks that broadcast news from Europe and the United States—have seen to that, as have travel and study abroad. By itself, this can't change everything in the nation, but it has caused the informed public to consider chauvinistic isolationism a bit of a relic of the past that is best left to our ancestors.

Nevertheless this is a very unhappy time since we currently live with a paralyzing fear of more hyperinflation. We also have a huge foreign debt that we can't pay. There's no easy way out; nor will the current efforts to replace the nation's heavily protected economy with a more open one bring instant relief. That's why one shouldn't celebrate Argentina's "getting in line" just yet. It's a line that it has been compelled to join and to which it remains unaccustomed. Moreover, if it doesn't generate the economic benefits promised by its advocates at home and abroad, we should expect a more characteristic expression of frustration through renewed public protest and defiance of other nations, if only to gain a little emotional gratification.

Well, enough said. I must get back to the office to listen to the minister of economy's speech. Maybe they've found enough oil to pay all our debts and make us rich again. More likely, he'll ask us to pay more for government services and start paying our income taxes.

I'll buy the coffee and *media lunas* next week and you can tell me what you Americans are doing with your budget deficits, failed banks, foreign debts, and white-collar criminals. Maybe we aren't so different after all.

2

The Price of Prosperity

It is tempting to blame Juan Perón for Argentina's woes, if only because so many Argentines do. But the country's economic infirmities and political rancor began much earlier. He exploited the hostility of the poor toward the rich but he did not invent it. The upper class had supervised the creation of a society over which they enjoyed immense social control well into this century. But as it changed and they did not, opposition to them grew, especially among nationalists in the middle class and the leaders of an alienated urban working class whose numbers increased rapidly in the 1930s. The oligarchy's stubborn refusal to share anything but the symbols of power with their adversaries is what gave Perón the opportunity to launch his provocative reformist effort in 1946. That they should have hung on so tenaciously is not all that surprising, however, given how much power they had accumulated while running the country for almost a century.

Enjoying a Late Start

When the Spaniards reached the sparsely populated prairies of the Río de la Plata river basin in 1536, they found none of the gold, silver, and abundant indigenous labor that had made Mexico and Peru so attractive to colonization and economic exploitation. Pedro de Mendoza established an outpost at what is now Buenos Aires only to abandon it promptly and settle up river in Asunción, the current capital of Paraguay. Few people followed him to the southern end of the New World during the next two centuries, however, and not until the early eighteenth century when the Treaty of Utrecht (1713) allowed the British to sell slaves and merchandise there and to export hides from the region did Buenos Aires become a trading post of some significance, rising to a population of 20,000 by 1776, when it was made a viceroyalty. But it would be another century before its economic development really got under way, several decades after independence in 1816 and two unsuccessful experiments in constitutional government in 1819 and in 1826 that were followed by a series of civil wars that did not end until 1853.[1]

Disputes over who would pay for the nation's development divided its citizens in the nineteenth century and still do today. Although they were happy to see their wool, hides, and salted beef sold in markets abroad, cattlemen did not want to expend their surpluses to build the nation's infrastructure or finance the immigration that would be needed to supply labor to the countryside for the development of grain production. Such "private-mindedness" set a standard of conduct that would become a way of life, inhibiting the creation of "public goods" from then until now. The elitist, constitutional governments that succeeded one another after 1853 tried to raise funds and build roads and railways, but their budgets were meager. So they turned to foreigners, who welcomed opportunities for investment when they saw how rapid markets for the country's grain and beef were growing in Europe. As consumption of its commodities abroad increased and railways were built ever farther from the coast into the interior, additional land was put into production, and by the turn of the century this isolated, sparsely populated country of feuding cattlemen was transformed into the breadbasket of an industrializing Europe, quickly becoming the most prosperous nation in Latin America and one whose per capita income surpassed those of most European countries at the time.

Argentina was blessed by land and climate that allowed it to produce an abundance of meat and grain using little technology, its *pampas* being one of the most fertile humid grasslands in the world. But it also had much more, most notably a small but ambitious landowning class that was able to adapt its cattle breeding and grain production to rising demand more swiftly than might have been expected from a people accustomed to modest success with sheep raising, breeding horses, and slaughtering low-quality native breeds of cattle for their hides and salted beef. Some had acquired their lands during colonial times, while many others took advantage of the Conquest of the Desert campaigns (1879–83) that cleared the interior of nomadic Indians and doubled the amount of available land on the *pampas*. The added territory was supposed to be distributed by authorities in modest parcels, but the plan was subverted easily by wealthy people who sought to expand their holdings or acquire new ones. As a result, when settlement was completed around 1914 nearly 80 percent of the *pampas* was owned by just 8 percent of the families who held property there. Production grew nevertheless, the area sown to grain increasing by 1,600 percent and the volume of exports by 2,000 percent between 1860 and

1914. Comparative advantage worked for the Argentine oligarchy, allowing the accumulation of great wealth from the exploitation of the nation's rich soil with the help of enthusiastic foreigners.[2]

New technology, like the refrigeration process introduced by the English River Plate Fresh Meat Company in 1883, made it possible to export frozen meat rather than salted beef. Soon cattlemen improved the quality of their stock using Herefords and Aberdeen Angus brought over from England. An added boost came with the invention of beef "chilling" in 1908, a process much preferable to freezing since it preserved more of the taste in the best meat. As processing and shipping (handled almost entirely by American and English companies) developed so did the division of labor within the beef industry, with cattle breeders starting production and "fatteners" completing it on their rich pastures near markets in and around Buenos Aires. As demand rose, herds grew steadily, and by 1920 stock had increased by 50 percent over the 1890 total.[3]

Grain production rose simultaneously thanks to an influx of immigrants who were eager to labor as tenant farmers on the still sparsely populated *pampas*. It also helped that Argentina had never been turned into a land of *haciendas* during colonial times because of the shortage of labor then. Had it, rapid adaptation to new export opportunities would not have been possible, but because cattlemen only needed immigrant labor to turn their lands into huge granaries, the transformation came easily.[4] Tenant farmers and cattlemen complemented each other perfectly. The latter needed their pastures upgraded to raise high-quality stock for slaughter and sale in European markets so they required tenant farmers to sow their holdings with alfalfa after raising grain on it under the standard three-year contract. Tenants leased from 240 to 600 acres, often through oral agreements which necessitated their sharing a specific portion of their profits with their landlord, generating investment-free income for the landlord while gaining access to some of the country's best land for themselves. Renting land was no substitute for owning it and grievances accumulated, but at the time it was a workable arrangement that swiftly transformed Argentina from one of the world's least developed pastures into one of its richest farmlands.[5]

Agriculture allowed some people to acquire great wealth very quickly much as minerals had done in other countries. People "struck it rich" because they held the right property. Land was a commodity that was retained for its value or leased and traded for profit much as gold and silver were. Even the tenants were not very attached to pieces of property since they had to move from region to region every few years to sustain themselves, seldom building homes or joining in the formation of permanent communities anywhere. Unlike places like Iowa or Illinois, where small towns sprung up and became county seats and service centers for farmers, in Argentina all government and trade were confined to Buenos Aires and a few provincial capitals. Even today, long after the emergence of a rural middle class, the visitor to the countryside is struck by how empty of towns it is.

Unlike the United States, where 63 percent of the farmers owned the land that they worked in 1914, only 40 percent did in Argentina. Had Argentines been allowed to acquire it more easily, their society would have become much different than it did. But without a large rural middle class leading movements for populist reforms this very agrarian nation entered the second quarter of the twentieth century under the control of a small but powerful rural elite who, along with their British customers, refused to share real power with those below them. Theirs was not the kind of society Alexis de Tocqueville described in *Democracy in America*, filled with yeomen farmers whose individualism was sustained by their access to new land; instead it was a productive economy owned and managed by a few thousand people who controlled the nation's primary source of wealth, people who resisted any innovation that threatened their social status and economic power. If social change were to come, it would not be in the countryside, where nothing resembling a large community of modern farmers with a stake in modernization developed until the mid-twentieth century.

It is necessary to appreciate how bound Argentina became to one source of wealth and economic development to understand why it never emulated the United States, a nation to which it was similar in natural resources. Everything depended on the *pampas* and its production, and other possible modes of development were either ignored or subordinated to it. In addition, just one city monopolized all decision making and communication with the rest of the country as well as the outside world. Argentina's ruling class had a good thing going, and the immigrants who came over had no choice but to subordinate themselves to them. The late James Scobie described it so well when he wrote: "It was as if, long before the Civil War, the South had emerged as the dominant and only area of United States expansion with its capital at Savannah or Charleston, an economy based entirely on cotton exported to British mills, and an oligarchy composed of plantation owners and merchants."[6]

The role the British played in all of this would become quite controversial, but to the oligarchy it seemed nothing less than natural. Never mind that the British had wanted to lay claim to the region's economies since colonial times and had sent a few thousand soldiers to liberate

Buenos Aires from the Spanish only to be roundly defeated not long before independence. Argentines evicted the Spanish on their own, but after they did they could hardly wait to welcome the British back, wanting all the trade and investment that Britain had to offer. It came slowly at first since Argentina had little to sell, but when their industrial revolution caused the British to look abroad for grain to feed its growing working class, it was to Argentina, among others, that they turned. Thanks primarily to British investment the railways grew from 6,500 kilometers of track in 1889 to 31,100 by 1914, and the national product rose at record rates. To all accounts it was a mutually beneficial partnership that fed British workers while making Argentine cattlemen and traders wealthy people. Argentines would one day change their minds about it all and rebel against British patronage, but that would not happen until after World War II, when the British no longer had much interest in shopping there.

A Nation of Strangers

North Americans pride themselves on being a nation of immigrants, a land where millions began anew after escaping the poverty and political persecution they suffered in their homelands. Argentina too was a nation of immigrants, the number of which is smaller than North America's, but as a proportion of the resident population it was actually much larger, nearly 30 percent in 1914 compared to 15 percent in the United States.[7] It is one of the seldom told stories of massive demographic change in the modern world. The Canadian and Australian experiences resemble it, but because Argentina's population was so small when immigrants started arriving in 1870—only 2 million—their demographic impact was enormous.[8]

When the Spanish conquered the River Plate region in 1553, an estimated 400,000 Indians lived there, half in the northwest (now the provinces of Jujuy and Salta) at what then was the southern tip of the Inca empire, and only 30,000 on the pampas. Just 1,200 Spaniards stayed behind after the conquest, but by 1778 their number had grown to 70,000. As happened elsewhere in the region, the indigenous population was decimated by disease and cohabitation with the Spaniards, and by 1850 about 70 percent of the population was mestizo or mixed blood. It was this largely mestizo society of 2 million people ruled over by cattlemen that the immigrants joined after 1880.[9]

They came in four waves, the first beginning in the 1880s, when cattlemen and land companies recruited colonists, tenant farmers, and people to harvest grain during the European winter and spring. Italy supplied most of them, giving Argentina the Italian veneer that it exhibits today, and Spain many of the rest, the annual number reaching a peak of 220,000 in 1889. Some were peasants, but most came from small towns. They did not consider themselves "Argentines" at first, many of them intending to accumulate wealth and then return to their native lands and set up a small business or buy a house. Eventually many would stay, but there was always a steady flow back to Europe; nearly one-fourth of those who arrived before 1915 exchanged their pesos and returned home.

Jews were among the members of the first wave, nearly all of them from Russia, some being brought over by the international Jewish Colonization Association in order to create farm colonies in Entre Rios and Santa Fe provinces, and others coming to make homes in Buenos Aires, where by the turn of the century they had created a large barrio several blocks square just north of the city's most prominent plaza. Today an estimated 400,000 Jews live in Argentina, most in Buenos Aires, where third-generation descendants of migrants are involved not only in industry and commerce but also in education, the professions, and politics. Their integration into society has not prevented charges of anti-Semitic persecution, the most recent being made when a military government ruled in the late 1970s. Jewish Argentines disagree about how seriously threatened they really are by anti-Semitism. Some Argentines delight in blaming Zionists for all of their problems, and a few use violence to make their point, but most Jews insist that there is nothing systematic or immanently dangerous about it. Yet, the mere fact that it troubles some of them indicates that anti-Semitism cannot be dismissed as casually as many people try to do.[10]

Economic depression in 1890 slowed the flow of immigrants to a trickle until a second wave began in 1904, again made up primarily of Italians and Spaniards, the largest number, 323,000, reaching Buenos Aires in 1912. Though some of them settled in the countryside as intended, two-thirds stayed in cities, where they set up small shops or worked in construction and on the railroads. By 1914, according to one source, the foreign-born owned 66 percent of Argentina's industries and 74 percent of its retail stores.[11] Immigration fell off during World War I only to pick up again afterward, albeit at a slower pace than before, with most people coming from Central Europe, especially Poland, and Russia, whose revolution many were fleeing. With little room left for them on the *pampas*, they were encouraged either to colonize the northeast to develop tropical fruit and lumber industries or to go south of the *pampas* to develop deciduous fruits in mountain river valleys. The last and smallest influx began after World War II, when a half-million fled the hardships created by the war in Europe. Nazi criminals like Adolf Eichmann were the most notorious of this group, but they were the exceptions. Contrary to popular mythology, Argentina never became a refuge for thousands of Nazis, most of its Germans having come earlier, forming a community of 45,000 by World War II.[12]

The Boom Ends

Good times were over far sooner than was expected. Reliance on agricultural exports for the achievement of economic development is always risky since customers can find other suppliers, natural disasters can wipe out crops, war can cut off trade, and tastes in food can change. The wisdom of hindsight makes the vulnerability of the Argentine enterprise obvious, but life was too good to believe that it would end soon. Not unlike oil-producing Third World nations in the 1970s, Argentines, after decades of meager development, had discovered that they had something that nations richer than themselves wanted, and they took full advantage of their good fortune. But the enterprise was never all that secure, being hit first by a world recession in the 1890s and then by World War I. But each time it was struck, the oligarchy rode out the recession, convinced that they would make up for their losses when better times returned. And they did for several decades, but in the 1930s it finally caught up with them.

The economy behaved erratically after World War I, its peaks and valleys coming ever closer together. For example, commodity prices fell when the war ended then rose again in 1922; a bad harvest followed in 1924 and world prices fell once more in 1925, only to rise in 1926. Still, Argentina managed to become the world's second largest exporter of wheat by the end of the decade (20 percent of the market), and the largest of corn (66 percent), linseed (80 percent), and meat (61 percent). Four cereal companies, owned predominantly by foreign capital, handled the grain trade, and five meat packers (three North American and two English) made sure that beef and mutton were sent in good condition to markets in Europe.[13] The operation ran well, absorbing occasional setbacks and then responding quickly to good markets when they appeared, convincing even doubters that Argentina could withstand the vicissitudes of the world market well enough to sustain its newly achieved high standard of living.

But economies do not always cooperate with those who direct them, and never less so than in 1929, when a depression that started in the industrial nations spread to the rest of the world. South American economies were especially vulnerable because of their heavy reliance on foreign markets and suppliers of industrial goods for their sustenance. The shock was unprecedented not only to their economies but to their politics as well. Ruling oligarchies panicked everywhere. After having tolerated the rise of urban middle classes and their political movements, they closed the door on them, fearful that they would permit economic disaster to provoke dreaded social upheavals, calling in the armed forces to keep order in Chile, Brazil, and Argentina.

After evicting the Radical party, whose election it had permitted fourteen years before, the Argentine oligarchy responded to the depression pragmatically, proving themselves capable of abandoning some of their most sacred free-trade doctrines when the preservation of their export economy required it. They begged the British not to abandon them and secured new trade agreements after granting their benefactors unprecedented concessions. Argentina was guaranteed a quota for chilled beef and the elimination of British tariffs on cereal imports in return for reduced tariffs on imported manufactured goods and a promise to spend sterling on goods and financial services from Britain. To complete the package the British helped Argentina create its first Central Bank.[14]

Essential to recovery was the government's initiating regulation of commodity markets and the sale of foreign exchange. A national meat board was created in 1933, membership on it being divided between public officials and cattlemen, and it was allowed to set minimum and maximum livestock prices, something previously forbidden by free marketers but now demanded by cattlemen as a means of protecting them against the world market and exploitative foreign meat packers. The grain trade was even more vulnerable with 70 percent of it exported, compared to only 33 percent of the nation's beef, so a grain commission was also created to operate much like the meat board. But instead of pushing up prices by withholding supplies from the market as the Canadians and North Americans were doing (a tactic prevented in Argentina by insufficient storage facilities), the Argentines chose to cover the losses borne by producers by financing the margin between the official and world market prices out of government profits on newly established exchange controls.[15] Thousands of vulnerable farmers were saved, and after declining by 11 percent between 1929 and 1932, the national product started growing again, helped by a drought in the United States that began in 1933 and lasted for four years, giving Argentina a virtual monopoly on the international grain market until the United States came back and caused grain prices to fall in 1937.[16]

Agriculture was not the only beneficiary of the rescue operation. Industry also profited. Manufacturing had been going on since before the turn of the century, and by 1920 it accounted for almost 20 percent of the national product. Enterprising immigrants and foreign investors had gone into food processing, and during the 1920s firms were added in chemicals, metals, and electrical products, some of them financed by North American investors bent on getting into the Argentine market.[17] Despite the ruling oligarchy's hostility to industry they had little choice but to tolerate its growth, and by 1940 its share of the national product had risen to 28 percent.[18]

Before Argentines had finished congratulating themselves on their recovery from the depression they were hit again, this time by World War II. At issue was whether Argentina should limp along, mixing a little more industrialization with continued reliance on the export economy, or devote far more public and private resources to industrialization. Finance Minister Federico Pinedo tried to settle the debate early by taking to Congress in 1940 a modest proposal designed to strengthen the country's economic position. He contended that massive industrialization was too expensive but some was necessary in order to increase economic independence. He argued for more food and textile industries and pursuing new markets abroad, especially in the United States. Unfortunately it was never tested since the opposition blocked its passage in the Chamber of Deputies largely on partisan grounds, the Radicals and their allies hoping to embarrass the incumbents as an election approached. But his ideas did not die; they merely languished until military politicians much less sympathetic to the oligarchy came along a few years later and adapted the notion of further industrialization to their own nationalistic objectives.[19]

A new generation of officers who were convinced that the oligarchy was losing touch with wartime economic realities took it upon themselves to prepare Argentina for its uncertain future, starting with their seizure of power in 1943. Untrained in economics and new at governing the country, they viewed development in basic, concrete terms, concentrating their energies on promoting the development of oil, iron, and steel industries. It was from among them that Colonel Juan Perón later emerged, taking the initiative away from his colleagues by using the support of the working class to put his notions of nationalism and populism to work in 1946.

A Society Divided

During all of this time, Argentine society was developing its current structure, one that is noted more for its divisions and antagonisms than its integration. The nation's founders had hoped it would be otherwise, of course. The oligarchy had always set the standard for good life in the country, giving it a reputation for extravagant wealth. Its members were rich, educated, and cosmopolitan. They owned three- and four-story villas in Buenos Aires that were overfurnished and overstaffed. When the heat of summer made the capital unbearable, they retreated to their chalets in the Córdoba hills and beach houses in Mar del Plata or vacationed in Europe.[20] With the help of English engineers and French architects, the oligarchy transformed Buenos Aires in a few years' time from a muddy old port town into one of the hemisphere's most elegant cities. They were a ruling class of agrarian entrepreneurs, who believed that Argentina was theirs to dispose of as they wished. Never did they doubt their right to rule over the several million immigrants who kept the enterprise going for them while they prospered.

The Argentine upper class lacked the cohesion characteristic of most elites in Latin America at the turn of the century. Although many old families increased their wealth in boom years, there was always room for others who made fortunes in real estate, banking, and trade. Competition among them for economic advantage was quite common. Rivalries grew, like the one between cattle breeders in the interior provinces and "fatteners" on the *pampas* near Buenos Aires, whom breeders accused of using their proximity to markets to rig them to the breeders' disadvantage. Similarly, fatteners contested with foreign meat-packing companies, which they claimed were always exploiting their oligopolistic control over the export market to deny fatteners fair prices. Gradually both were challenged by industrialists who resented the economy's direction by free-trading agrarian elites.

Labeling the upper class an "oligarchy" might seem wholly inappropriate given their diversity and lack of affection for one another. Yet calling them anything else risks ignoring their strength as a ruling class that defended its power quite successfully until World War II. They were elitist to the core, convinced of their superiority to those beneath them socially, and were always willing to go to great lengths to protect their privileges. Their economic competition and disputes over government policy were intense, but the oligarchy seldom allowed them to stand in the way of defending their kind against critics in the middle and lower classes who sought larger shares for themselves. Tariff policies, commodity prices, and trade strategies were legitimate issues for dispute, but the redistribution of real power never was. The oligarchy tolerated the election of candidates from the middle-class Radical party in 1916 only because they knew that the Radicals understood the rules of the game well enough to abstain from tinkering with the wealth and power of the rich. When the world depression struck and Radical control over the protesting masses weakened, members of the oligarchy once more united long enough to direct the armed forces to evict the Radicals and return the government to the upper class for another decade.[21]

The oligarchy's panic and grab for political control in the 1930s proved very costly to the country's maturation. Coming after the middle class had begun to accumulate some power of its own, it deepened antagonisms between the two classes. Nothing that happened during the first half of the twentieth century did more to retard the development of a politics built on accommodation for mutual advantage that is so important to democratic government. At the precise moment that the society's growth and increasing diversity made a broad political consensus essential to political stability, the oligarchy chose to solidify divisions among social classes and increase middle- and lower-class resentment of their exclusion from politics. The result was a renewed provocation of an interclass conflict that the populist Juan Perón would rush to exploit before his rivals on the Marxist left could do likewise. By the time World War II arrived, Argentines did not need to be told that their subjugation by an unpaternal upper class would persist unless a more aggressive effort was made to end it.

The wealthy are not the only ones who are blamed for the failure to fashion stable, constitutional governments after 1930. Many fault the middle class and its habit of emulating the rich rather than reshaping society along bourgeois, moderate lines. With prosperity and immigration, the middle class had grown rapidly; by 1920 nearly one-third of the nation's urban dwellers were in the middle class. They never enjoyed much cohesion as a social force, however, sharing as they did little more than a desire to "make it" in the New World much as the upper class had done. The fact that the middle class was large and its members were of diverse origins made collaboration difficult. Despite the leadership of the Radical party, it proved weak and ineffective as a governing class, exhibiting the kind of woeful division and vacillation that now seems endemic to the Argentine political scene.[22]

Perhaps it is too much to have expected the middle class to fashion a democracy in such an elitist society. Immigrants learned quickly to live by the existing rules of the game. For many it was a small price to pay for what they gained materially, some of them becoming quite affluent in their new home. It was an exciting place to be for the immigrant accustomed to the immobility of traditional European village life, since few restrictions were placed on how he earned a living. Buenos Aires was truly the city of opportunity at the turn of the century, and taking advantage of it was all that preoccupied many people until they had settled in and discovered how little power they really had. As one Spanish observer noted on a visit to the Argentine capital in 1910, "The city is forever remaking and altering itself and everyone seems to live in a constant state of alert as if at war, stimulated by the preoccupation of enriching himself as quickly as possible."[23]

Today Argentine society resembles European ones more than it does others in Latin America. Its upper and middle classes are large and culturally sophisticated, and its working class has become one of the most urban and highly organized of any in the hemisphere.

Today only a minority of the upper class derive their income from the land, most having turned long ago to finance, commerce, and industry. They store much of their wealth outside the country and remain as worldly as before, traveling frequently to Europe and the United States to be among equals. Most still believe in their superiority to the rest of the nation, being as certain as their grandfathers that the country needs to be under the firm control of an enlightened elite in order to prosper. They have little good to say about the politicians who have ruled the country during the past forty years, and though more accepting of the armed forces and the necessity of their policing an unruly population, class differences make it impossible for them to welcome middle-class officers into their social circles. In short, they know that too much has changed since Perón came on the scene to allow them to control everything again, but that does not prevent their retaining substantial wealth and social prestige with the help of the investments they make abroad in more prosperous and reliable economies.

Just how many people are wealthy no one can say with any certainty, for nowhere do people disguise their lack of wealth so successfully. Argentines take great pride in pretending that they are more affluent than they really are; for them faking prosperity is not a sin, but a talent much admired. The worst examples of such pretensions have a seedy, rather pathetic quality to them, but the best are hardly distinguishable from the real thing. It is because so many of them are so good at exhibiting a veneer of affluence that Argentines seldom seem to suffer as much as they should from deep recessions and other calamities. It is hard to believe that the people one meets on the streets of Argentina's largest cities are members of a nation whose per capita income is only $2,000. Income is higher in cities than small towns, of course, and a visit to working-class suburbs and the poorest provinces makes one less incredulous, but discovery of the nation's regional poverties takes nothing away from the fact that there are few peoples anywhere who are more adept at convincing one that affluence is their normal condition.

The middle class is larger and more diverse ethnically and professionally than it was a half-century ago. Most of middle-class Argentines eat well, own homes or apartments, and drive their own automobiles. Although they are among the nation's most productive farmers, the vast majority work in small businesses, government bureaucracies, or as professionals in cities. They take their recreation in private clubs, wear the latest fashions, and avoid all forms of heavy labor.

Many of them strive for personal economic independence, inspired by examples from the past—the cattleman's enrichment and the immigrants' success in business. It is to become a *propiocuentista,* or owner of the firm, that many enterprising people work so hard. Because of them, small businesses abound throughout the country. In difficult times many of them go bankrupt, but that seldom stops the ambitious from trying time and again. They are economic survivalists, forced to invent creative methods to operate as independent entrepreneurs, often taking great pride in their dexterity and defiance of the odds. Society pays a price for it, of course. The *propiocuentista* does not want to be reined in by anyone, dedicated as he is to retaining independence by avoiding social control. Civic responsibility holds little appeal to a mentality that fears the consequences of conforming to standards set by authorities with societal concerns. Government can serve as a necessary protector and provider by giving business to entrepreneurs who are unable to make it on their own in unregulated markets, but few *propiocuentistas* believe they incur obligations to return the favor by paying taxes or obeying regulations intended to benefit the larger community. As far as they are concerned, Argentina is the land of opportunity not conformity. After all, that is why their ancestors came to this faraway land in the first place.

When it comes to politics, members of the middle class exhibit little coherence or consistency. They are downcast and pessimistic one moment and hopeful and cautiously optimistic the next. Many things bother them, from the imagined and real conspiracies of oligarchs and foreigners to the belligerence of a proletariat whose militancy earns it rewards at the expense of the middle class. They occasionally appeal to the armed forces to defend their interests, but they are fickle collaborators, welcoming protection for a time and then demanding that government be returned to them before the military has completed its assignment. In brief, the middle class is an essential part of the nation's power structure, one that supplies most of its bureaucrats, party leaders, and military officers, as well as the people who manage most of its businesses, yet it cannot run Argentina by itself. The nation's upper and lower classes have made certain of that.

It is the power of the working class that has grown the most in the past half-century. During the construction of railways and the building of metropolitan Buenos Aires, immigration changed the composition of the working class and rapidly increased its size. Industrialization added even more to its ranks. Just before the turn of the century, labor unions began forming to defend working-class interests, led primarily by European immigrants, who brought their proletarian ideologies with them. For a time they met repression, but migration to the cities from small provincial towns created a working mass living in close proximity, thus facilitating organization and political mobilization. It was General Juan Perón, and not the socialist and syndicalist leadership, that did the organizing, however, and Argentine labor has remained powerful and ideologically nonconformist ever since.

Nowhere else in Latin America has organized labor become as aggressive and politically potent nor labor's confrontations with authorities as routine. It is true that many Argentine workers do not belong to unions and that the 3.4 million who do lose as often as they triumph when they challenge the economic power structure. Nevertheless, nobody can rule the country for long without blue-collar collaboration, since so many of the nation's public and private enterprises depend on a highly skilled work force for their operation. That is why today few things preoccupy authorities more than finding ways to secure the conformity of a still dissatisfied work force.

Taken together, Argentina's social classes form a nation whose members share no common understanding of what membership in a national community demands of them. The wealthiest members of society look abroad for their sustenance and comfort. The middle class would like to follow them, but its members must instead devote their energies to dealing rather atomistically with permanent economic insecurity. And the working class relies on its power of intrusion as an organized force to extract just rewards from employers and the nation's governments. The country is more European in ancestry than any Latin American country except neighboring Uruguay, yet its economic development has fallen far behind that of the once-poor countries from which its immigrant population came. And, though Buenos Aires is one of the world's most Caucasian, middle-class cities, Argentina's poorest provinces resemble poor regions of Chile or Colombia more than they do those of Spain or Italy. Regionalism survives within the country despite a pretense of nationality. Argentines love the same flag and proudly sing the same anthem, but the sophisticated Buenos Aires *porteño* has no doubts about his superiority to his provincial compatriots.

Demographically life has changed little for some time. Most people live in cities, 83 percent of them in towns with over 2,000 people, and 47 percent in cities of more than 500,000, the three largest being Buenos Aires (10 million) and Córdoba and Rosario (1 million each). By Latin American standards they are a well-educated people, though not as well educated as they pretend: only 32 percent of those over fourteen years of age have completed primary school, 10 percent secondary school, and just 3.3 percent have university degrees. The Argentine middle class, though proportionately the largest in Latin America, is not really a highly educated one, but rather one that has profited from the nation's scarcity of skilled labor, abundance of public employment, and the low cost of such necessities as food.[24]

Argentine women are the most educated in Latin America. In 1980 almost half of the university graduates were women, among them one-third of those from law school and one-fourth of the new doctors. Many women work full time and now compose 27 percent of the national work force, spread nearly equally among domestic employment, office work, schoolteaching, and sales. Is this evidence of the Argentine woman's "liberation"? Not really, since male dominance remains strong in the home as well as almost everywhere else in society. The scarcity of labor opened the door to female employment long ago, and economic decline and lower real wages in recent years have made two incomes more necessary than ever in order to maintain the standard of living previously enjoyed by middle- and lower-class families. Some women are trying to promote greater equality between the sexes and it is no longer considered as alien an issue as before, but progress is slow.[25]

Argentina today is a remnant of its glorious past and much more, a nation that has continued to mature economically and change socially despite losing much of its momentum fifty years ago. Its people are proud of their past, but they do not revel in it the way Mexicans do. They have no roots in an ancient pre-Columbian culture, nor did they fight a revolution that gave them a new political purpose in the twentieth century. Monuments to those who led the war for independence are evident in most city plazas, but there are no large museums of real quality anywhere in the country or "statues of liberty" that celebrate the arrival of millions of immigrants. For a long time those who came to its shores had trouble making up their minds about whether to settle there, and today their descendants seem too worried about the future to devote much time to celebrating their ambiguous past. When they tell their history, they do so in a very partisan manner, each version filled with short lists of heroes and long ones of villains. The Radical party faithful claim credit for breaking the oligarchy's monopoly and worship the memory of Hipólito Yrigoyen, the first Radical president (1916–22), and for them democracy's founding father. Peronists, in contrast, have little use for Yrigoyen, believing as they do that popular democracy began with the liberation of the working class by patrons Juan and Eva Perón in 1946. And not to be left out, conservative members of society show no respect for either view of history, convinced as they are that Radicals and Peronists have done more harm than good to what was once a rich nation. In short, they all love their country but can agree on little else.

An Aversion to Legitimacy

Argentine politics mystifies foreigners, who cannot comprehend why so many literate and sophisticated people find it so hard to live in peace with each other. They insist that abundant food, high employment, and a large middle class should guarantee greater civility and accommodation. The Argentines know otherwise, yet they also know that their politics is not as chaotic as it appears to people unfamiliar with it. Although military and civilian governments rise and fall according to no constitutional plan, the nation's power structure has changed very little during the past four decades. As a result, politics is quite repetitive, the military coming and going at almost regular intervals and civilian governments doing much the same. It is as if Argentines designed their own way of doing politics many years ago, and though it seems bizarre to others, they have stuck with it because it is what they know best.

When change has come it has been in the form of additions to the national power structure rather than subtractions from it. Periodically a movement has risen up, moved in, and ruled for a time before being forced out of office. There were three of them during the first half of this century, the Radicals governing for more than a decade starting in 1916, the oligarchy returning in 1930 and staying the same length of time, followed by the Peronists from 1946 until 1955. Each thought itself superior to its rivals only to be deposed by them with the military's help before consolidating control over society. The oligarchy engineered the removal of the Radicals in 1930, the Radicals celebrated the eviction of the oligarchy in 1943, and both of them cheered when Perón was tossed out in 1955 (see Table 2.1, p. 32).

After they sent Perón into exile, his enemies within the armed forces set out to destroy his movement by forcing the working class into other parties. But the masses would not permit such house cleaning, and when elections were held again in 1958 and Peronist candidates

2.1   Elections and Presidents, 1916–89

Year	President	Party	Percentage of Popular Vote
1916	Hipólito Yrigoyen	YCR	45
1922	M. T. Alvear	UCR	48
1928	*Hipólito Yrigoyen	UCR	57
1931	General A. Justo	Concordancia	39
1937	*Roberto Ortiz	Concordancia	54
1946	General Juan Perón	Laborista	52
1951	*General Juan Perón	Peronist	62
1958	*Arturo Frondizi	UCRI	45
1963	*Arturo Illia	UCRP	25
1973	Hector Campora	Peronist	49
1973	*General Juan Perón	Peronist	62
1983	Raul Alfonsín	UCR	52
1989	Carlos Saul Menem	Peronist	47

*Government overthrown by military coup

Party Identifications:

> UCR = Unión Civica Radical (Radical party)
> UCRI = Unión Civica Radical Intransigente
> UCRP = Unión Civica Radical del Pueblo

Sources: Cesar Reinaldo García, *Historia de los grupos y partidos politicos* (Buenos Aires: Sainte Claire, 1983); and *La Semana*, November 3, 1983, p. 69.

were prohibited from participating, the exiled Perón instructed his followers to vote for Radical candidate Arturo Frondizi without pledging their loyalty to him. Frondizi promised Perón that he would legalize Peronism after his election in defiance of military wishes, a bold gesture that caused many within the Radical party to bolt and form their own separate People's Radical party (UCRP) to contest the election with Frondizi's Intransigent Radicals (UCRI). Frondizi won easily with Peronist support, but he lost Perón's backing immediately afterward over his choice of economic austerity measures that were damaging to the labor rank and file. Nevertheless, despite military opposition, he went through with the legalization of Peronism, inviting the movement's candidates to contest with his own party in gubernatorial elections in March 1962, which they did, triumphing in the largest provinces and provoking another coup by anti-Peronist officers.

What to do next was determined after a year of conflict within the military between legalists who wanted to give elections another try and others who aspired to some form of permanent military rule. The former prevailed and authorized new elections in mid-1963, though again they prohibited the Peronist party's participation. This time UCRP candidate Arturo Illia won, though with only 25 percent of the popular vote since many Peronists cast blank ballots in protest of the entire process. Illia governed for three years, suffering congressional losses to Peronists when he too legalized them in 1965. A year later the military took over once more, though this time they did so inspired by much more ambitious objectives. Encouraged by many in the business community who longed for less politics, the same "legalist" officers who had called for elections in 1963 deposed Illia and took complete control for themselves, creating an authoritarian government devoted to accelerating the nation's economic growth and reorganizing its politics from the bottom up. Politicians were made unwelcome while military officers and civilian technocrats ran the nation, delivering on their promises to accelerate economic growth. But in mid-1969 the public protested massively, shaking General Juan Carlos Onganía's government to its foundations. A year later his colleagues removed him and began a slow process leading to the holding of new elections in 1973.

The temptation to invite Perón back to subdue the country's contumacious labor movement was great in 1973. The seventy-five-year-old exile cultivated confidence in his ability to restore order and was brought home after eighteen years abroad to lead his party to victory in the 1973 elections. Prohibited from candidacy himself, he endorsed stand-in Hector Campora, who won easily only to be pushed aside so that Perón could be elected president six months later. The elderly general's tenure was brief as he died of natural causes before his first year had ended, leaving the presidency to his wife and vice-president Isabel. Argentina reached a low point during the next two years as terrorism grew while the economy plummeted. To no one's surprise and to the relief of almost everyone the armed forces took over again in mid-1976.

Service commanders, as they had done in 1966, promised to reconstruct the nation's economy and politics, convinced that it was the only way to avoid repetition of the Peronist disaster. While their civilian advisors went to work on the economy they unleashed a brutal, secret war against terrorists and leftists of almost any stripe. They kidnapped and killed over 9,000 persons and boasted of having saved the nation from destruction while their subjects cowered in fright. But when General Jorge Videla turned the presidency over to General Roberto Viola in 1981 as planned, the authoritarian edifice began to crack. Protests against its punishing economic policies grew in the business community, and confidence in the government dropped when foreign debts rose astronomically and the peso collapsed in value. An attempt to shore up the regime was made in late 1981 by General Leopoldo Galtieri, but when he went to war in the Falklands and lost, he took military dictatorship with him. In 1983 officers departed for their bases and gave civilians a chance to start all over again.

A bemused but troubled Argentine observer summed it up well when he concluded, "We have created a system that permits all sectors to alternate in power despite continuous interruptions of the formal political process. It is as if there is a tacit agreement that no government should be allowed to endure. In this each sector can take its turn in power without ever having to share it."[26]

But there was no real tacit agreement on how or when to exchange office, only determinations by each "sector" to avoid succumbing to its rivals entirely. The result was a cyclical politics in which civilian and military governments rose and fell at regular intervals without anyone planning it that way. The regularity is stunning: during the last twenty years there were two civilian governments that lasted three years, each time separated by two military ones that ruled for exactly seven years each.

If the country's political history is marked by additions and cycles, it also reveals an obvious irresolution of fundamental problems of political legitimacy. Time and again Argentines have found it impossible to agree on how they are to be governed. It started with the oligarchy's desire to make politics a reflection of the distribution of economic power in the country rather than allow it to become a means by which those less well off could compensate for their economic disadvantages. When they finally allowed the middle class into the government in 1916, it was understood that the latter's elevation was only to be a partial one. It was also a brief one, for the oligarchs returned in 1930, trying harder than ever to rig elections and exclude the masses from politics. However, their doing so provoked a rebelliousness that would remain long after they were evicted in 1943. Thereafter it seemed that anyone who governed the country invited rebellion whether or not he ruled repressively, succumbing to opposition before his tenure had expired.

Argentines cannot help but wonder why they have gone through all of this. There was nothing inevitable about it. Mexicans have not suffered a military coup in seventy years, and after a century of dictatorship the Venezuelans adopted a multiparty democracy that has operated without interruption since 1959. Even Brazil, after two decades of military government, found the restoration of constitutional politics a smoother and more dignified process than the Argentine military ever has.

Compromise and consensus have not come very easily in Argentina at any time in its history. Those who ruled the country when its modernization began were averse to sharing real power with those below them. And when the oligarchs were finally forced from office in the 1940s by the Peronists, they were shown little more respect than they had shown their victims previously. And on it went, with the Peronists popularizing authoritarian politics and reinforcing antagonisms in society and partisanship in government. How they managed the feat and what it has meant to contemporary politics is our next subject. Juan Perón tried twice to transform his country, once beginning in 1946 and again in 1973, but he came up short each time. His death in 1974 ended his quest, but his politics survive him, a little weakened by the loss of its founder but still enthusiastically embraced by millions.

Notes

1. For a compact summary of the nineteenth century, see James R. Scobie, *Argentina: A City and a Nation* (New York: Oxford University Press, 1971), chs. 1–4.

2. Detailed accounts of development on the *pampas* are given in James R. Scobie, *Revolution on the Pampas: A Social History of Argentine Wheat 1860–1910* (Austin: University of Texas Press, 1964); and Roberto Cortes Conde, *El progreso argentino, 1880–1914* (Buenos Aires: Sudamericana, 1979).

3. Horacio Giberti, "Granos, carnes, y tierra," *Primera historia integral 42* (Buenos Aires: 1980), p. 35. Demand for Argentine beef rose when hoof and mouth disease in France cut live shipments from there to Great Britain and British involvement in the Boer War increased demand at home for frozen beef.

4. Scobie, *Revolution on the Pampas*.

5. Jorge Federico Sábato, *La pampa prodiga: Claves de una frustración* (Buenos Aires: CIESA, 1980), chs. 1–2. Immigrants were also attracted to the countryside by land developers who tried to create new enterprises outside the *pampas* region. In Córdoba, Entre Rios, and Santa Fe, land companies established colonies in the 1880s and attracted Europeans to them by advertising abroad. See Manuel Bejarano, "Inmigración y estructuras tradicionales en Buenos Aires," in *Los fragmentos del poder: oligarquía a la poliar44ía argentina*, ed. Torcuarto Di Tella and Tulio Halperin Donghi (Buenos Aires: Jorge Alvarez, 1969), pp. 101–147.

6. Scobie, *Argentina*, p. 232.

7. Oscar Cornblit, "Inmigrantes y empresarios en la política argentina," in *Los fragmentos del poder*, pp. 394–401.

8. Gobierno Argentina, Dirección de Estadisticas y Censos, *Censo-Serie B*, 1983, pp. xi–xx.

9. Ibid. It has been estimated that in 1870 Indians formed 12 percent of the population, mulattoes 14 percent, and pure Europeans only 3 percent, the other 71 percent being mestizo.

10. For a recent history of Jewish migration to Argentina, one should consult Eugene F. Sofer, *From Pale to Pampa: A Social History of the Jews in Buenos Aires* (New York: Holmes & Meier, 1982). The most recent controversy over anti-Semitism was touched off by journalist Jacobo Timerman, editor of *La Opinión* newspaper, when he was jailed and tortured by the armed forces and then released under foreign pressure and allowed to migrate to Israel. Timerman blames anti-Semitism for his persecution and criticizes Argentine Jews for pretending that the problem does not exist in order to get along as best they can. Many of them, in turn, complain that Timerman glorified his own suffering by

cloaking the whole episode with memories of the Holocaust. After Alfonsín's election he returned to Argentina in 1984 to edit the daily *La Razón*. See his *Prisoner Without a Name, Cell Without a Number* (New York: Knopf, 1981).

11. Cornblit, "Inmigrantes y empresarios en la política argentina," p. 405.

12. Dirección de Estadísticas y Censos, *Censo-Serie B*, 1983. The data on German residents are taken from Ronald C. Newton, *German Buenos Aires, 1900–1933: Social Change and Cultural Crisis* (Austin: University of Texas Press, 1977).

13. Arturo O'Connell, "La Argentina en la depresión: los problems de una economía abierto," *Desarrollo económico* 23, no. 92 (January–March 1984): 479–488.

14. Javier Villanueva, "Economic Development," in *Prologue to Peron: Argentina in Depression and War: 1930–1943*, ed. Mark Falcoff and Ronald Dolkart (Berkeley: University of California Press, 1975), pp. 56–82.

15. See Gary W. Wynia, *Argentina in the Postwar Era* (Albuquerque: University of New Mexico Press, 1978), pp. 26–27, for more details.

16. O'Connell, "La Argentina en la depresión," pp. 488 ff.

17. Villanueva, "Economic Development," pp. 67–68.

18. Livio Guillermo Kuhl, *Una política industrial para la Argentina* (Buenos Aires: Club de Estudio, 1983), p. 73.

19. Juan J. Llach, "El Plan Pinedo de 1940, su significado histórico y los orígenes de la economía político del peronismo," *Desarrollo económico* 23, no. 92 (January–March 1984). Llach argues that the "internal market" strategy advocated by Peronists at their formation in 1944 was an adaptation of the ideas put forward by conservative Pinedo three years before. Pinedo was appalled by the Peronists' abandonment of free trade, but that did not stop them from turning his critique of the primary product export economy and advocacy of industrialization into a nationalist and protectionist justification for industrial development.

20. Scobie, *Argentina*, p. 173.

21. On divisions within the rural oligarchy, see Peter H. Smith, *Politics and Beef in Argentina* (New York: Columbia University Press, 1969); and on politics during the 1930s, Peter H. Smith, *Argentina and the Failure of Democracy: Conflict Among Political Elites: 1904–1955* (Madison: University of Wisconsin Press, 1974); and Mark Falcoff and Ronald Dolkart, *Prologue to Peron*.

22. Scobie, *Argentina*, p. 175.

23. James R. Scobie, *Buenos Aires: Plaza to Suburb, 1870–1910* (New York: Oxford University Press, 1974), p. 232.

24. Dirección de Estadísticas y Censos, Censo B.

25. Ibid.

26. Guido Di Tella, *Perón–Perón 1973–1976* (Buenos Aires: Sudamericana, 1983), p. 319.

3

The Peronist Invention

"I am a Peronist, fanatically Peronist," Eva Perón loved to tell anyone who would listen. And when she did she spoke for millions of Argentines who were equally proud of their newly found fanaticism. Together they helped Juan Perón create a politics that was impatient with complexity and suspicious of foreigners and oligarchs and one that revered the *descamisados* (shirtless ones), as Perón called his masses. No labor movement in Latin America has become stronger or more contentious than Argentina's, not even those in "revolutionary" Mexico or highly industrialized Brazil. That is why authorities who persecute the working class continually fail to subdue it.

A General's Ambition

Juan Perón was an enterprising politician who wanted to make Argentina a powerful nation at a time when its future was in doubt. He was not a revolutionary but an audacious opportunist, whose personal ambition and good timing led him to use the working class to break the oligarchy's grip on the nation. But it was the oligarchy's profits and not its property that the Peronists confiscated, committed as they were from the outset to making the state the patron of entrepreneurs and workers alike rather than the nemesis of either. Their failures were many, and the country is still paying for them, but however great and costly they were, few Peronists regret what they did.

It is not hard to understand why something like Peronism would arise in postwar Argentina. The nation's spectacular economic boom had begun to taper off before the 1929 depression. Conservative efforts to patch up the economy during the 1930s were moderately successful, but they did not dispel concern about the country's economic vulnerability or prevent rising anxiety about how to cope with the adverse effects of a new world war. On the political front things looked even less inspiring. The Radical party, plagued by internal division and embarrassed by its collaboration with the ruling oligarchs before the war, seemed to have lost its drive and originality. And ruling conservatives inspired little confidence in their ability to offer anything new when conditions demanded it.

Argentina was changing but no one appeared ready to meet the challenge. Industrialization had progressed substantially after 1930, supplying more of the national product than agriculture by 1940. With the growth of industry came a larger working class, causing a new political concern for military officers who were determined to prevent its radicalization by socialist and anarchist intellectuals and labor leaders who led the attack against capitalism. What to do about all of this was unclear at first, nationalist officers having decided only that it was a problem far beyond the capacity of the lethargic oligarchy to solve. Finally the armed forces took it upon themselves to set things right, deposing the ruling oligarchs in June 1943.

Their objectives were never very clear, and that is why it was relatively easy for one among them to seize the initiative and offer solutions of his own. Juan Perón adroitly exploited fear of working-class radicalization, offering to take care of the nation's proletariat if others would give him the authority he needed to accomplish the task. No one fully understood where it would all lead, but that was to Perón's advantage, as it would be in virtually everything he did. He was determined to win the allegiance of organized labor and use it to the state's advantage as well as his own. If it worked, the government would become the patron rather than the oppressor of a compliant working class that had discarded its revolutionary ambitions in exchange for a host of new economic and political privileges. It would require substantial change in the function of government, beginning with its transformation from just a regulatory mechanism into a beneficent provider that guaranteed the economic security of those in its care. But Perón managed it, needing only three years to make his way to the presidency and three more to win over millions of people who were delighted by the attention and affection he gave them.

Argentines will never agree about how much Perón actually accomplished. Too much is at stake, even today, to permit anything resembling objectivity. Even scholars are not certain about the politics he practiced, some finding it fascist in character, others simply *caudillismo* in modern dress, and some an innovative version of populist democracy. Fascination with it is matched by frustration with its refusal to fit neatly into familiar categories of politics. But its ambiguity and unconventional character was of no concern to Perón; he delighted in being unique, seeing himself as the creator of an innovative political synthesis that he boasted was neither capitalist nor socialist, neither authoritarian nor liberal democratic.

It was his political practice and not political theory that distinguished Perón from his peers, however, for his grand synthesis was always more something of mind than deed. He was a military officer who liked politics, one who matured in an organization whose fatuous nature tutored its members as much in bureaucratic conspiracy as in weaponry. He was also the kind who believed that leadership involved commanding the loyalty of people much like the general did his troops by leading them in conquest and sharing its bounty with them afterward. There was always something Romanesque about him, no doubt due in part to his admiration for the style of Benito Mussolini, whom he observed at first hand while stationed briefly in Italy just before the war. He was not the country's first military politician, nor would he be the last, but he quickly proved himself to be the most adroit at outwitting civilians at their own game.

There was nothing in Perón's early life to predict his becoming the nation's most powerful leader. His grandfather was a physician and senator, but his father turned to farming, never rising above the middle class. Born in the small town of Lobos in Buenos Aires province on October 8, 1895, Perón was of Sardinian, Basque, and Scottish ancestry, nothing at all unusual in this country of European immigrants. He went to school in Buenos Aires, his parents hoping that he would become a physician, but when the time came he chose the military academy, claiming later that he did so primarily to stay with friends. An average student, he received his commission as a second lieutenant in 1913 and began what should have been a normal career in the increasingly professionalized, German-trained Argentine army.[1]

He rose through the ranks without particular distinction, developing a reputation for industry, lack of pretension, athletic ability, and success as a teacher of noncommissioned officers. It was to teaching and writing military history that he devoted his energies during the 1930s, spending some time as an instructor at the military academy, where he became a lecturer admired by students for his ability to simplify complex matters of history and military strategy for audiences lacking in university educations. This experience served him well when he later chose to become the nation's "instructor" from the presidential podium, the first leader ever to speak directly to the working masses in language inspiring to them, at his most effective when appearing before them as the enthusiastic officer intent on leading them into battle against the oligarchy and British imperialists.

Critical to Perón's political education was his being stationed in Italy from July 1939 until December 1940, where he watched Mussolini and the Italian fascists at work. He was not so naïve as to believe that he could simply imitate the Italians back home, but the idea of building a stronger nation using bold and popular leadership to mobilize people and resources was quite appealing to him and seemed to be exactly what Argentina needed at the time. Many people worried about the economy's decay after the war, and in his militaristic way Perón convinced many of them that he, like Mussolini, could cure the nation's ills by mobilizing its people for the pursuit of common objectives much as the fascists had done in Europe a decade before. He was not the first to take his inspiration from such sources, of course. Lieutenant General José Uriburu, the leader of the coup that removed Radical party president Hipólito Yrigoyen in 1930, also believed that fascism was the answer to depression-related problems, and only the oligarchy's fear of losing control over him prevented Uriburu from carrying through with his plot. But in 1943 the military had turned against the oligarchy, and to many people, frustrated as they had been by a long depression and a slow recovery that had revealed their frightening vulnerability to decisions taken in European capitals by bankers, generals, and prime ministers, Perón's bold approach to the country's reconstruction was inspiring.[2]

He started his quest a few months before the coup, when he and some colleagues formed the Grupo de Oficiales Unidos (GOU), a secret military "lodge" intended to bring officers of like mind together to formulate their solutions to the nation's problems and prepare a strategy for securing their implementation by military superiors should they take over the government. Lodges had been common within the army for a couple of decades, serving as secret seminars for would-be conspirators, most of whom were devoted more to advancing each other within the army than to political matters.[3] The creators of the GOU had both objectives in mind, but it was their political ambitions that would distinguish them. To begin with, they were disturbed by the army's loss of public esteem as a result of its close association with the corrupt and increasingly incompetent Castillo administration, itself the unexpected result of the more tolerant Roberto Ortiz being forced by illness to relinquish the presidency to his reactionary vice president Castillo in 1940. Equally influential was their fear that Castillo or his soon-to-be-elected pro-British successor would yield to U.S. pressure to end Argentine neutrality, something nationalists like Perón abhorred doing. Some of them favored the Axis powers, but whether they did or not, they felt Argentina had more to gain by staying out of the war than it did from endorsing either side. And finally, they were concerned that a decade of the oligarchy's repressing the working class would prompt communist and syndicalist mobilization of the urban masses toward the achievement of radical change, something that they, committed as they were to the essentials of mixed capitalism, could not tolerate. Since the conservatives had lost their touch, they had to go, but their eviction in 1943 was never intended to allow anything but the creation of a new ruling class that was even better equipped to prevent the radicalization of national politics. Even Perón agreed with that. What his colleagues lacked at the outset was a concrete plan for accomplishing the task, and it was to creating one that he devoted himself while superiors took charge of the nation's governance.[4]

His three-year assault on the presidency was the kind from which legends are made, and the Peronists love to recite it.[5] It was indeed a spectacular triumph, but there is little in his good timing and tactical maneuvering that envious politicians would find all that mysterious. He was just better than they were at taking advantage of the anxieties caused by the country's isolation during the war and its hostility toward Great Britain and more adept at exploiting the desire of the working class for recognition and favor than some of its own leaders were. He knew that Argentina would never be the same again after the war regardless of who led the nation. But he, more than most, had some idea, albeit a very crude one, of where the nation might go in the postwar years. Most important, he knew how to communicate his popular message to everyone who needed to hear it, using some of the same talents that had made him a popular teacher of noncommissioned officers.

Peronizing the Proletariat

The coup's leaders rewarded Perón with an undersecretaryship of war, a position which he exploited to advance his GOU colleagues within the army, but it was his work in the obscure labor secretaryship that contributed the most to his political triumph. His strategy was daring though quite simple. Rather than repress organized labor as the conservatives had done, or allow them to be led by parties on the left, as would surely happen if the country were governed democratically, he set out to incorporate labor leaders into ruling circles, making the federal bureaucracy their patron and them wards of the state. The idea was not new; European fascists had tried it and so had Mexico's revolutionary leaders like Lazaro Cárdenas a decade before. The scheme was corporatist in nature, based on the linking of private economic interests in capitalist economies to the state in an organized and centrally supervised manner in order to save capitalism from self-destruction.

The labor movement was not eager to sign up at first. Perón was a stranger to them, an officer with no obvious affinity for unions that had been led for over fifty years by civilian anarchists, socialists, and syndicalists. They were born when working conditions were deplorable and wages low, prompting agitation for reform. In 1895 there were 23,000 industrial enterprises in Argentina, primarily in furniture, food, printing, metalwork, and construction, which employed 170,000 persons. Most of the latter were foreign born, having migrated there a few years before, bringing their proletarian ideologies with them from Italy and Spain. Typographical workers were the first to organize in 1877, but it was not until 1901 that a group of unions launched the country's first national labor federation. Their exclusion from politics by the ruling oligarchy and maltreatment by their employers made revolutionary doctrines popular among workers. But they were divided from the beginning over matters of political strategy, some preferring the Socialist party practice of accommodation and others mass protests intended to force concessions by authorities. Neither strategy achieved a great deal, however, since authorities, be they Radicals in the 1920s or conservatives after 1930, refused to concede much to the working class. Typical was the way acclaimed populist Hipólito Yrigoyen, elected president by the Radical party in the country's first real democratic elections in 1916, responded to his working-class critics. When strikes escalated into unprecedented mass protests in 1919, Yrigoyen turned the police loose on them. Then he signed legislation granting them the eight-hour workday and pension programs, promising the working class more if they would stay in line and accept his paternal rule over them. It was a mixed blessing, obviously, but never enough to compensate for their losses after being hit by economic depression, unemployment, and renewed repression in the 1930s.[6]

Disputes among its ideologues also weakened the labor movement during the depression years. Nevertheless, socialists and syndicalists united long enough to launch a new national federation in 1930, the General Confederation of Labor (CGT), modeling it on the French CGT, then Europe's most prominent labor organization. It was dominated initially by the railway workers and included only a few industrial unions, but by taking advantage of proletarian discontent with the oligarchy's heavy-handed ways, its leaders converted many to the cause of mass protest against capitalism itself. Though their ability to affect the government's behavior was slight thanks to its power of repression, fear of their mobilizing the working class toward such ends worried military officers like Perón as much as it did the nation's wealthy when they witnessed unprecedented growth in the industrial work force as the country entered the 1940s.

The migration of thousands of unskilled laborers to Buenos Aires during the war had created an immense base for mass organization. Laborers in some of the new industries were incorporated into existing unions, but most remained unorganized during their first few years of employment. The challenge for anyone eager to take the proletarian cause away from its more radical champions was to deal with unorganized labor before CGT unions did while at the same time dividing and weakening the CGT. It was a monumental task, and few in the Argentine bourgeoisie could even conceive of its being done, let alone carry it out. Laborers were not sitting outside their factories waiting for a Perón to lead them. They had organizations eager to mobilize them that were led by men with a half-century of experience, albeit a rather disappointing one, but one that had taught them what they were up against in the nation's well-entrenched and reactionary upper class. Still, Perón, undeterred by the odds, went after the labor movement and did not stop until he had completed one of the greatest robberies anyone had seen. It is doubtful that even he knew exactly where it would end or the tactics that he would employ along the way. But the more his presidential ambitions rose and his success at wooing labor leaders grew, the more confidence he gained in his ability to ride them to the top.

There were many "critical moments" in Argentine history when decisions were made whose consequences are still felt today, but few were more consequential than a little-known event that occurred on May 24, 1944. Until that time most labor leaders had spurned Perón's overtures, making it clear that they had no intention of cooperating with the military regime. Some among them, including the leadership of the two largest organizations, even went so far as to announce a "liberty march" to be held on May 1, 1944, to protest the government's authoritarian ways. But just as they were preparing for their protest they received invitations from the government to join with it in the celebration of a national independence day on May 24. It was a clever move aimed at dividing the labor movement and securing for the government whatever popular support its seduction of labor bosses could deliver. To the government's delight it worked. Union leaders found themselves trapped between a call for a demonstration of their patriotism and their desire to represent class interests. By a vote of six to four they chose to call off their protest, allowing their co-optation by authorities then advised by Perón.[7]

Perón solidified his ties with labor by securing for them government decrees that guaranteed the members of responsive unions retirement benefits, social security programs, paid vacations, and the like. He also appealed to their nationalism, adroitly attracting wartime neutralists away from the socialists and communists who campaigned for taking the side of the Allies. Step by step he drew one union after another from its old ideological stance to a new, pragmatic one that put them under the supervision of an increasingly paternal state. In doing so he also elevated labor leaders long ignored and persecuted by authorities to membership within the government. It meant a great deal to the working class, not just because they had so long been denied respect, but also because it was obvious that their inclusion within the government meant that they, as a political force, would attain the power needed to guarantee their remaining at the center of national politics thereafter.

Winning the Prize

The cultivation of working-class support was only one part of Perón's presidential campaign. He also had to prevent his military colleagues from blocking his quest, a distinct possibility since he and his GOU friends were a small faction whose ambitions were resented from the outset by senior officers. Though Perón secured appointment as vice president in July 1944, rival officers did not give up their attempts to stop him until he had defeated them in a direct confrontation fifteen months later in October 1945. Fearful that his popularity among the working class would catapult him into elections planned for 1946, they had him arrested in mid-October and carted off to prison on Martin Garcia Island just offshore from Buenos Aires. Unfortunately, they allowed him to bid farewell to his followers over radio just before departure, touching off unprecedented labor protests that culminated on October 17, when thousands came out of the working-class suburbs to concentrate before the Casa Rosada to demand that then president Edelmiro Farrell release Perón from prison, which he reluctantly did. The army always finds it hard to deal with mass demonstrations; they can break the back of union strikes but popular rebellion frightens them, so on October 17 they yielded, bringing Perón to the presidential balcony to receive the cheers of the masses, as he would do often during the next decade.[8]

U.S. paranoia and the Radicals' high principles also contributed to Perón's triumph four months later. From the outset foreigners appeared to be more worried about him than most Argentines were. The U.S.

government feared after war broke out in Europe that Germany would extend its influence into South America if no resistance was put up by local authorities. Argentine neutrality had frustrated their efforts, and the creation of a government whose members exhibited sympathy for the Axis powers seemed to confirm their worst fears in 1943. The latter was encouraged by the dispatches of sensationalist correspondents like Ray Josephs, who warned Americans about Perón, insisting that his

> strong sense of showmanship, his Goering-like uniforms and his constant smile hide a relentless drive which insures getting him what he's after. . . . The colonel's speech bore the old Nazi-flavored refrain that employers, workers and the State were the parties to all social problems and that they and nobody else would arrange the solution "avoiding the useless squandering of energies and values."[9]

He continued:

> His methods have a familiar ring; he believes in striking the enemy with audacity, taking advantage of his opponents' errors, gaining time and then advancing quickly. He speaks the language of the *calle* [street], likes good eating and hearty living, and goes to workmen's *boliches* [bars] to talk to them and convince them he is their true pal.[10]

Hardly the portrait of an Adolf Hitler or Benito Mussolini, yet one that nevertheless was cause for worry in Washington. No matter that Buenos Aires was farther from New York than was Paris; anyone who was not a U.S. ally was a potential enemy that might give strategic advantage to the Germans in a war that included battles for control of the Atlantic, North and South. But such reports, when read in Argentina, were just what Perón needed to promote nationalism. Nothing helped him more than U.S. Ambassador Spruille Braden's delivery of the same message. Braden had made up his mind before arriving in Argentina in mid-1945 that Perón had to be stopped, convinced that he and his military colleagues were "bred by the Nazis." At his urging the State Department issued a "Blue Book" just two weeks before the 1946 election warning Argentines of the mistake they would make by electing him. Characteristically Perón turned it to his advantage, blaming the Americans for trying to replace Great Britain as Argentina's subjugator.[11]

The Radical party was the only remaining obstacle. It was the nation's largest organized party prior to 1945 and one that expected to triumph over conservatives when elections were held. Perón's opponents within the military knew this and were tempted to conspire with the Radicals to lend them the help they might need to assure victory.

But true to their high principles, the Radicals refused military over-tures, a decision no doubt bolstered by unjustified confidence in their ability to defeat the newly mobilized Peronists. When they finally real-ized that their chances were not good they had no choice but to turn to the conservatives and several minor parties for help, forming an elec-toral alliance behind a Radical presidential candidate that called itself the Unión Democrática. But it was too little and too late: when the votes were counted 52 percent had gone to Juan Perón.[12]

The Peronist State

Mobilizing the working class against the nation's powerful oligarchy hardly seemed the best way to unite the nation. But the contradiction never bothered Perón, for it was really a mock battle that he fought with the oligarchy. He had set out to prevent a class struggle rather than advance one, and winning the favor of labor and then taming it was how he intended to do so. Critical to success was his making the "*oligarquía*" the enemy while promoting industrial development by lending as-sistance to private industry. He and Evita railed against the rich, attack-ing their ostentatious wealth, ridiculing their love for private clubs and horse racing and their affection for the British, feeding the *des-camisados* (shirtless masses) on the illusion that they were taking control of the country from its richest members. Actually, nothing of the sort occurred. What he took from the oligarchy was its government, not its property. It was good populist theater, not revolutionary politics, and ten years later, when Perón fled, the oligarchy was still there, bruised and vengeful, but not seriously damaged by Peronism.

The Peronist state never became as corporatist as Perón wanted, nor did it unite social classes as much as he intended. It was partisan and favored the working class while advancing Argentine capitalism by making government as much the benefactor of industry as organized labor. Its organization began with the formation of the Partido Laborista and its nomination of Perón for the presidency on October 24, 1945. Labor leaders organized the party, but they were joined in it by dissident Radical party politicians from the Unión Cívica Radical–Junta Reno-vadora, many of them critics of their own party's leadership for its collusion with the ruling oligarchy during the late 1930s. The Centros Independientes formed the party's third constituency, including within its ranks people from all over the political spectrum, among them provincial conservatives who detested the Radical party and die-hard nationalists who hoped that Perón would become a New World fascist.[13] Its organization left much to be desired, but that did not matter for the numbers were there. Later he would reorganize it as the Partido Peronista, transforming it into an instrument of personal control. Ostensibly a democratic party that drew its authority from its grass-roots *unidades basicas*, or basic units, it was actually a hierarchy commanded by Perón in the role of supreme leader. Military concepts, not democratic ones, defined its operation, with "tactical commands" being made responsible to "strategic commands." Unlike the Radical party, which was created by outsiders who used it to agitate and campaign their way into the government, the Peronist party became primarily the instrument of authorities, who drew on their control over the state and the resources it allowed them to keep the party going.

Essential to Perón's success was his sustaining control over organized labor after it had elected him president. It was never automatic since labor leaders occasionally found themselves torn between their deep, and often radical, political ambitions and the conformity Perón demanded of them. He insisted that they forsake their old ideological motives for more pragmatic ones that fit into his design for the country and that they remain loyal to a military officer who lacked their proletarian origins. Not one to take chances, Perón had secured the decree of a new labor law in October 1945, a law that would prove invaluable to his domination over unions in later years. Modeled on Mussolini's legislation, it forced a concentration of power within the labor movement and thrust government into the supervision of its compliance with a very politically motivated plan of reorganization. In essence it required that authorities recognize only one national labor organization in each industry, effectively eliminating dissident unions that defied the orders of the "official" ones. Some resistance to him remained within the CGT, however, and it was not until February 8, 1947, when he secured the removal of Luis Gay from the secretary generalship of the confederation, that he felt secure. Though supportive of Perón, Gay had resisted complete subordination to him, committed as he was to an "independent" labor movement in principle. Perón gave up on winning Gay's allegiance and replaced him with a more subservient Aurelio Hernández, thus finishing the creation of his "verticalist" command structure within the CGT.

The government's domination over the CGT, though great, was never as complete as Perón would have liked, despite his best efforts to assure it. It is no secret that he had to intervene many times to terminate unauthorized strikes by locals, whose leaders took it upon themselves to improve salaries and working conditions. But, each time they defied him, Perón struck back, jailing rebels and replacing them with new leaders whom he authorized to reward loyal members with more pesos. Such methods corrupted and divided the labor movement often, always presenting union bosses with difficult political choices. Their loyalty to Perón and the unity that it gave the entire movement were sources of immense power which they needed to defend themselves in a society where most power had been concentrated at the top. However, it was often in their own interest, especially after Perón fled, to ignore his orders and pursue a more self-aggrandizing strategy aimed at satisfying their own political and economic needs, sometimes by cooperating with governments he opposed. There would never be an easy way out, for even though unity brought power, it invited the kind of subjugation that many individual unions found disadvantageous to their local interests.[14]

Eva Perón added something special to her husband's arsenal of instruments for staying popular. She was the perfect populist propagandist, thriving on the adoration of the masses:

> To her followers, she was Evita, a selfless woman who worked tirelessly to improve the lives of workers, destitute women, and needy children, totally dedicated to the downtrodden because she was born poor like them, and so committed to them that she sacrificed her life on their behalf. To her enemies, however, she was only an ambitious actress, a trollop who rose to the top by using countless men, a hypocrite interested in money, jewels, and luxurious clothes, and a vengeful woman intent on accumulating power to make Argentine society pay for the shame heaped upon her because of her background.[15]

Her political career began just before his election in 1946. They had met a year before when they participated in fund raising for victims of an earthquake in the northern provinces, she a twenty-four-year-old actress of very modest fame, and he a forty-eight-year-old widower and rising power within the army. She moved in with him and watched as his campaign for the presidency began to develop, and then joined the protest when he was arrested in October 1945. She did not march the masses from their homes to the Casa Rosada as myth would have it, but was one of several from the general's inner circle to speak up for his release. It worked and they were married four days later.

He took advantage of her oratorical skill and sudden fame, making her a special liaison with the masses. For her fans she became a direct link to authorities, one that allowed them to bypass the CGT hierarchy whenever she agreed to carry their messages to cabinet ministers. She also was a very unique social worker, the director of her own Fundación Eva Perón, from which she launched projects for the young, aged, and poor in barrios around Buenos Aires. She was especially fond of holding court with poor ladies who would stand in line for hours to make their requests to her and receive money or goods in return. The Fundación's responsibilities and capital grew rapidly. By 1950, it was constructing schools, workers' resorts, and union headquarters and was one of the biggest spenders in the government. Many people benefited from its projects, but its value was always more symbolic than substantive, for it reinforced the notion that the masses had acquired benefactors whose name was Perón.[16]

Evita's projects brought inspiration to the needy, especially women, but her goal was never their "liberation" as understood by feminists today. While she thrived on the masses' adoration, she always subordinated herself to Perón publicly. He was her leader as well as theirs, she told women when she launched the Partido Peronista Feminina, the party's women's branch, in 1949. She encouraged political activism among women, but insisted that it not come at the expense of their fulfilling their duties to their husbands. This message of devotion to the masculine leader was sent into schools through the required reading of her book *La Razón de mi vida* (The Purpose of My Life), which called on children to be as dedicated to him as she was. Always feigning a humility that was transparent to all but her most devoted followers, she delighted in playing the role of the humble companion of the greatest man Argentina had ever known.

Her death in 1952 hurt Perón and his government. But it would be incorrect to blame his downfall on her absence. The working class remained loyal to him until the end, and the officers who eventually overthrew him made their first try in 1951, when she was still alive. It did take some of the glitter away, however, at a time when the economy was in trouble and he was forced to impose austerity on his supporters to deal with the crisis. For many it was like a movie ending with a tragic finish while life carried on. At the same time it gave Peronist propagandists the material for a legend of great and tragic proportions with which to remind Peronists of their origins and purpose. It was for Evita as well as themselves that they had to fight on, if only to justify her faith in them and vindicate the price that she had paid for her people. It was powerful stuff and the Peronist leadership knew it. The military's theft of her embalmed body and secret transport of it to Milan, Italy, in 1955 only helped the mythmakers who made the return of their saint a cause for unifying the flock. And it eventually paid off: Evita was brought home in 1974 when the Peronists ruled again.

A Populist Paradise Never Reached

Perón's nationalism and his populist economics were not simply the wild ideas of an unscrupulous politician out to accumulate mass support.

There was much to be concerned about in Argentina at the end of World War II. After recovering some from the depression, the country's economic future remained in doubt. Great Britain was gone as a trading partner and capital was needed to advance the nation's industrialization, but Argentines were not certain where it would come from after the war; moreover, Radical party politicians and the military opposed relying as heavily as before on foreigners to supply it. Nor were they certain how much of the European market they could capture at war's end, especially if the United States took it upon itself to supply the damaged nations the grain they needed. Some even warned of another world war that would isolate Argentina again, this one fought by the United States and the Soviet Union. Because Argentines did not want to be caught unprepared for more isolation, they felt compelled to strengthen their position economically as best they could.

Perón chose to prepare the country for the unknown by making it more independent of its trading partners with additional industrialization fostered by mass consumption. His approach was akin to that of the American New Deal except for his greater reliance on the expropriation of foreign-owned utilities and market regulation. Backed by substantial gold reserves built up during World War II, he used his authority to turn the state into the economy's manager. Crude in design and execution, the approach consisted of taking over most utilities and all banking, purchasing railways from their British owners, imposing state control over the export of commodities, and supervising labor-management relations. He also raised tariffs to protect industries from foreign competition and stimulated domestic consumption by raising real wages almost 50 percent between 1946 and 1948. In essence, he made the state more responsible than ever before for public welfare, increasing its powers and inflating its budget, guaranteeing the nation thereafter a budget deficit in which nearly everyone developed a stake.[17]

The operation relied on the country's farmers and cattlemen to finance import substitution industrialization. Cleverly adapting to his nationalist needs the system of production and price controls created by the conservatives during the 1930s to protect producers from the vicissitudes of the international market, Perón confiscated some of the farmers' profits and used them to pay for the subsidization of industry, the employment of thousands of his supporters in government jobs, and the building of the nation's infrastructure. He required farmers to sell their grain to the government at prices lower than those paid in the world market, keeping the difference to pay for his projects. The rural sector became his unwilling collaborator, and as long as they kept producing and prices stayed up, it worked. But it made him the farmers' prisoner, for by relying so much on them he placed the fate of his effort in their hands. Like all Argentine presidents after World War II, Perón wanted to exploit the country's most valuable resource in order to rebuild the economy. And like them he learned how risky this "easy road to development" really was, discovering the hard way how agriculture, though rich and bountiful, could never live up to the exaggerated demands that urban politicians placed on it.

In the short run he needed to sell grain at good prices in order to finance his scheme, but, as feared, increases in U.S. exports cut into potential markets, especially after the Marshall Plan began in 1948, when the Truman administration sent an abundance of grain to help allies in Europe with their recoveries. Then two successive droughts in Argentina reduced farm production, making it impossible to take advantage of the rise in world demand for commodities touched off in 1950 by the Korean War and economic recovery in the industrial nations. This especially hurt since income from exports was desperately needed at the time to pay for increased imports of capital goods and raw materials for industry. Consequently Argentina staggered after 1950, failing to "take off" as Perón had wanted. Peronism had brought a three-year boom, followed by a bubble that burst before it had achieved its primary objectives. In the end it was Perón who had to adjust, backing away from his nationalism and inviting foreign firms into the country again while taking away many of the workers' income gains in order to deal with unwanted recessions.

Was the Peronist solution a colossal bungle, done in by policies totally inappropriate for Argentina? It was certainly ill-timed, for at the moment that the world economy was beginning a thirty-year period of incredible growth that opened hosts of new opportunities for trade, he was coddling an industry whose high costs denied it a chance to advance through the export of manufactures, making the mistake of fighting an economic war using battle plans more appropriate to past ones.[18] Nevertheless, his making the state a grand economic patron was not really all that unique. Brazilians, Chileans, and Mexicans were doing much the same thing at the time, though a bit more efficiently than Perón did. In each country the defense of a highly protected industry became synonymous with industrialization per se; no one was concerned about its costs since the mere fact of industrialization brought so much with it, not the least of which were greater independence from the industrial nations and the employment of an expanding work force. That protection would one day make industrial exports less competitive in world markets was the least of their concerns when they started.

Ironically he proved more adept at compensating for adversity than at creating new wealth. When expansion ended he responded with tough austerity measures in 1952 that gradually restored an equilibrium of sorts and led to 5.5 percent average growth rates during his last two years. Moreover, he persuaded workers to put up with the real decline in wages induced by his stabilization policy. It is the latter that sustained the belief, even among some non-Peronists, that only he could ever get the working class to conform to austerity measures in the future and contributed to the military's bringing him home to pacify his followers in 1973.

The Peronist experiment left Argentina with a host of new problems. The public sector was bloated and the Argentine upper and middle classes even less willing than before to pay their tax bills. Industrialization had proven far more expensive than expected, and Peronist farm policy had discouraged the expansion of production at a time when ever increasing amounts of foreign exchange were needed. And infrastructure deteriorated when the Peronists found themselves unable to carry through with their construction plans after 1950. But most important, people lost what little confidence they had in government during the Peronist era, all of them, that is, but the die-hards of the Peronist movement, who would never lose theirs. Instead of bringing a new coherence to society, Perón deepened old conflicts and added new ones. Government was intensely partisan before he had come along, and was even more so after he left. The notion that authorities governed for the entire nation, balancing one interest against another, favoring some but not to the total exclusion of the others, never had taken hold in Argentina before 1945, and Perón and his successors saw to it that it did not thereafter either.

How Fascist Was It?

Histories of Perón's government abound, but satisfactory descriptions of the exact nature of Peronism remain scarce. Some contend that its original design was largely fascist, among them Marxists who see Perón as the instrument of a bourgeoisie that used him to establish state control over the proletariat in order to prevent its radicalization.[19] They are correct to some degree, for he and his military colleagues began with the idea of making the state the patron of unorganized laborers in order to block their mobilization by revolutionaries. But Marxists try too hard to demonstrate that because many of his cabinet ministers were from the middle class and were supported by small business and tenant farmers his regime was under the control of the bourgeoisie. What they neglect to note is that people from the middle class were on both sides of the Peronist divide, more of them opposing him and his scheme than joining it once its true character was known.

Others, among them prominent political sociologists, emphasize differences between the Argentine social structure and those of European nations, arguing that what distinguished Peronism was its greater reliance on the working class for its power than on the petite bourgeoisie, as was the case in fascist Europe. Had the Argentine social structure been farther along in its development, Peronism might have taken the form of European fascism; as it was, the closest that it would come was in its desire to replace the bogus liberalism of the oligarchy with a corporatism in which a strong central government imposed itself on all social sectors.[20]

There may be an even simpler explanation of what Perón wanted to do if one recalls that he took inspiration from Mussolini not Hitler, having observed the latest Italian renaissance at first hand just before the war. Italian fascism was always a bit nebulous, and the state that it established was built as much on words as it was on deeds. Of course, it did exhibit a mania for spectacular projects, most of them made from cement and steel, but what made it work as long as it did was Mussolini's determination to turn a disorderly and weak Italy into a proud and strong nation run by a popular authority. To someone like Perón who rejected bolshevism and had lost what little confidence he had in liberalism, Italy's rebirth under Mussolini was enviable and worthy of imitation. If the Italians had made a mistake, it was in going to war, something that he had no intention of doing. Working out the details of Argentina's renaissance and its corporatist organization did not really concern him much at the outset; instead, what mattered was getting the whole process started, which is what he thought he was doing when he marched Argentina forward in 1946.[21]

His treatment of opponents was as repulsive to democrats as Mussolini's had been. He drew the masses into a single party, mixing radical rhetoric with conservative, autocratic methods of direction, and when frightened by his opponents, encouraged its thugs to rough them up, steadily raising the cost of criticism and protest. The intervention of hostile newspapers and the burning of churches whose priests protested his legalizing divorce and prostitution became commonplace during his second term. Still, his operation was even less well organized than Mussolini's had been. It was, as most political innovations in Argentina are, a hastily contrived and deficient imitation of the original.

Especially frustrating was his failure to win the full confidence of entrepreneurs whom he thought he was regulating for their and the nation's own good. But they were never desperate enough to accept him as their savior, and only the most economically vulnerable and opportunistic saw advantage in going along with him. Equally troublesome was the fickleness of his colleagues in the armed forces. He had tried to penetrate the services and create a hierarchy loyal to him, but no president had managed it before and he was no exception. Nor did he find it advantageous to challenge them directly by creating an Argentine SS, fearful as he was that so provocative a step would surely prompt direct retaliation. In the end he had little choice but to rely on military friends, whom he never entirely trusted, to keep their colleagues in line.[22]

Perón was always less comfortable working on policy with the nation's industrialists, farmers, and laborers than Mussolini had been. A corporatist in spirit, he was never much of one in practice. Instead, he preferred to be everyone's commander, who ruled over them in the country's best interests. Doing otherwise was too much work and involved too many people in high circles for his taste.[23] Nevertheless, he went through the motions, twice creating government councils on which private interests were represented. But fearful of their interfering with his supervision of the country, he ignored them when critical decisions were made, preferring to rely almost entirely on conventional fiscal, monetary, and regulatory devices to induce desirable behaviors.[24]

Ambiguity not consistency characterizes Peronism as a political phenomenon. For example, Peronists competed in elections with other parties, winning a free one in 1946. But that did not stop them from abusing the rights of their critics, forcing some to flee the country and others to go underground. They favored organized labor in disputes with industry, yet they protected industry from foreign competition and came to its rescue when the economy went sour in 1952. They attacked the oligarchy and took some of the farmers' profits from them with taxes and price controls, yet they took none of their land away. They talked of corporatism, claiming to be a movement whose goal was the unification of the nation for a common purpose, but they divided it even more than before. And though Peronism was born within the military establishment, it was the Argentine army that sought to stop Perón's ascendancy in 1945, staged unsuccessful coups against him in 1951 and 1955, and finally deposed him later in 1955. He lived off ambiguity, determined to succeed in a society where a constitution and popular support did not guarantee him tenure. The oligarchs had struck back in 1930 to end the life of an elected government, and it was quite conceivable that either they or one of the opposition parties would work with the armed forces to do so again. That is why Perón's treatment of the opposition is not really surprising; he wanted to prevail in a society where one dealt harshly with one's rivals before they were able to retaliate.

It was not only popularity with the masses and intimidation of the opposition that sustained Peronists in power. To keep their powerful machine going, Peronists also relied heavily on the state's resources. It is easy to forget that Peronism was not a spontaneous phenomenon but something created by people in government to keep themselves there. As such, it relied on the government's resources as much as on union dues to sustain its operation. The idea of becoming just another political party competing in a democratic system was alien to the movement's founders. In their view the government belonged to them, and they expected its prompt return after it was taken from them in 1955.

Peronists were rapacious monopolists when they ruled the nation, never as neat or well organized as fascists are supposed to be, but nearly as disrespectful of their critics. Still, despite their verbal and physical intimidation of opponents, they never came close to taking real control over Argentine society. And throughout it all Perón worked not just for his own glory, but also to make Argentina powerful and more widely appreciated, determined to recover the respect lost when authorities had gone begging to the British after the depression. He also created the country's first welfare state, which, if not as massive as he promised, was enormous for a nation of Argentina's public resources. The country would never be quite the same again, though it was not until several presidents had tried and failed repeatedly to dismantle his highly regulatory welfare state that his achievement was fully appreciated.

The New Generation

Life did not cease for Peronists after the 1955 coup, even though their party was closed, many of its leaders were jailed, and most CGT unions were intervened in by military officers. As one of his first objectives, General Pedro Aramburu had set out to purge the CGT of Peronists, hoping to superintend the election of less politically ambitious union officials in their place. But individual federations resisted, and a new generation of Peronists emerged to lead most unions in a prolonged effort to resist persecution. With Perón gone they had to rely on their own devices to survive, developing new political strategies and tactics. Standing their ground against hostile authorities became the order of the day, as they tried to buy enough time to reorganize and mobilize the masses in campaigns to secure Perón's return from exile. It would be eighteen years before they succeeded, however, and in the interim this new generation of labor leaders learned to play a new game, opposite the one Peronists had played in the past. Now, they defended the working class against the government, and frequently mobilized union members to undermine the authority of non-Peronist presidents. It was never easy, but they fought hard and long, weakening some governments and disrupting others until the armed forces had little choice but to invite the old general back, in 1973, to restore order to the nation.[25]

The Peronists' strength came as much from their numbers as from their tactics. It is worth recalling how massive a movement Perón had created when he reorganized the CGT. By 1950 the employees of nearly all but the smallest enterprises had been drawn into the organization, and with the government's assistance, they built huge treasuries from funds extracted from employer and employee alike. In the 1960s nearly one-third of the nation's labor force still belonged to unions, far more than in any other Latin American country.[26] Of even more importance politically, more than half of the union members lived in or around Buenos Aires; this concentration facilitated mobilization for strikes and protests against authorities. Although size and concentration were no guarantee of victory in conflicts with governments that fought back, they did serve to make the complete subjugation of labor unions impossible.

What Perón's absence cost the CGT was not its power but the unity it had enjoyed while he was there to discipline rebels in its midst. No one but he could enforce the principle of *verticalidad* on the labor movement. Without him the various federations of the CGT had to settle their differences on their own, something that never came easily to so aggressive a group of labor leaders. Disagreements arose over how to respond when their party was excluded from elections and over what to do about government efforts to co-opt unions into alliances that dealt harshly with those that did not join. As a result, divisions within the CGT became common, and it was often impossible to know exactly who commanded the confederation. This pattern of fragmentation emerged as early as 1957 at the CGT convention that Aramburu had called to launch his de-Peronization effort. Although Aramburu failed, divisions did result, as federations that had never enjoyed being party to Perón's exploits rushed to escape Peronist control. When the convention ended there were three factions instead of one. The largest, calling itself the "62," claimed loyalty to Peronism. A second, the "32," separated itself from Peronism and expressed a commitment to less politicized unionism. The third faction was formed of a few remaining federations whose leaders said that they were Peronist but called themselves "independents" to indicate their desire to escape the control of Peronist politicians. During the next two decades anywhere from 50 to 80 percent of the nation's union membership belonged to the "62," sustaining its leadership of the largely Peronist working class, even though it too was often torn apart by disputes among its own members.[27]

Typical was the rivalry that arose between José Alonso, leader of the garment workers who was elected secretary general of the CGT at its convention in February 1963, and Augusto Vandor, head of the nation's powerful steelworkers union. Alonso was committed to the CGT's old line, espousing loyalty to Perón and his cause as the movement's unifying principle. Vandor, in contrast, was more independent, never entirely separating himself from Perón, but always reaching out to non-Peronist unions to form alliances devoted more to the immediate interests of labor than to the long-term ones of Peronism. He reminded one of Luis Gay, the CGT secretary whose defiance caused Perón to remove him in 1947. Calling his faction the "Azopardo" (after the street on which its headquarters was located), he charted his own strategy, ignoring orders from Perón in Spain when they conflicted with this own intentions. For example, when loyal unions decided to aim for some accommodation with the military regime that took over in 1966, Vandor led his followers into battle with the armed forces, staging massive strikes which provoked a violent response from authorities that broke their back and resulted in the government's intervention in Vandor's metallurgical workers union. Later, in 1969, he was assassinated by terrorists determined to liberate workers from their "bourgeois" leaders; Alonso was killed a year later by the same people, but their deaths only led others to sustain divisions within the movement that owed more to a growing independence among member federations than to rejection of Peronist ideals.[28]

Conflicts between individual unions and CGT leaders also resulted from changes caused by the country's further industrialization in the 1960s. Large enterprises that manufactured automobiles, chemicals, and plastics were built with the government's encouragement, most of them owned by multinational corporations. Many were placed inland, some as far north as Córdoba, where workers were housed in neighborhoods alongside factories. Their cohesion as communities was greater than was traditional in the older, leader-dominated unions, and being new and distant from the capital, they demanded more autonomy organizationally, often moving to the left ideologically to distinguish themselves from the old CGT in Buenos Aires. Some of them participated in the massive protests that occurred in Córdoba in May 1969 against the military regime; protests which, though put down by the army, led to the armed forces pulling out of the government and letting the Peronists back in four years later. The rebellion gave the Córdoba unions a new sense of power that would make them increasingly defiant of the CGT, as Perón would discover when he returned to the presidency in 1973.[29]

Whether united or working separately, labor leaders concentrated their attention as much on confrontations with authorities over their policies as on collective bargaining at the local level. This was natural since wages were so much affected by government interventions in the economy and by the implementation of successive anti-inflation stabilization programs. It also followed from the CGT's determination to make governing the nation impossible for anyone who attempted to exclude it. Using a "rubber band" strategy, which had them yielding to hostile governments one minute and then fighting back the next, CGT leaders managed to keep most governments on the defensive, making it impossible to build any foundation for post-Peronist politics. They were simply too numerous to be destroyed by force of arms and too consumed by a desire to restore Perón to power to roll over and die as a movement.

In other countries similar persecution might have radicalized the working class, but this never happened in Argentina. Most unions refused invitations from the left to vent their frustrations on capitalism itself. Perón's popularity had something to do with it, but very practical political considerations were just as influential. Peronism had given labor leaders a taste of power and it remained the shortest route to regaining it. To forsake it for more revolutionary causes would remove them even further from their objective; moreover, alliances with ideologues would have proved uncomfortable for the organization men of the CGT. The Peronists were power politicians who knew what they wanted. And it was not socialism or communism but control over the social services and wage policies that populist politics had given them. Theirs was the narrowest of visions but that was no embarrassment to them, and the more ideologues on the left attacked them for selling out the proletariat, the more stubborn they became in defending themselves. Their success in denying Marxists and anarchists access to the working class has never been complete, but it is remarkable nevertheless and remains a source of great pride to regulars in the labor hierarchy.[30]

While all of this was going on, Peronist white-collar politicians, many of whom had been senators, deputies, judges, and cabinet officers, busied themselves discovering ways to buy time until they, too, would return to power. They worked hard to assume a new respectability, although, since they were from middle- and upper-class families, this did not require much on their part. Often they went into business, helped by the entrepreneurs whom they had made wealthy when they were in office. They retained friendships with military officers who shared their nationalist beliefs, each helping the other to advance economically while plotting with and against the other politically. In short, Peronist entrepreneurs and professionals clung to their positions at the edge of the national economic establishment, advancing as best they could while waiting for Perón to come home. When they were assaulted, it was by the youthful left and not by anti-Peronist authorities. Increasingly after 1969 they were terrorized by extremists who resented their very bourgeois behavior. To defend themselves, they joined labor bosses in creating little armies of their own, which made war on terrorists, initially just out of public view. By the early 1970s, however, this violence had spilled over into the streets. With the situation getting out of control, it seemed that only Perón could bring peace to a nation in which both sides claimed to be fighting in his name. Thus it was to Perón that the nation turned in desperation in 1973.

El Retorno

The decision to let Perón return was a long time in coming. Only after military officers intent on imposing order on the country failed to do so after six years of trying did they decide to call elections. But even then it was not their intention to stand by and watch a Peronist replace them in the Casa Rosada. Instead, they hoped that either a new party led by a military officer would hold the Peronists off or that, if this failed, a coalition of non-Peronist parties would do the job. But neither alternative attracted much support, and when elections were held in March it was Juan Perón who would prevail one last time.

He campaigned for his FREJULI party, first from Spain and then during a brief visit home at the end of 1972. He promised national unity not division this time, claiming that after years of battle between the government and organized labor, only he could end the fruitless struggle and bring everyone back together again. But that was not all; while preaching unity he promised each interest that appealed to him for support exactly what it wanted: order for the military; a healthy investment climate for business; and a social revolution for the strident Peronist Youth. It was all rhetoric and everyone knew it, yet they wanted desperately to believe that he would deliver on all of his promises. Even some in the armed forces resolved that the time had come to give the seventy-seven-year-old populist a final try at ruling his people.

In retrospect it looks preposterous, of course, the old, ailing general coming home and making everything right again. But Argentines longed for order, and after nearly two decades of failing to subdue one another, Perón was all that was left, it seemed. That is why 49.5 percent of them voted for his stand-in candidate Hector Campora in March. A runoff was required, but the second-place Radicals with only 21 percent conceded and it was all over. As expected, the working class had voted Peronist, as had some in the middle class. The more laborers there were in a district and the lower their average income, the more it went Peronist, just as in the old days. The only difference this time was the addition of many young persons from the middle class who saw Perón as a vehicle for reform.[31]

Campora's presidency began on May 25, but it lasted only fifty days. He did make the most of it, however, to the displeasure of the party's old guard. He took Perón's call for reconciliation more seriously than was intended, declaring an amnesty for all "political prisoners," turning loose 370 persons, some of them well-known terrorists. A military that had seen some of its prominent members assassinated by those released took a dim view of the exercise, as they did Campora's authorizing the destruction of police files. Orthodox Peronists were no happier, fearing that Campora was starting something that he would not be able to control. So when Perón returned on June 20, they demanded Campora's removal and he gladly complied.

On July 13 Campora was ousted and Raul Lastiri, then president of the Chamber of Deputies, announced new elections for September 23, which Perón then won with 62 percent of the vote. Peace did not follow immediately, however. Instead José Rucci, secretary general of the CGT, was assassinated by terrorists who accused him and his CGT colleagues of betraying the proletariat with their bourgeois unionism. Perón did nothing at first, demanding peaceful reconciliation by all of his friends, but within a few weeks he lost his patience and turned the police and the military loose to battle with the terrorists.[32]

It was on the economic front that the Peronists seemed most at home when they began. Even before Perón returned to assume the presidency, Campora's advisors were preparing another neocorporatist solution for handling conflicts over policy among rival economic sectors. Its design was the work of nationalist businessman José Gelbard, leader of the General Economic Confederation that had been founded in the 1940s and authorized by Perón to represent the nation's entrepreneurs before his first government. Gelbard believed that orderly policy-making required advanced agreement between labor and management in all sectors of the economy. Concretely he proposed a *pacto social,* or social contract, that called a truce over wage and price policies for two years while authorities worked to reduce inflation, then hovering around 70 percent, prior to dealing in any significant way with progressive income redistribution, Peronism's most fundamental economic goal. To induce labor's cooperation he raised wages by 20 percent while freezing all retail prices. It worked, and reluctantly CGT leaders signed on, as did skeptical business leaders and representatives of most farmers' organizations.[33]

When Perón was elected in September, confidence in the *pacto* rose briefly. But it soon became obvious that even he was no match for the forces working against its completion. Labor unions had changed during his exile, many of them having secured greater independence from the CGT's leadership. As we learned, they had spent almost two decades on the defensive, fighting authorities who tried to discipline them, and now they had no intention of becoming docile again, even when the general demanded it of them. Moreover, some labor leaders, especially the younger ones from more recently industrialized cities like Córdoba, did not really trust him, having become convinced that he had compromised himself with the nation's economic elite and armed forces in order to be allowed back. Even conservative labor leaders were suspicious of him, fearful that he had neither the will nor the stamina to lead them against a revolutionary left that was challenging their control over the proletariat at the time of Perón's return. Whether he could have passed the test of either we shall never know, for just as he began to assert himself he died of natural causes on July 1, 1974, a year after coming home.[34]

They had done well economically during their first year back. The economy grew by 6.5 percent in 1973, slightly faster than the previous year, and the rate of inflation was cut in half. But the price and wage freeze lasted too long, impairing business profitability and discouraging investment, eventually causing shortages of all kinds. Equally disturbing was a sudden scarcity of foreign exchange, a consequence of the Peronists' overheating the economy while maintaining a fixed exchange rate. Moreover, import prices rose by 35 percent in 1973 and in 1974, while export prices remained constant. And, unfortunately, the European Common Market decided to add to the country's woes by banning meat imports in July 1974 in order to protect its own beef industry.[35]

Perón's death could not help but set off a power struggle within the government, given his failure to pick successors or create the means for others to do so, but it could not have come at a worse time for a *pacto* that needed renewal. His wife and vice president, Isabel, succeeded him, but she relied heavily on close friend and Social Welfare Minister José López Rega for guidance during the next months. López Rega was Perón's personal secretary in Spain, an eccentric, conservative Peronist, known by Argentines as Isabel's unscrupulous "Rasputin" for his reliance on astrology to justify his capricious and vindictive behavior. He was tied to a cadre of Peronist businessmen, some of whom wanted organized labor brought back into line, using as much force as necessary. Most labor leaders, even an old guard whose affection for the rebels in their midst was no greater than López Rega's, wanted no part of it. Neither did the Peronist Youth, themselves an obvious target for persecution given their deep penetration by revolutionary cadres. Campora had allowed each of these groups a free rein after his inauguration, but Perón, acceding to the demands of conservatives and labor bosses, had begun purging the movement of its radical youth a few months before he died, forcing many of them underground. That left a struggle for power between the movement's right wing and rebel labor leaders, a conflict that might have been avoided had it not been for López Rega's personal ambition and overconfidence, as well as his desire to make conformity with austere economic policies the test of loyalty to the movement.

He started by dismissing most of Perón's cabinet, including *pacto* designer José Gelbard.[36] That set the stage for a confrontation with the most aggressive labor unions over the renewal of the *pacto* in June 1975, one that López Rega sought and was convinced he could win. It began with the appointment of Celestino Rodrigo, a fellow member of the Peronist right wing, as economy minister. Rodrigo announced an orthodox economic stabilization plan, not unlike the one Perón had forced on his people back in 1952, aimed at taming inflation, which then was shooting up to an annual rate of 335 percent. Prices were freed, government spending cut, and wages kept under control. It was exactly the opposite of what laborers wanted after two years of *pacto* wage controls. When they protested, Rodrigo, on López Rega's advice, offered a "take it or leave it" 50 percent wage increase. But that was not enough: labor leaders balked at the insult and declared war on the government, touching off an all-out fight with López Rega and Isabel Perón. Who the winner would be was never in doubt to anyone but López Rega and his inner circle. Labor leaders mobilized the rank and file and nearly shut down the entire country from July 4 to July 8 at the cost of $66 million per day to the economy. Peronist deputies in Congress gave their support to the unions, and suddenly Isabel and López Rega found themselves isolated from the movement they were supposed to be leading. Isabel had no choice but to relent, and when she did her cabinet resigned and López Rega fled the country on July 18, not to be seen again in Argentina.[37]

Isabel Perón's government never recovered the authority that it lost from its defeat by the CGT. Efforts were made to patch up the economy but conditions only became worse, as did the level of violence caused by the intensification of warfare between terrorists and the government. By early 1976 no one was really in charge anymore. Peronism was a movement without direction, a collection of rival factions whose leaders had lost what little respect they had for each other. Everyone in society began to take cover as the country came apart, counting the days until the military took over on March 24, 1976.)

The Montoneros and Liberation

The greatest tragedy of Perón's return was not his flawed economic policy or the self-destructive battles fought between labor leaders and the Peronist right but the violence that arose before his return and escalated after he died. It had never been his intention to lead his people into a civil war or even to provoke others to fight one. But he contributed to one nevertheless by encouraging young revolutionaries to believe that they could use him to advance their own cause of true revolution. When they finally realized that he was more their enemy than friend, they went to war against Peronism as well, lumping together the Peronist "forces of occupation" with their bourgeois coconspirators and military protectors as objects for clandestine persecution. The struggle that followed was a bloody one, and Argentina is still recovering, a decade later.)

The violence that Argentines lived with in the 1970s was truly unprecedented. To be sure, political conflict had always been intense and brutality not uncommon, but never before had it bred so much personal insecurity, fear, and madness. Even in the last years of the first Peronist regime, when protests and repression rose, most people left their homes confident that they would return to them at the end of the day to spend a quiet night with their families. It was quite different in 1975 and 1976, when they feared becoming innocent victims of terrorist bombings or police reprisals. Violence had been infecting politics for some time, encouraged by the success of riots in bringing down General Juan Carlos Onganía's dictatorship in the late 1960s. Young and affluent recruits to leftist political causes embraced it with unprecedented fervor, determined to provoke a complacent society's rebellion against militarism and strong-arm Peronism. Their vision of the mass insurrection was romantic and naïve, but that did not make them any less dedicated to pursuing it by terrifying a society unaccustomed to bombs exploding in public places.

The Montoneros sprang from this new generation of idealistic, self-disciplined terrorists.) On May 29, 1970, they introduced themselves to the nation by kidnapping and killing General Pedro Aramburu, the president who had tried unsuccessfully to de-Peronize the masses in 1955 after Perón fled. They were punishing him for his misdeeds, they claimed, among them his authorizing the execution of twenty-seven Peronists and his hiding Eva Perón's embalmed corpse in Milan, Italy. But they also wanted recognition, letting the world know what they would do to the enemies of Peronism if they did not let Juan Perón back into power. Who these strange people were and why they claimed Peronism as their cause was something of a mystery at first, even to Peronist leaders, who denied any association with them.

Guerrilla warfare was not entirely new to the country, of course. As early as 1962 the Marxist-Leninist Armed Forces of Liberation (FAL) was trying to wage a rural war, and in 1967 the Che Guevara–inspired Revolutionary Armed Forces (FAR) set up its own *"foco"* in northwestern Argentina. Not long thereafter the Trotskyite Revolutionary Workers' party launched an armed unit called the People's Revolutionary Army (ERP), which functioned well into the 1970s. By the time the Montoneros came along each of these groups had tried to mount a war against Argentine authorities. Yet, it was obvious that none had met with much success as long as they were devoted to replicating rather classical guerrilla strategies.[38]

The Montoneros intended to do things differently. To begin with, they were very few in number, no more than twenty persons who operated in utmost secrecy at the time of the Aramburu operation. They had come together in 1968, some of them right-wing nationalists with fascist ideals and others advocates of their own versions of Christian liberation. Initially intent on little more than destroying authority in its existing forms, they would eventually claim revolutionary goals aimed at creating a new society, one built on the replacement of capitalism with a socialism untarnished by old-fashioned populism or the crudities of modern communism. But to do that they needed power and that is where their support for Peronism came in. Though it would later prove to be their undoing, at the time it seemed a reasonable strategy.

Like Peronist nationalists they saw Argentine history in simple terms, as a struggle between its landed oligarchy and the masses. The Peronists had led the masses into battle with the oligarchs only to be stopped by the latter's counterrevolution in 1955. To return to power the masses had to become more revolutionary than before, inspired by the likes of the Montoneros and other radical forces. The Montoneros had no illusions about winning the masses from their less revolutionary Peronist leadership overnight, but they believed that somehow they could expropriate them from Peronism, turning what had become a rather unrevolutionary, self-interested proletariat into a revolutionary force that they would lead toward the destruction of capitalism and the social structure that accompanied it. In the meantime they had to rid the country of its military government, and that required their devotion to the Peronist effort to achieve Perón's return. Short-term objectives not ultimate ones controlled their behavior initially, giving them no choice but to devote themselves to working with a Juan Perón who had no intention of releasing the masses to their care. For him they were not competitors but instruments to be used to undermine the authority of a ruling military and force their accepting his return to the presidency as the only way to restore order and legitimate government to the country. Liberation was his cause, too, but his version had little to do with socialism or revolution as Montoneros understood it.[39]

But that does not explain the Montoneros' preference for terrorism over the direct mobilization of the masses. It seems that their choice of tactics also derives from very practical considerations as well as a degree of romanticism. Little insight was needed to recognize that most workers were heads of families who could ill afford the personal sacrifices required to wage real war against the state. If battles were to be fought, less compromised youth would have to wage them, people in their twenties, some of them students. Moreover, Argentina was an urban country and it was in the cities that authorities had to be confronted; and it was there that terrorism worked best since it allowed sudden strikes followed by the perpetrators' immediate blending back into society, undetected by the police. The age of rural warfare was over in 1970, the victim of repeated defeats in Tucuman during the 1960s and the shock of Che Guevara's fiasco in Bolivia in 1968. A new kind of warfare was called for, one that could destroy authority by demonstrating the government's incapacity to protect its own members from violence. Evidencing an incredible vision, the Montoneros were convinced that by humiliating the oppressors of the working class they could win the latter to the cause of liberation no matter how bloody and disrupting their attacks on authorities became.[40]

Their daring kidnappings, robberies, and attacks on military installations as well as their celebrating the martyrdom of colleagues who "fell" to military bullets earned the Montoneros the attention they desperately sought in 1971 and 1972. They were also helped by the military's massacre of sixteen terrorists who had escaped from the Rawson Prison in August 1972. When the fleeing prisoners did not make it to an awaiting hijacked aircraft at nearby Trelew Airport in time to board it, they were captured, taken back to prison, and shot by officers embarrassed by their escape. Unintentionally, authorities made heroes of the men and women they killed, and they could do nothing but watch as Perón, seizing on the event for personal advantage, sent flowers from Spain to honor the victims.[41]

But just when the Montoneros' war was getting under way, it ended, at least temporarily. In mid-1972 General Alejandro Lanusse announced his intention to hold free elections the following year, giving the Peronists a chance to return to the offices from which they were evicted eighteen years before. When they won the election and Hector Campora was inaugurated on May 25 the Montoneros, now a few hundred in number, were among the celebrants, cheering wildly at the release of their imprisoned colleagues by the new president. It was a bizarre occasion, even in the annals of Argentine history, as the members of terrorist organizations danced in the streets, celebrating the inauguration of an elected government while the armed forces and the police they had been assaulting for over two years quietly looked on. Almost overnight the once reclusive Montoneros had become participants in constitutional politics, 8 of their members taking seats among the 145-person Peronist majority in the Chamber of Deputies.

What to do next was never all that obvious, however. Victory in elections for the cause they supported took them only halfway home, creating an opportunity to work directly with the masses without any guarantee that the new government would allow them to carry through with their plans. Moreover, they were trained in secretive, terrorist activities and not mass mobilization. To come above ground suddenly and lead the crowds did not come automatically to them. But they tried anyway, starting by rapidly expanding their influence within the Peronist Youth movement, itself the depository of a new generation of Peronist leftists. The Montoneros showed exceptional skill at recruitment, and they quickly captured leadership posts in the youth organization, to the displeasure of the government's more conservative Peronist leaders, who feared competition from a rival organization commanded by ideologues with whom they had little in common other than apparent concern for the working class. The more the Peronist Youth called on its members to "stamp on the old union leadership as if they were cockroaches," the more upset the latter became.[42]

It was obvious that the Montoneros' triumph was more apparent than real: they were heard within the new government but they were excluded from all of its most powerful posts. To compensate they threw their enthusiasm into organizing grass-roots social movements all over the country, in slums and university campuses, linking them together with something called the Tendencia Revolucionaria, an organization whose leaders promised to force the government to deliver on its revolutionary promises. But in doing so they invited an open conflict with the Peronist old guard that would doom them before they were prepared to go into battle. Peronist right wingers started the fight the day Perón returned, staging a shootout with the banner-waving Peronist Youth at Ezeiza Airport on June 20, 1973. Led by Jorge Osinde, a former security chief, Peronist thugs fired on their youthful rivals, killing 30 and wounding 300 more. Their message was clear: no matter how much Perón had egged them on before his return, revolutionaries were unwanted in the movement now that he was back.[43]

After he became president, Perón immediately declared war on the Trotskyite People's Revolutionary Army (ERP), always more avowedly anti-Peronist than the Montoneros. He also wanted to send a message to the Peronist Youth, making it clear that the time had come for them to get in line under his leadership, leaving their zeal for "liberation" behind them. But the message did not penetrate the Montoneros armor, and they continued with their calls for mass action, somehow convinced that when Perón discovered the magnificence of their efforts he would accept their achievement. The old general's patience with them was wearing thin, and then it ended abruptly at a mass rally on May Day 1974. After being interrupted several times by youthful chants of the names of slain Montoneros, Perón

lost his self-control, abandoned his national unity speech, and unleashed an attack on the Peronist Left which amounted to a declaration of war. After just fifty seconds of praise for the quality of Argentine trade unionism, hearing slogans against union leaders from the Left, Perón made his first reference to "those stupid idiots who are shouting"; but the Tendency at first did not react. Peron continued, "I was saying that through these [last] 21 years, the trade unions have remained intransigent, yet today some beardless wonders try to claim more credit than those who fought for 20 years." Soon after, having heard Montonero propagandistic slogans about two assassinated labor leaders ("Rucci, traitor, say hello to Vandor"), Perón referred ominously to "comrades who have seen their leaders assassinated without punishment having been implemented yet." He lambasted the Revolutionary Tendency as "infiltrators who work within and who in terms of treachery are more dangerous than those who work outside."[44]

At long last it became clear to the Montoneros that Perón had abandoned them. If any doubts remained, López Rega dispelled them after Perón's death when he sent his own neofascist terrorist organization, the Argentine Anti-Communist Alliance, or Triple A, after them, instructing his men to liquidate suspected Montoneros. As part of its crusade the government closed the Montoneros' newspapers, denied them permission to hold rallies, and fiercely broke up their demonstrations. Locked out of the government and denied any opportunity to influence it, the Montoneros decided to go back underground in September 1974. Drawing on the reservoir of support they had created during the previous year among students and the poor, they began a new campaign of terrorism, commanding one of the mightiest urban guerrilla organizations ever to exist in Latin America.[45]

They raised money by kidnapping wealthy businessmen and holding them for ransom, securing $70 million in 1975, and then purchasing the weapons they used to assassinate labor leaders and right-wing Peronists. In mid-1975 they expanded operations to include attacks on military installations and police stations, and during 1976 killed or seriously injured 300 persons. Retaliation came, as they expected, but it was not until the military took over in March that it began to overwhelm them with its ruthlessness. In the past when terrorists were caught they were sent to prison, where they were tortured but usually kept alive. Not any longer. On orders from the highest command, military intelligence and paramilitary units abducted whomever they wished (averaging fifteen per day during the last quarter of 1976), took them to secret concentration camps, tortured them for information about their colleagues, and then killed them without even recording their deaths. Many of their victims were not terrorists but young people who had participated in the social works of the Tendencia Revolucionaria when the Montoneros had gone above ground to mobilize their mass movement during the first months of the Campora government. Some were also Montoneros who revealed the location of their colleagues while under torture, making it possible for the armed forces to rip their organization apart in one year. In early 1977 those who remained at large gave up, nearly one thousand of them fleeing abroad, most taking refuge in Mexico City, Havana, and Caracas.[46]

Many lessons were learned from the painful experience. The Montoneros knew that they had naïvely overestimated their ability to win Perón to their side and had waited too long to admit their mistake. They had also underestimated the average Argentine's aversion to terrorism of any kind and how easy it would be for the armed forces to convince even the working class that its acts of repression were all that separated society from chaos and destruction in 1976. Peronists also learned many things, the most obvious of which were the costs of forming alliances with people much more radical than themselves. Radical revolutionaries are incompatible mates for the rather bourgeois Peronist leadership. Most labor leaders are part of the nation's diverse and disjoined political "establishment," threatened as much as merchants and bankers by a radical redistribution of power. They will use whomever they can to reconquer government when they are excluded from office but once back they will not share power with such allies. The Montoneros, in their zeal to fashion an innovative kind of liberation, one that was supposed to join Peronist nationalism with their version of mass revolution, never accepted such realities of power and interest until they had been destroyed by their illusions.

An End and a Beginning

Perón's last presidency was the victim of its own contradictions, the most destructive of which was between his desire for political reconciliation and his need to promote political conflict in order to force the military to bring him back. He could not turn political violence on and off as he had done many years before. From exile he had promoted the growth of two conflicting movements, one run by labor leaders devoted to protecting their privileges and the other by youthful ideologues who wanted to give real power to workers. Always confident of his Machiavellian wisdom, Perón played with both, convinced that he could draw on their energies at will. But his political habits were those of another era, totally inappropriate for a new age of much more extremist politics. He had rediscovered a country that was beyond his power to govern. It was a land in crisis, both economic and political, one wracked by a war between the left and right, and one without a ruling class with enough power to restore order. Old age and ill health slowed Perón down, but it was Argentine society that defeated him in 1974, as it would have any other Peronist who tried to govern under such circumstances.

The Peronist return in 1973 proved a debacle for Argentina. It was also a boon to the movement's opponents within the upper and middle classes and to military officers determined to reconstruct the nation's politics according to their own design. The latter had tried and failed in 1966, but that did not weaken their desire to try once more in 1976. Why people in uniform should be so ambitious for themselves and their nation yet perform so badly each time they try to govern it is a question that cannot be answered without a closer look at the country's *partido militar.*

Notes

1. Joseph Page, *Perón: a Biography* (New York: Random House, 1983), pp. 22–23. Page's lengthy biography is the best compilation of events in Perón's political career yet available.

2. Ibid., pp. 34–35.

3. On the origins of lodges in the Argentine army and the purposes they served in the 1920s and 1930s, see Robert Potash, *The Army and Politics in Argentina: 1928–1945* (Stanford: Stanford University Press, 1969).

4. The controversial GOU is examined in ibid., chs. 7–8; and Page, *Perón,* ch. 5.

5. The most notorious example of such legend building was *La Razón de mi vida,* a book ostensibly written by Eva Perón that was made required reading in all schools. In it Eva tells of Perón's magnificent rise to power to serve the Argentine masses and of her complete devotion to him and his cause, making herself an example of the loyalty expected of everyone else. Thousands of copies were burned by his enemies when Perón was overthrown in 1955, but reprintings in later years make it available today.

6. Hiroschi Matsushita, *Movimiento obrero argentina: 1930–1945* (Buenos Aires: Siglo Veinte, 1983).

7. Ibid., pp. 273–298. In his book Matsushita offers the most thoroughly documented study yet of labor politics before and during Perón's rise. He stresses the importance of fundamental changes in posture by the government and the old labor leadership in May 1944, claiming that opportunism won out over ideology on both sides and established the basis for Perón's capture of the labor movement during the following year.

8. Few events in Argentine history have more written about them than those that occurred in October 1945. Probably the most complete account is Felix Luna, *El 45* (Buenos Aires: Sudamericana, 1971). Also see Nicholas Fraser and Marysa Navarro, *Eva Perón* (New York: Norton, 1980), ch. 4.

9. Ray Josephs, *Argentine Diary: The Inside Story of the Coming of Fascism* (New York: Random House, 1944), p. 261.

10. Ibid.

11. Relations between the United States and Argentina between 1943 and 1946 were obviously more complex than described here, as recent research into State Department records reveals. See Carlos Escude, *Gran Bretaña–Estados Unidos y la declinacion argentina: 1942–1949* (Buenos Aires: Belgrano, 1983); and Mario Rapoport, *Gran Bretaña, Estados Unidos y las clases dirigentes argentinas: 1940–1945* (Buenos Aires: Belgrano, 1980).

12. On the election campaigns, see Luna, *El 45.*

13. Alberto Ciria, "Peronism and Political Structures: 1945–1955," in *New Perspectives on Modern Argentina* (Bloomington, Ind.: Latin American Studies Program, 1972), pp. 1–7.

14. Ruben H. Zorrilla, *El liderazgo sindical argentino: desde sus origenes hasta 1975* (Buenos Aires: Siglo Veinte, 1983), pp. 28–39.

15. Marysa Navarro, "Evita and Peronism," in *Juan Perón and the Reshaping of Argentina,* ed. Frederick Turner and José Enrique Miguens (Pittsburgh: University of Pittsburgh Press, 1983), p. 15.

16. Ibid., pp. 18–25. Also see Fraser and Navarro, *Eva Perón.*

17. On Peronist policy, see Gary W. Wynia, *Argentina in the Postwar Era: Economic Policy Making in a Divided Society* (Albuquerque: University of New Mexico Press, 1972), pp. 47–80.

18. This point is made very effectively by Guido Di Tella, "La Argentina economica (1943–1973)," *Criterio* (navidad 1982): 746–763.

19. The latest attempt to portray Peronism as the fascist enemy of real proletarian revolution is Juan José Sebreli's *Los deseos imaginarios del peronismo* (Buenos Aires: Legasa, 1983).

20. See Gino Germani, "Fascism and Social Class," in *The Nature of Fascism,* ed. S. J. Woolf (London: Weidenfeld, 1968); and *Política y sociedad en una epoca de transición* (Buenos Aires: Paidos, 1968).

21. I am grateful to Paul Johnson's insights into Italian fascism for this comparison. See *Modern Times: The World from the Twenties to the Eighties* (New York: Harper Colophon Books, 1985), pp. 96–103.

22. This comparison draws heavily on descriptions of European fascism offered by Renzo de Felice in *Interpretations of Fascism* (Cambridge: Harvard University Press, 1977), ch. 1.

23. Wynia, *Argentina in the Postwar Era,* pp. 52–61.

24. Ibid., ch. 2.

25. Marcelo Cavarozzi, "Unions and Politics in Argentina, 1955–1962," Wilson Center Working Paper, no. 63, pp. 4–12.

26. Data on employment are taken from Kuhl, *Una política industrial para la Argentina,* p. 117; and on labor membership from Zorrilla, *El liderazgo sindical argentino,* p. 129. The high percentage of union membership is explained in part by Argentina's lack of a large rural labor surplus.

27. Zorrilla, *El liderazgo sindical argentino,* p. 129.

28. Ibid., pp. 60–68.

29. On labor during this period, see Ruben Rotondaro, *Realidad y cambio en el sindicalismo* (Buenos Aires: Pleamar, 1971).

30. I am grateful to Eldon Kenworthy's comments on the Cavarozzi paper for having pointed out this retention of perspective and its causes. See Cavarozzi, "Unions and Politics in Argentina," p. 18.

31. José Enrique Miguens, "The Presidential Elections of 1973 and the End of an Ideology," in Turner and Miguens, *Juan Perón and the Reshaping of Argentina.* Also see Manual Mora and Peter Smith, "Peronism and Economic Development: The 1973 Elections," in ibid.

32. The eventful year of 1973 is neatly summarized in Gerardo Lopez Alonso, *Cincuenta años de la historia argentina* (Buenos Aires: Belgrano, 1982), pp. 270–285.

33. The program is described in some detail in Guido Di Tella, *Perón–Perón 1973–1976* (Buenos Aires: Sudamericana, 1983), ch. 3; and Horacio Maceyra, *Campora/Perón/Isabel* (Buenos Aires: Centro Editor de América Latina, 1983), ch. 4.

34. On dissent within the Peronist movement during Perón's last months, see Jorge Luis Bernetti, *El peronismo de la victoria* (Buenos Aires: Legasa, 1983).

35. Guido Di Tella, "The Economic Policies of Argentina's Labor-Based Government, 1973–1976," Wilson Center Latin American Program Working Paper, no. 47, p. 14.

36. Maceyra, *Campora/Perón/Isabel,* ch. 7.

37. Lopez, *Cincuenta años de la historia argentina,* pp. 324–327; and Maceyra, *Campora/Perón/Isabel,* ch. 7.

38. The history of these and other guerrilla organizations is summarized in James Kohl and John Litt, *Urban Guerrilla Warfare in Latin America* (Cambridge, Mass.: MIT Press, 1974), ch. 4.

39. Celia Szusterman, "Review and Commentary," *Journal of Latin American Studies* 16 (1984): 157–170.

40. Ibid., pp. 79–84.

41. Kohl and Litt, *Urban Guerrilla Warfare in Latin America,* pp. 333–334.

42. Richard Gillespie, *Soldiers of Perón* (New York: Oxford University Press, 1980), p. 121.

43. Kohl and Litt, *Urban Guerrilla Warfare in Latin America,* p. 333.

44. Gillespie, *Soldiers of Perón,* pp. 149–150.

45. Ibid., pp. 160–163; Montonero leader Mario Firmenich announced their war against Peronist authorities at a secret press conference on September 6, 1974.

46. Ibid., p. 251.

4

El Partido Militar

Argentines were never less fond of their armed forces than in 1983 when they paused to contemplate what their soldiers had done to them during the previous decade. At least 8,000 citizens had been killed by military and paramilitary personnel, most of them in secret after being tortured in detention centers all over the country. And as if that were not enough, the military government went to war with Great Britain only to suffer a humiliating defeat and the loss of 712 soldiers and sailors, most of them draftees. In 1983 many people wanted their military to vanish, but it was not to be. When democratic governments tried to subdue and shrink them, they held their ground, rebelled a little, and survived with most of their organizations intact. Obviously the *partido militar* was too much a part of the nation's politics to disappear so quickly.[1]

Nor should we expect it to vanish, for the military's political involvement is just as much a part of national life as party politics are. To begin with, officers

> have taken power repeatedly for the simple and actually rather banal reason that the civilians have not managed our affairs of state very adequately. Military coups are like artillery projectiles, which explode not on their own account but because of those who load and fire them. Thus our present [in 1981] "authoritarian" situation is not the responsibility of the military but of all of us.[2]

Politicians for years had readily accepted corporals, generals, and admirals as "colleagues" in a complex and at times byzantine game.[3] The script and the cast of characters changed often, but at one time or another members of the lower, middle, and upper classes, as well as leaders of labor, industry, and agriculture, have turned to the armed forces for help in the solution of political and economic problems that they could not solve by themselves. The military once responded cautiously, acting like the reluctant partner in an unsought courtship, but when officers carried out their first coup on September 6, 1930, they accepted new responsibilities, thereafter becoming a self-proclaimed "guardian of the constitution" that considered itself above civilian law. As if to make their point, they have deposed six constitutional presidents since 1930—four of them after 1955—as well as six of their own de facto ones; and they have supplied the nation with presidents during eighteen of the past forty years.

Professionalism the Argentine Way

Military officers were not supposed to become politicians. The oligarchs who created the nation's modern armed forces wanted a professional military able to defend the country while leaving the affairs of state to them. That is why a president like Domingo Faustino Sarmiento, intent on "civilizing" the country, founded its first military college in 1870 and a naval academy soon thereafter. At the turn of the century a war college was added and a German colonel appointed its acting director. Professionalization requires expertise, institutional autonomy, internal control, and the creation of a sense of corporate identity. Formal rules must prevail over informal ones, while quality of performance and seniority serve as the basis for promotion. It was to achieve these ends that German instructors were hired, compulsory military service for twenty-year-old males made law, and statutes developed to regulate military careers, from recruitment through promotion and retirement. It seemed to work at first, and officers soon developed a real sense of professional purpose, performing initially as loyal servants of civilian authorities.[4]

While the army was taking its instruction from the powerful Germans, the navy emulated the British, then ruler of the Atlantic. Argentina's first admirals purchased English ships and copied British organization. Considering themselves more sophisticated technically and more worldly than army generals, they recruited the sons of wealthy Anglophiles to their service. Their elitism has declined some with time, but they retain a very separate identity and still enjoy a rivalry with the larger army.[5]

Professionalization did not keep soldiers out of politics very long, however. The Radical party, excluded from office by ruling oligarchs at the turn of the century, recruited individual officers and soldiers to participate in the several unsuccessful insurrections that they staged to drive the oligarchs from office. Later in 1916, when the Radicals finally were allowed to govern, President Hipólito Yrigoyen repaid his rebellious military allies with reimbursements of the salaries they had lost when forced into retirement as punishment for having cast their lot with the Radicals. When charged with politicizing the military with such payoffs, Yrigoyen defended his right to do so, claiming that he was doing little more than rewarding officers who had understood that their "primordial obligations to country and constitution [were] far superior to all military regulations."[6] When officers removed Yrigoyen a decade later they would make the same claim, to his dismay and everlasting regret.

What unity there was within the services disappeared in the 1920s as officers disagreed over the propriety of the Radicals playing politics with them. Yrigoyen frequently sent the army to intervene in provinces and remove opposition officials, ostensibly to eradicate corruption, and many officers resented being used as if they were members of the president's political fraternity. At the same time, some among them devoted their energies to political debate within secret lodges formed by officers who were concerned about defining the military's role in society in more activist ways. It was from such lodges that a new generation sprang to the aid of oligarchs who had grown petrified by the Radicals' ineptness in dealing with the depression that struck Argentina in 1929. Led by retired General José Uriburu, they plotted for three months in mid-1930, some of them inspired by Uriburu's proposal to replace constitutional politics with fascism. The coup came on September 6, 1930, but Uriburu lasted only a short time, his fanatical nationalism and dreams of corporatism being too much for an oligarchy that felt more comfortable with their old constitutional charade.

The coup set a precedent that would be emulated many times afterward. By stepping in and taking it upon themselves to "organize" the nation's affairs, the armed forces became a legitimate participant in the nation's politics, one that every interest would thereafter consider a potential ally. They had in effect become the *partido militar,* a political organization with commitments that obligated future generations of officers to assume responsibility for the nation's governance whether in office or not.[7]

Officers opposed to Uriburu's extremist politics replaced him with more moderate General Agustín P. Justo, whom the oligarchy then elected president in a rigged contest. But divisions among officers over the country's direction persisted. At one extreme were so-called legalists, who preferred constitutional government. Their convictions were strong enough to cause them to launch unsuccessful coups against Justo in 1932 and 1934. They were opposed by authoritarian "corporatists," who had backed Uriburu only to lose out to Justo. Most officers positioned themselves between these two extremes, however, content either to help the oligarchy defend its fraudulent democracy or to stay out of politics altogether.[8] Political division within the military did not end in the 1930s, but has persisted to this day. Legalists supportive of constitutional democracy have reappeared in every generation, as have authoritarians. This is why a military that seems entirely fascist in its objectives can be heard to praise the virtues of democracy. Their chameleonlike political behavior reflects honest differences among them, as well as the preference of many for leaving the nation's supervision to civilians, fearful that their involvement in politics will breed internecine conflicts that will undermine their operating as a professional organization.

Until 1943 the oligarchy was served well by the armed forces, but the marriage was doomed to failure by the incompatibility of the military's ambitions for the country's economic modernization and the oligarchs' inertia. In the 1930s the officer corps doubled in size and so did their ambitions. Secret lodges thrived during World War II, as soldiers debated diplomatic posture and economic strategy just as civilians were doing. When the war began, seventeen of thirty-four general officers in the army had undergone training in Germany, making most of them pro-Axis in sentiment and insistent on a policy of neutrality in the face of British and U.S. pressure on the civilian oligarchy to declare war against the Germans.[9] Discontent with the oligarchy's flirtations with the Allies grew within some lodges, as did a feeling of descent into helplessness in the face of war-induced economic isolation. Nationalistic officers wanted a strong Argentina and became convinced that the armed forces would have to take it upon themselves to change the nation's direction. Never in complete agreement over what direction to take once in charge, they put the lessons they had learned in 1930 to work, organizing a coup to evict the oligarchs in June 1943.

Two competing military factions joined in the conspiracy, one liberally inclined and the other corporatist. While liberals dominated the coup's original leadership, they were never completely in charge afterward. Both factions found places in the new cabinet and contested for influence over the nation's course. Two issues, one domestic and the other foreign, divided them. The former involved a choice between holding free elections or creating a "permanent" authoritarian government of some kind, and the latter between staying neutral or declaring war on the Axis powers. There was no easy way out of the dilemma, and President Ramirez vacillated as long as possible, finally breaking relations with Germany in February 1944 and announcing elections for later that year. But the triumph of the pro-Allies liberals was only temporary, for while they did get the election they wanted, it was won not by a liberal but by nationalist Juan Perón.[10] What really disturbed Perón's rivals within the armed forces was his defeating them at their own game by mobilizing enough popular support to win a free election, something it was thought the nationalists, with their disdain for democracy, could never do. They tried to block Perón's ascent, as we learned in the previous chapter, but showed themselves most inept in doing so, effectively giving up when they released him from prison and turned him back to his *descamisados* on October 17, 1945.

Why rival officers did not just leave Perón in jail and put down the demonstrations violently is not self-evident. No doubt disagreements among service commanders over his imprisonment weakened their ability to stand firm. Moreover, he had many allies within the government who argued against taking on the workers directly in what was sure to be a bloody confrontation with lasting effects on the military's political legitimacy. Officers fear the masses and have never welcomed a war with them. They want to be respected for their leadership as well as their power and were desperate in 1945 to avoid contributing to the alienation and radicalization of the working class. In the end Perón gave them a way out, one that was preferable to continuous conflict between military authorities and the masses, even if risky.[11]

He glorified the armed forces, giving them a prominent position in the manufacture of weapons and in the creation of a steel industry. But the country's soldiers were never at home with his personalistic politics and conspiratorial ways; nor did they warm to the demagogic power accumulated by Evita, becoming most offended when Perón suggested her for the vice presidency in 1951. That same year his opponents in the army, with substantial support from the navy and air force, attempted a coup against him but lost when most of the army remained loyal. He punished the conspirators with imprisonment, but that did not deter more plotting against him, much of it picking up momentum during his battle with the Catholic church over the legalization of divorce in 1954. In June 1955 another coup was attempted, only to fail, but three months later the military succeeded, driving Perón into exile without his asking the masses to go to the streets to defend him.

Anti-Peronist Crusades

Perón's overthrow put the armed forces deeper into politics than ever before, increasing among them the conviction that they were all that stood between the nation and its self-destruction. One does not remove the leader of the country's most popular party and turn its governance over to the minority easily, even less so in an Argentina where Peronists believe that they alone are the nation's only legitimate rulers. Nor was it realistic to expect that his flight would spell the end of Peronism as a cause or political force. Yet that is precisely what General Pedro Aramburu and his cohorts set out to accomplish once they were firmly established by the end of 1955. But doing it proved more difficult than they had anticipated, and when a CGT convention was finally held in 1957 its members elected a new generation of leaders loyal to Perón, leaving the military where it had begun.

The Peronists' stubborn resistance to dismemberment left the armed forces with another political dilemma from which there was no easy escape. They wanted to create a civilian government able to direct the nation, one that was neither Peronist nor too feeble to deal with the Peronist opposition. When they began planning for the restoration of constitutional government they found themselves with just three options, none of which was satisfactory. They could hold free elections and accept a likely Peronist victory. Or they could hold elections and exclude them from participating, allowing the creation of a weak, minority government to whose destruction the Peronists would undoubtedly commit themselves. Or, finally, they could govern by themselves, something they were not yet convinced they could do satisfactorily. Not surprisingly they chose the second option, knowing full well that they were inviting Peronists to reject the entire constitutional process by excluding them. Claims that the Peronists' undemocratic behavior necessitated their exclusion were convincing to officers and the heads of other parties who wanted the government for themselves, but the working class would have none of it, declaring that any government so created would be illegitimate and the object of protests.

The script was written in 1958 and the charade acted out during the next eight years. Arturo Frondizi, the Radical party's candidate, won the presidential election that year, helped out by making an agreement with Perón that brought him votes in exchange for his promise to legalize a Peronist party during his tenure. But the CGT soon turned against Frondizi, depriving him of anything resembling majority support. He legalized its party nevertheless, only to be defeated by it in gubernatorial elections in 1962 and then deposed by the military for having permitted a Peronist triumph.

What to do next touched off a bitter conflict between factions within the armed forces that ended only after blood was shed by both sides. Army Commander Juan Carlos Onganía led one group, called the Azules, most of whom came from the cavalry and claimed the restoration of constitutional government as their cause. In rebellion against them stood anticonstitutionalist Colorados, who drew on the infantry, the engineer corps, and the navy for their support. Each wanted to decide what the armed forces' politics would be over the next few years.

For nearly six months they maneuvered against one another, eventually moving troops into positions and engaging in brief battles on a few military bases. With the critical support of the air force the Azules finally gained the upper hand, but not before retired General Benjamín Menéndez, a leader in the 1951 coup attempt against Perón, had led a last Colorado charge.[12] Colorado marines sent by the navy took over much of the city of La Plata just to the south of Buenos Aires as well as portions of the port in the capital. Simultaneously sailors on the Punta Indio and Puerto Belgrano bases announced their rebellion against Azule authorities. Azule armored units struck back, subduing Punta Indio but only after absorbing blows from naval air attacks. The Colorados gave up finally, and the Azules went ahead with their plan for elections in 1963. They also devoted themselves to unifying the armed forces once the dust had settled.[13]

The Azules prohibited Peronist candidates once again when elections were held in 1963, this time giving the victory to Radical Arturo Illia with only 25 percent of the popular vote. For the next three years the CGT harassed Illia's administration, gradually discrediting its authority and provoking another coup in 1966. Ironically the same officers who had fought within the armed forces to assure that constitutional government and military professionalism were restored led the coup against Illia in 1966, General Juan Carlos Onganía himself becoming president afterward. Illia's brief tenure had actually given Onganía the time he needed to unite the military in preparation for its trying to govern the country by itself. Military officers cannot run the country if they are at odds with each other. But once united by common convictions and purpose their chances of success are vastly improved, or so they believed when they set out to remake Argentina in their own image on June 28, 1966.[14]

Why Bureaucratic Authoritarianism?

The creation of military regimes in Brazil in 1964 and Argentina in 1966 devoted to ruling indefinitely was unprecedented and demands some explanation. Unfortunately, scholars have yet to agree on exactly what caused this strange departure from past behavior.[15] The most popular account views it as a political consequence of incomplete industrialization and class conflict in highly dependent countries. For two decades they had been modernizing their economies using a strategy of import substitution industrialization. But early in the 1960s the momentum generated by the creation of consumer goods industries had faded, putting pressures on authorities faced with rising expectations of a working class that had grown powerful with industrialization. Conflicts over too few goods grew, and civilian governments tried to patch them over with pacification measures that proved inflationary and economically destabilizing. Eventually it became obvious that in order to produce more and import less, industrialization had to be "deepened" with the addition of basic industries. That could be accomplished, however, only with the participation of multinational corporations, who were reluctant to invest in countries wracked by social conflicts that their leaders seemed too weak politically to resolve. Something more powerful was needed and bureaucratic authoritarianism was one source of such power. Advised by civilian and military technocrats devoted to attracting new capital from at home and abroad, officers took over and did as they were told, making it clear that they would govern their countries until they were satisfied that they had changed society enough to guarantee transition to orderly and highly disciplined civilian rule.[16]

There is a certain plausibility to such a story, at least in the Argentine case, since it describes the obvious conflicts generated by populism and insufficient and inconsistent economic growth. The efforts of the Onganía government to attract foreign investment after it took over lends further credibility to it. But one risks oversimplification by looking only at economic causes of such political change. Politics is conditioned and constrained by economic realities, but it is seldom caused by them alone. The officers who evicted Illia in 1966 had more on their mind than just economic growth. Equally influential was the political impasse into which they had put the country in 1955 and the frustration it had bred among them and much of the nation's upper and middle classes. The "Peronist problem" was very real to them, especially after watching the CGT use its *plan de lucha* to harass the Illia government, making it seem helpless before the country's fundamental political problem. Another solution had to be tried, and governing by themselves until they had de-Peronized the nation was all that was left.[17]

If they needed grand ideas to help them justify their new crusade, Onganía and his colleagues found it in the national security doctrine that had been maturing in the region's war colleges during the 1950s and 1960s. The Brazilians had advanced it the furthest, having taken their inspiration from President Truman's anticommunist containment strategy and the counterinsurgency doctrines advanced by the French in their efforts to put down rebellion in Algeria. An added incentive came from Fidel Castro's triumph in Cuba in 1959 and the threat that Castro-inspired insurgents posed to militaries all over the hemisphere. To avert a similar fate Brazilian officers concentrated their energies on designing a war plan aimed at defeating the radical left in their midst.

The result, as prepared and taught at its war college, became the national security doctrine.[18]

Onganía appreciated the homework that the Brazilians had done for him. In early August 1964 he warned during a visit to the U.S. Military Academy at West Point that it had become the mission of Latin America's militaries to protect their countries against "exotic ideologies" that could upset authority in their republican systems. Back in Argentina the general's warnings were taken more seriously than they were at West Point, and it was not long before conservative magazines were predicting that he was on his way to becoming "an Argentine de Gaulle."[19]

The doctrine was an approach to politics that specialized in the identification of man's enemies. Marx was one of them, and Freud, the destroyer of families, another. Neither belonged in the loyal, patriotic society that the military wanted. But even they were not the source of the problem, just manifestations of it. More fundamental were flaws in human nature that had allowed excessive passion and aggression to go uncontrolled by reason. According to one Brazilian military theorist,

> . . . The general and growing insecurity in which distressed mankind is struggling today is the venomous opium that gives rise to and feeds these awful visions, able meanwhile to become a monstrous reality. The insecurity of citizens within the nation and the insecurity of the State facing other States, the omnipresent vision of war—civil war or subversive war or international war—dominate the world of our times and explain the neurotic distress with which panic-stricken crowds and the helpless persons, the disillusioned and afflicted peoples, and finally humankind rises up and complains and struggles, ready for slavery if some lords or tyrants offer them on a dish of lentils a little security and peace.[20]

To General Golbery, the author of this statement (and advisor to Brazilian military presidents after 1964), people were consumed by a "venomous opium," reality was "monstrous," and crowds were "panic-stricken," and "helpless and disillusioned" by "war." When confronted with social tension people became "neurotic victims" of it, always yielding to aggressors who threatened their safety or promised to feed them. People were weak and vulnerable and, therefore, had to be protected by those stronger than themselves, the best of them being military officers educated in these "truths" at war colleges and sworn to the nation's protection against itself. That soldiers might appear to be as uncivilized as society's worst enemies when they were at war with them did not concern Golbery, convinced as he was that the repression they practiced was more than justified by the ends that they pursued.

The Christian faith also compelled the military to action. To them the newer theologies of liberation, then popular at the grass roots all over Latin America, betrayed the beliefs of traditional Catholicism, subverting hierarchical authority in the church as well as in society. Without his own armies to do battle with betrayers of the faith, the Pope needed all the help that he could get from secular militaries, they rationalized, convinced that their defense of a medieval Christianity moralized their effort. Communism was the enemy of Christianity and capitalism, so those who criticized either were taken to be communist and deserving destruction. It was an old refrain, but to military officers who had watched Fidel Castro put their Cuban colleagues to the firing squad in 1959 and then pronounce himself a communist, it was a very persuasive one, especially in Argentina and Brazil. But even more important, it served as a convenient rationalization for a new kind of military intervention, one that sought to demobilize organized labor and the proponents of radical reform simultaneously. Proletarian resistance to authority had to be ended, as did all other sources of conflict, and the doctrine told everyone why their survival as nations depended on its being done.[21]

An Authoritarian Experiment

The Argentine military is wedded to political simplicity, so when it took over in 1966 it announced that it was going back to basics, telling the nation,

The Armed Forces, interpreting the highest common interest, assumes the responsibility, not to be relinquished, of guaranteeing national unity and making general welfare possible, incorporating into the country the modern elements of culture, science, and technology. By so doing, they make a substantial change that raises the country to the place that it deserves, given the intelligence and human values of its inhabitants and the wealth with which Providence has endowed its territory.[22]

"Responsibility, not to be relinquished" was the key phrase, a reminder to everyone that the military would thereafter remain the judge and jury in national politics, whether in office or not. Onganía and his colleagues were as convinced as General Uriburu had been in 1930 that "only the armed forces, with their code of honor, patriotism, and superior sense of organization and discipline, could provide the leadership necessary to bring about a national revitalization."[23] Politics, as traditionally practiced in the country, was no longer affordable. Argentina had known enough of opportunism, disorder, demagoguery, and immorality. To eliminate such vices Onganía offered two solutions, one visionary and the other quite concrete. The vision was of a new social order, more coherent and socially integrated than before, and one in which something called "spiritual unity" replaced egoism as the principal determinant of human conduct, establishing a community ethic to replace individual ones. At its worst, it reflected a pathetic craving for the conversion of Argentina into the homogeneous and unified society that it never had been.[24]

The vision also had a longitudinal dimension, one that viewed the world's salvation as a progression that went through at least three separate stages. Having learned in the war college how economic, social, and political forces were related, officers knew that each had to be changed in order to affect the other. Onganía wanted to begin with the economy, then turn to the social and political structures to complete the nation's transformation. Somehow, once basic economic problems were solved, conversion of the populace to a new community ethic that bred consensus and harmony would follow, yielding conflict-free politics. It was as if officers had read texts about the coherence of a British or German society and thought that it could be replicated through their autocratic direction, ignoring for the time being that their authoritarianism would breed its own antithesis of opposition and protest.[25]

Onganía's concrete objectives were of a more familiar kind. He closed the legislature, outlawed all political parties, and took over the General Confederation of Labor, cutting off all channels of protest until his economic program was completed. Then he delegated immense authority to Economics Minister Adalbert Krieger Vasena, an internationally respected economist who had served in previous military governments. Krieger Vasena contended that the Argentine economy was plagued by incredible inefficiencies in the private as well as the public sector, most of them induced by excessive subsidization, overextended welfare programs, and an undisciplined working class. Accordingly, he announced a series of policies aimed at reducing the public sector deficit, raising taxes, cutting import tariffs, establishing wage controls and voluntary price controls, and allowing foreign investors easier access. And before long it seemed to take effect: inflation fell to its lowest level in three decades; investment rose; and the protests of organized labor were successfully repressed. Moreover, by enticing some union leaders into cooperating with the government while repressing others it seemed as if Onganía and his advisors had at last outmaneuvered their toughest opponent.[26]

But working-class docility was only temporary, and in May 1969 the government was wracked by an outburst of public protests, later known as the Cordobazo. They began slowly, escalating as violence increased on both sides, starting on May 15 when confrontations between university students and police during a protest against increases in cafeteria prices in the northern province of Corrientes resulted in one student's death. Two days later another student was killed when sympathetic students in Rosario also protested, and then one more on May 21, the latter only fifteen years of age. Indignation spread, but it was only when students in the interior city of Córdoba organized mass demonstrations with workers in the auto industry, themselves frustrated by Onganía's repression of organized labor, that it turned into a major assault on the president's authority. On May 29 workers left their factories to march on the city, challenging police as they did, putting up barricades, burning automobiles, foreign-owned businesses, and anything else they could find, defying authorities as long as they could. Finally the army was sent in, killing 12 persons in two days and injuring at least 100 while taking hundreds prisoner, including prominent labor leaders, whom it sentenced in military tribunals. In the end the army won, as the protestors knew it would, but peace had been broken and with it confidence in Onganía's reconstruction of a new nation. He tried to pass the blame to others, even dismissing the highly successful Krieger Vasena, but the damage done was irreparable. He had done the one thing that no authoritarian military president can afford to do in Argentina: he had allowed his people to demonstrate his failure to subdue them as he had promised to do.[27]

It may seem strange that a government as strong as Onganía's, one that had successfully put down the Córdoba riots, would allow the event to induce self-doubt. But it happens often among officers, and no amount of chest beating seems sufficient to overcome their fundamental political insecurity. They know how difficult subduing a society of which they are a contributing member really is. Too many forces have accumulated too much power and skill in wielding it to yield easily to their would-be oppressors. The working class is among them. Because their conformity with government policy is so essential to its success, no government can endure working-class defiance for very long. Officers were aware of all this, having witnessed Perón's mobilization of the working class and General Aramburu's failure to "de-Peronize" it after his expulsion. General Onganía and his colleagues had also watched the intensely partisan CGT vengefully devour the Radical party governments created in 1958 and 1963 in elections from which Peronist candidates had been excluded. When they took over in 1966 the armed forces had no "solution" to the problem, aware as they were that repression alone could not keep as powerful an organization as the CGT under their control. They chose to divide and conquer, meeting labor protests head-on and ruthlessly suppressing them, at the same time inviting selected unions to ally themselves with the government as long as they refrained from protesting its policies. It was always touch and go, and disagreements among officers over Onganía's tactics existed from the day he began. The Cordobazo riots and Onganía's use of the army to crush them irritated his critics within the armed forces, and his refusal to listen to them hastened his overthrow. Arrogant to the end, he hung on for another year until the plotters could marshall enough support within the army to depose him in May 1970.

The Military's Political Problem

It was not only events like the Cordobazo that weakened military governments, but also their inability to progress beyond the crudest authoritarianism in a nation that required more sophisticated leadership. They claimed to know the nation well, but they actually knew little about designing and implementing national policies. Their approach to governance was always rather simplistic, stressing their notions of good and evil, order and disorder, but that seemed crude to civilians who were aware of more complexity and subtlety in the world around them. It was never enough to take over and demand that everyone obey the junta's orders. Of course they did find civilian technocrats to help them, but this alliance was seldom anything more than a marriage of convenience between two types of people whose interests only superficially complemented each other. Moreover, it never made up for the military's inability to create institutions that could resolve the more delicate political and economic conflicts that plagued the nation. Instead, they only provoked an immense sense of exclusion from power among citizens.[28]

Military governments need more than a few civilian advisors to accomplish their objectives. They also require public support. This may sound strange given how powerful they always appear to be, but it is far easier to stage a coup and close down political parties and labor unions than it is to reconstruct the nation's political process or revive its economy. Many people must cooperate, most especially the members of the middle and upper classes who manage and finance the nation's most powerful public and private institutions, but military officers are ill-prepared and uneasy about dealing with competent civilians who often question their judgment. It is hard for them to decide when to abide by civilian advice and when to ignore it at the risk of alienating the people whose cooperation they need in order to govern effectively. Nor do they understand that a public that is impressed by their initial achievements will always withdraw its support after a year or two. Governing a nation like Argentina may require a strong executive that can maintain order over partisan objections, but it also needs one that understands the subtleties of its politics, that can handle the demands placed on authorities by the people whose collaboration it needs. Yet officers distrust civilians and do not always know what to do with them, and civilians develop very little confidence in officers.

The officers also did not understand that very few of the people who welcomed them when they imposed order on society were very fond of the military itself. In fact, most of their civilian suitors usually turned out to be fickle allies who eventually turned against their military rescuers. Civilian support for military intervention was usually motivated by rather narrow, short-term self-interests rather than philosophical convictions. Rampant inflation, working-class protest, terrorism, or a bad business climate frightened people and alienated them from floundering civilian governments, prompting them to accept military intervention as a necessary evil in times of crisis. This gave the military a certain legitimacy, but it was a highly instrumental kind that lasted only until order was restored or the military proved itself incapable of solving fundamental economic problems. In either case, demands for the restoration of civilian government arose within a few years of the coup as career politicians, after a brief retreat, became eager to get back to work serving the interests of their patronage-hungry constituents. Officers ignored them at first but public disaffection with their authoritarian ways always occurred. After a time officers began to disagree over how to respond to such discontent, feeding impressions of their losing control over one another, which in turn encouraged their critics to believe that added pressure would cause them to give up their enterprise rather than risk serious conflicts within or among the three services. There was no simple solution to the dilemma they faced: holding firm might work for a time, but it also would reinforce the public's perception of a regime fearful that its authority was dissipating rapidly. Perhaps they could have sustained themselves in government had they actually created new political institutions to replace their autocratic ones, and allowed enough civilian involvement to placate or co-opt their critics. But they were always incapable of such creativity. Instead, they retreated and eventually gave up.

Onganía's failure to prevail over the nation as he had planned demonstrated how unwilling Argentines were to have the nation reconstructed by so isolated a military authority. It also showed how hard it was for the military to progress beyond the first of its three stages of reconstruction. Yet the most obvious features of political life are not always the best understood, especially where compulsion to ignore them runs deep. So it was when General Jorge Videla and his colleagues decided to give authoritarianism another try in 1976, confident that then, more than ever before, Argentines would appreciate what the armed forces could do for them.

Combat without Rules

Exhibiting a somber formality characteristic of officers when they take on the chore of ruling the nation, the junta that was created on March 24, 1976, pronounced constitutional government a failure. Argentines needed discipline not liberty and now they would have it. As officers saw it, politicians had become too partisan, labor leaders too selfish and corrupt, businessmen too slovenly and unproductive, and themselves tired of trying to set things straight by meddling in elections and threatening coups for nearly two decades with little success. Economic debauchery had reached its limits and the time had come to restore discipline using the laws of supply and demand as well as political repression. Much like Puritans intent on punishing people for their sins, they demanded that the evils of populism be replaced by the cold rationality of the marketplace. It all seemed rather utopian at the time, but that did not reduce its appeal to many Argentines who were themselves exhausted by political stalemates and economic crises. For them it was time to take on the nation's "Italianized" way of life and purge it of its licentious, populist ways.[29]

General Jorge Videla seemed the right man for the job, having risen up the hierarchy as a student and teacher of the army's national security ideology. When the military evicted the oligarchy back in 1943 Videla was in his final year at the Colegio Militar, nineteen years of age. He started his career as an infantry second lieutenant in 1944, ending his first decade of service in 1954 as an instructor in the Colegio. Then he went on to study in the Escuela Superior de Guerra, Argentina's war college. In 1956, not long after Perón's overthrow, he began his "international" education, serving as aide to the chief of Argentina's first delegation to the Inter-American Defense Council in Washington, D.C., returning home in 1959 to teach military intelligence courses until 1961, when he took over as head of cadets at the Colegio Militar. Any officer who aspires to lead the army must become a military politician operating within the Defense Ministry's hierarchy, and in 1962 Videla moved into the army's command, where he observed the conflict between Colorados and Azules that erupted that year. In 1964 he went abroad again, this time to study counterinsurgency tactics under U.S. instructors at their school in the Panama Canal Zone, then in its heyday as part of the U.S. effort to help Latin American armies prevent more Castros. The following year he joined with colleagues to teach strategy in the Centro de Altos Estudios, an organization for advanced study devoted to preparing colonels for their responsibilities as the nation's guardians at home and abroad. It was no coincidence that Videla later drew much of his presidential staff from colleagues and students he had known at the Centro. But that would come later; in 1973 he was given the highest honor for the consummate "professional" when he was appointed head of the Colegio Militar. From there he went on to become the army's commander-in-chief in 1975, and then president after the coup a year later. No officer plots a career intended to end in the presidency, but had one been designed for an officer planning to lead a war against terrorism, it would have looked like Videla's.[30]

He went to work right away, unleashing the three services' intelligence and counterinsurgency units to make war on the Montoneros and the ERP guerrillas, who were waging their own war against the most powerful members of the national establishment. It went quietly and methodically, with no boasting about arrests or killings. Videla was a professional and not a politician, one who had a job to do and did it brutally and efficiently without concern for what any but his fellow officers thought about it. For him the terrorist was the lowest form of life, a mixture of delinquent, mentally insane, and Marxist mercenary. To reward terrorism by neglecting to combat it was tantamount to treason.[31] He did not ask civilians whether they agreed, confident that their fright and passivity was endorsement enough if any were needed. Most people pretended not to notice what he was doing, going about their lives assuming that it would all be over quickly. But many others, most of whom had never committed acts of terrorism, lived in fear, worried that they too might be taken away from their homes in one of the government's infamous, unmarked, gray Ford Falcons, never to be seen again. The intelligence arms of the three services and the police took several "suspects" daily to the 280 prisons that they had secretly created, most of them on military bases in or near the nation's largest cities, where they tortured and killed them and destroyed records of their having been arrested. That the Nazis had done such things in Germany everyone knew, but Argentina was not Germany, nor was its military "Germanic" in character any longer. That is why it all seemed so unbelievable at first; but as disappearances and deaths accumulated, it became obvious that the country was being raped by its own kind.

A decade later most Argentines would deny having known at the time how far the military was going with its "war," but its deeds were never entirely hidden from public view. Though it was not until investigations completed in 1984 revealed how many lives were actually taken that the severity of the repression was documented, people knew that some among them were disappearing, perhaps for good. Many in fact, especially in the business community, were active supporters of the military's crackdown, ostracizing those among them who objected to cleansing the country of its youthful "undesirables." And very few in the nation's political parties or its most prominent institutions spoke out against the barbarity, resigning themselves to living with it for the time being, watching silently as those who did protest, like *Buenos Aires Herald* editor Robert Cox, were chased into exile. As a result, they now must come to terms with their own consciences, coping in individual ways with the moral scar that their military's crimes and their tolerance of them have left, knowing that no number of show trials will ever remove it entirely.[32]

An Unwelcome Economic Crusade

There is something paradoxical about authoritarians becoming the advocates of economic liberty, but it never bothered them. As they saw it, politics and economics each had their own logics and power structures, so there was no need to connect them as liberalism had once done, making freedom in each dependent on its existence in the other. While Videla's policemen were secretly pulling up to houses and kidnapping whomever they pleased, wealthy businessman José Martínez de Hoz, a collaborator with previous military governments, worked on the liberation of the nation's troubled economy. He had persuaded the junta that what Argentina needed was a massive dose of economic liberalism that aimed at transforming its highly subsidized and overregulated enterprises into ones that lived or died by the dictates of supply and demand in national and international marketplaces. Like Krieger Vasena during the Onganía years, Martínez de Hoz was convinced that Argentina languished because of the inefficiency of enterprises that relied far too much on a protected national market for their survival. With production for the domestic market reaching its natural limits, real growth in the future would have to come from exports. And because commodity exports were not, by themselves, sufficient to sustain rapid growth, industry would have to do the job. But that would not come easily for, in order to compete with Third World industrial product exporters like Taiwan, Korea, and Brazil, Argentina would have to reduce the prices of its industrial products substantially by cutting labor costs and achieving higher industrial efficiency. And the only way to do that was to force domestic firms to compete with lower-priced imports by reducing tariffs even if it led to the failure of local industries that could not compete.

Martínez de Hoz did not write the final chapter in Argentine economic history during the next five years, but he did produce one of the country's most controversial ones. He was well known inside and outside the country, born into a wealthy old family with substantial interests in land and industry. He was the modern oligarch: articulate, well acquainted with business leaders in Europe and the United States, and always available to assist any Argentine government that would entrust the economy to him and his sophisticated colleagues. He had served briefly as economics minister in 1962 in a military government, had supported the efforts of Krieger Vasena during the Onganía years, and had made his proposals known to military officers before the 1976 coup. His appointment as economics minister was never automatic, however; none of them are. Generals are not closely acquainted with most civilian economists. When they create a government they often screen candidates for positions in it, listening to their proposals and then deliberating among themselves before announcing their choices. Martínez de Hoz was especially appealing in 1976 because of his connections with bankers in New York and London at a time when the country was being overwhelmed by its foreign debt. Videla also hoped that this wealthy entrepreneur would persuade Argentina's rich to bring their money home after three years of capital flight under the Peronists. Still, the new minister's internationalist economics, with its emphasis on free trade and receptiveness to foreign investment, frightened some officers, many of them reluctant to abandon their nationalism for what seemed a risky reentry into the world economy on foreigners' terms. Their distrust of Martínez de Hoz put many obstacles in his path later on, most of them coming when he tried to reduce the size of the public sector and its many military-directed enterprises.[33]

It is popular in Argentina today to believe that it was greed more than economic philosophy that motivated Martínez de Hoz. It is not easy to separate the two ever, and even harder when the philosophy espoused favors the minister's social class more than it does the others. But to stress personal motives is to ignore the economic ideas on which his programs were founded, ideas then popular in Chile and Uruguay as well as Argentina, inspired by monetarists in the United States and their students who had returned home to their respective Latin American countries in the 1960s and 1970s to advocate the restoration of market economics to countries where populism had produced an undisciplined work force, a bloated public sector, and a class of industrialists who survived primarily because they were protected against foreign competition. This economy of protection and speculation, they insisted, had to be transformed into one of production. As they saw it, the logic of their analysis was quite compelling.[34]

Businessmen were totally unprepared for what followed. Complaints against their inefficiencies had been made before but seldom had they been punished for them, and they had no reason to expect that their nationalistic military would allow it to happen this time. But the new minister was determined to break the cycle by making local manufacturers compete in an open market that included cheaper imported goods. Well-financed, capital-intensive industries could adapt to the challenge, but for the vast majority who had survived through protection, tariff reduction brought the threat of disaster. It was not just a matter of large firms versus small ones or foreign versus domestic, for many large foreign enterprises had come into the Argentine market in order to get under the country's tariff barriers, and once in place they were no more eager for liberalization than anyone else.[35]

The plan was composed of three essentials: first, tariff reductions to invite competition from imported products, something which would be achieved gradually over three or four years, forcing reductions in costs and less inflation along the way; second, the freeing of capital markets previously controlled and subsidized by government, allowing supply and demand to determine interest rates again; and third, reductions in the public sector deficit, which had reached 16 percent of the gross domestic product, by cutting wages, increasing taxes, and selling hundreds of public enterprises[36] (see Table 4.1).

4.1   Phases of Economic Policy, 1976–81

Phase 1	Orthodox stabilization (April 1976–February 1977)
Phase 2	Unorthodox "price truce" (March–August 1977)
Phase 3	Credit squeeze (September 1977–November 1978)
Phase 4	Application of "convergence" (December 1978–February 1981)

But plans, no matter how well designed, cannot be implemented while everything else is "held constant." Argentina was caught in a crisis in 1976, with the rate of inflation rising to almost 600 percent annually and foreign debts in need of immediate renegotiation. Martínez de Hoz was forced to adopt emergency measures as well as long-term ones, beginning immediately with a set of orthodox stabilization policies. They were accompanied with a relaxation of price, financial, and marketing regulation and improved export incentives, while wages were controlled, causing a sharp decline in real wages. In 1976 alone the salaries of public employees dropped from 16.2 percent of the national product to 9.8 percent, helping to reduce total public spending by 6 percent.[37] A renegotiation of the foreign debt followed agreements with the International Monetary Fund on short-term financing, and thanks to a bumper wheat crop, the trade balance improved soon thereafter. At the same time tariff reductions were begun, albeit slowly, but enough to induce substantial competition from imports by the end of 1977. On balance, conditions improved in 1977, exports and foreign exchange reserves rising, gross domestic savings increasing by one-fourth, and the government deficit cut almost in half.

Inflation forced him to set aside the war against regulation for a brief period in order to call for a "price truce" starting in March 1977 that asked the country's 800 largest corporations to freeze prices for 120 days in the hope of breaking the dynamism of inflation long enough to cause people to alter expectations and change their price-setting behavior. Then in June 1977 the government announced a major financial reform aimed at attracting deposits into the banking system. For almost three decades interest rates had been administered and kept negative, denying the financial system an important role in the transfer of resources in the country since depositors, facing high inflation and negative interest rates, invested only in very short-term assets. He decontrolled interest rates and removed restrictions on the creation of new financial institutions, causing lending rates to become positive eventually, which in turn caused a rapid expansion in banking. Businessmen borrowed heavily, taking their chances on interest rates not rising significantly more and on business improving enough to make their borrowing profitable, and short-term foreign depositors took advantage of the removal of restrictions on running money in and out of Argentina. For a while it looked as if the government had built a new financial system almost overnight.

Authorities made what would become a fateful decision in December 1978. Frustrated by inflation's resistance to treatment, they decided to go after it using foreign exchange policy. It was something like returning to the gold standard without gold, in which the government would set exchange rates, declaring devaluations at scheduled intervals, but doing so at a rate that overvalued the peso enough to make imported goods less expensive than domestic ones. What this would do, it was hoped, was induce slower price increases at home under the pressure of competition from imports, bringing the rate of inflation down as it did. To no one's surprise the peso was soon overvalued by as much as 50 percent, and by 1980 visitors to Buenos Aires were finding it one of the most expensive cities anywhere while middle- and upper-class Argentines were buying cheap dollars and using them to travel all

over the world, bringing home with them the latest in consumer electronics and designer clothes. Meanwhile, after almost going to war with
Chile over islands in the Beagle Channel claimed by both countries, the
military also went shopping, adding expensive items to its weapons
arsenal. Argentines simply went on a buying spree that turned their $2
billion current account surplus in 1978 into a $5.7 billion deficit by
1980. Yet even that seemed manageable at the time since high interest
rates were attracting enough dollars to the country to finance the
negative commercial balance.[38]

In capitalist systems economists try to induce desired behavior
using the incentives and regulations allowed them by law and tradition.
They make assumptions about profit motives and try to design policies
that take advantage of them while achieving societal objectives. So it
was when Martínez de Hoz went to work on the economy. He wanted
desperately to force Argentine entrepreneurs to adapt their expectations
to the discipline imposed by greater competition, ending their reliance
on government subsidization of their operations. It was an audacious
effort that required time to work and enough incremental success to
build confidence in its permanence. But suspicious Argentines had
heard it all before and were as skeptical of his ability to work miracles as
they had been of his predecessors. Their perspective is short term and
quite rational, educated on generations of policy failures that teach one
always to be prepared for the worst. They waited and watched in 1978
and 1979, and sure enough, things did not turn out as they were
supposed to. For one thing, bankers quickly got carried away with their
new freedom, overextending themselves by taking in far more deposits
than they could service adequately. That they did so was due in part to
the incomplete nature of the new financial reforms. While interest rates
were freed, the government's 100 percent guarantee of deposits was not
ended, prompting new and old commercial banks to bid aggressively for
deposits and accumulate an abundance of risky portfolios. When some
very large banks suddenly collapsed in 1980, the government was
forced to bail them out, along with some of the large manufacturers that
were also technically bankrupt. By June they had seized 13 percent of
the deposits in private banks. But the bailout led to rapid monetary
expansion and new pressures on prices.[39]

The overvalued exchange rate made things even worse. Here the
issue of public confidence is critical since the more the currency is
overvalued the more people expect its devaluation and act accordingly.
Only the fool neglects to protect himself by purchasing as many dollars
as possible before the inevitable devaluation makes dollars even more
expensive. And Argentines are not fools: while Martínez de Hoz assured

the public that he would not abandon his system of incremental devaluations no matter how much capital fled the country, everyone ran for cover, buying scarce dollars at ever higher prices on the black market. At the same time conditions went sour for business. They had borrowed heavily after the financial reforms, and private sector indebtedness had tripled during 1979 and 1980, but high and variable interest rates and a recession that began in 1980 caught many of them overextended, inducing record bankruptcies and a financial crisis.[40]

As disappointing as all of this was, few things frustrated Martínez de Hoz more than the resistance of the public sector to surgery. At first substantial progress was made. Tariff reduction and the liberation of capital markets reduced the influence of the state over private business substantially, and his freezing public-employee salaries brought down the deficit as a percent of the national product from 16 to 5.6 percent in only two years. Moreover, he managed to replace Central Bank financing of the deficit by making government securities attractive in the open market. But that only scratched the surface. More important over the long haul was the sale of public enterprises, a campaign designed to reduce substantially the government's operation of deficit-ridden ventures. But little progress was made, the government selling off only its smallest firms. The larger, less efficient ones were no more attractive to the private sector than they were to the people who wanted to sell them. Nor was the military enthusiastic about reducing the size of the government since they enjoyed their role in its expansion and management.[41]

Argentines will always debate, as will economists elsewhere, whether or not trade liberalization was the primary cause of the government's failure. That it affected the performance of industry is undeniable: the output of import competing firms fell by 9 percent and the size of the industrial work force dropped by 20 percent.[42] But regardless of such "achievements," it was doomed to failure by the mismanagement of the rest of the program. Budget cuts were blocked by military officers trying to prepare for war against Chile, and overvalued exchange rates made it impossible to keep dollars in the country. And when price controls were abandoned, foreign exchange made available, and labor subdued, businessmen who wanted to take advantage of such incentives often found themselves stymied by variations in relative prices and interest rates and uncertainties about how long the government could sustain its overvalued exchange rate in the face of foreign debt pressures. Bankruptcies rose almost fivefold between 1976 and 1980, reaching the equivalent of about $1 billion in liabilities (roughly equivalent to 3 percent of total sector liabilities), too much to sustain confidence in the government's program. Nor did their borrowing abroad do the country that much good in the long run. Of the $35 billion that was lent Argentina between 1976 and 1983, little if any was used to finance additional investment. Thus it was that officials who were determined to stabilize market behaviors actually touched off new instabilities and prompted waves of speculation. Their whipping of the wild stallion, it seems, just made it buck more after a temporary pause.[43]

They, like the Chileans and Uruguayans who tried to remake their economies in much the same way in the late 1970s, were the victims of a very superficial understanding of the reasons for the success of Japan, Korea, and Taiwan, whose industrial export growth they had hoped to replicate. Their elitism caused them to place emphasis on firm government leadership and good relations with "good" industries, but those were only two parts of the Oriental success story. Even more important were their exceptionally high rates of capital formation, a high degree of labor discipline, and an unswerving entrepreneurial dedication to quality control and to the aggressive pursuit of export markets, all of which are usually missing in the Latin American economies. Once again, it seemed, the neoclassical economist's frustration with the status quo and his own inability to make basic changes in the private sector caused him to try another short-cut approach, which, by its partiality, was doomed to fail from the beginning.[44]

When General Roberto Viola succeeded Videla as scheduled at the end of March 1981, he was greeted by indebted Argentine businessmen who demanded that Viola dismiss Martínez de Hoz and stop opening the nation's economy to freer trade. Without much argument, Viola gave in and replaced Martínez de Hoz with some of his opponents in prominent industrial and agricultural interest groups. But conditions only became worse thanks to a world recession that struck Argentina in 1981, causing its GDP to fall by 6 percent that year (and manufacturing by 14 percent) (see table 4.2). Recognizing that the overvalued exchange rate was inflicting serious damage on the country's productive base and was leading to unsustainable losses of foreign exchange, Viola announced a series of large currency devaluations during his first six months, suspended the tariff reduction program, reintroduced export taxes and import licensing, and reduced public expenditures, the net result of which was to push several overextended producers into bankruptcy.

Army commanders soon concluded that Viola was losing control over the nation that they were trying to discipline, and in December 1981, less than a year into Viola's term, the commander of the army, Leopoldo Galtieri, evicted him and took over as president. Eager to appear bolder and more resolute than his predecessor, President Galtieri

4.2 Economic Performance, 1976–83 (annual percentage change)

Year	Total Investment	GDP Growth	Wholesale Price Index
1976	6.4	−0.5	498.7
1977	19.4	6.4	149.0
1978	−15.2	−3.4	149.4
1979	7.9	6.7	149.3
1980	7.2	0.7	75.4
1981	−23.1	−6.2	109.6
1982	−15.3	−5.1	256.2
1983	−8.4	3.1	360.9

Source: *Clarín*, economic supp., January 13, 1985, p. 11.

appointed one of the nation's best known free-market advocates, Roberto Alemann, to restore some order to the economy, promising to back him no matter how painful his prescriptions were. But before Alemann had a chance to test his rescue plan, Galtieri leaped into disaster.

An Unwelcome War

General Leopoldo Galtieri went to war on April 2, 1982, just four months after he had replaced General Viola, though he always claimed that war had never been his intention when he sent his troops to the Falklands/ Malvinas Islands, located 400 miles off Argentina's southeastern shore, to easily overcome resistance by a few dozen British marines.[45] In Buenos Aires people danced in the streets while the rest of the world watched in amazement. The festivities were brief, however, for a few weeks later the British replied with force, and after 937 lives were lost in combat (712 Argentines and 225 British), a humiliated Argentine army returned to the mainland in defeat on June 14.

It is not hard to understand why reclaiming the islands was popular in Argentina or why the British refused to allow it. The first recorded landing there was made by English mariner John Strong who was driven off course by violent winds in 1690; he named the islands after Viscount Falkland, then the Royal Navy treasurer, and sailed away. After settling on the mainland the Spanish listed the islands as theirs, but it was a Frenchman, Louis Antoine de Bougainville, who established the first settlement in 1764, and named them the Iles Malouines, from which the Spanish later took the name that Argentines use today, the Islas Malvinas. A year later British Commodore John Byron surveyed the islands and claimed them for King George III, setting up a small colony on Saunders Island at Port Egmont. Meanwhile the Spanish protested the French intrusion, and after some negotiations the French agreed to depart. The English were less accommodating, however, so the Spanish evicted them by force in 1770. They were allowed to return in 1771 only to leave voluntarily three years later, leaving behind them a plate inscribed with their claim of ownership.[46]

The independence of the Río de la Plata region in 1816 forced the Spanish to exit South America, leaving it to the new Argentine nation to assert its authority over the Malvinas, but it made no serious effort to do so until 1826 when the government demanded that the North American seal hunters who had set up camp there pay taxes to Argentina. Angered, the U.S. consul in Buenos Aires immediately dispatched the USS *Lexington,* then visiting the Argentine capital, to liberate the hunters. The Americans won easily and went home. And that is where the British came in. Seizing the new opportunity, they returned, intending to provide themselves with a base for whaling and to facilitate sea trade with Australia via the Straits of Magellan. But it was the shepherd and not the whaler who moved in when the Falkland Islands Company was created in 1851 and purchased 60 percent of the land for sheep grazing. A century later most of the 1,800 people still on the islands lived in company housing and did their shopping at a company store while law was enforced by a governor appointed by the British Foreign Office.[47]

The Argentines never ceased demanding the return of the islands, but it was not until 1965 that they began to make some progress, starting with U.N. General Assembly Resolution 2065 which called for a binational negotiation leading to decolonization and the return of the islands to Argentina.[48] Nevertheless, discussions between diplomats from the two countries made little progress because the British simply refused to address the sovereignty issue, claiming as before that since there was no native population on the islands, it had never been a colony.

The idea of seizing the islands by force was not suddenly dreamed up in 1982. Planning actually began in the early 1970s, led by navy Captain Jorge Anaya who gained prominence when, after becoming an admiral, he was made a member of the junta that appointed General Leopoldo Galtieri president at the end of 1981. Impressed by how easily the Indian government had seized the Portuguese colony of Goa in 1961 and how little the rest of the world had protested the invasion, Anaya had often tried to convince other officers that they could do likewise in the Malvinas.

The plan surfaced again in 1981 just as the military was losing its control over the economy and civilians were launching a new multiparty campaign for free elections. After General Galtieri became president

Admiral Anaya convinced him that his presidency and the armed forces had much to gain and little to lose from retaking the Malvinas since it would be so popular throughout the country. Anaya's case was not hurt by the way the British were already cutting back their forces in the South Atlantic in order to reduce their naval budget.[49]

Galtieri and his colleagues were well aware that their invasion would be controversial, and they knew that taking Britain's Falklands would provoke more hostility in Great Britain than the loss of Goa had in a weaker Portugal. Nevertheless they wanted to believe that the British were no more likely to go to war over the islands than the Portuguese had been. Had they believed otherwise, they might not have acted as they did. Moreover, Galtieri did not want a real war; instead, he sought to force the British to negotiate recognition of Argentine sovereignty by drawing the attention of nations that he hoped would pressure the British to concede. As he saw it, holding the Falkland Islanders hostage was the only way to get the British to negotiate and agree to do what many people in their own Foreign Office had been urging the prime minister to do for some time.[50]

Immediately after the invasion the Argentines went to the United Nations in order to diffuse predictable British efforts to mobilize world opinion against them. They sought to block the British in the Security Council and then secure mediation in their favor. Though intensely anticommunist, Argentine officers were confident that they could secure a Russian veto of any hostile British resolution since they had become a major supplier of grain to the Soviet Union after the United States cut off its sales in reprisal for the Soviet invasion of Afghanistan in 1979. Two days before the invasion, on March 31, Argentine Foreign Minister Nicanor Costa Mendez had asked the Soviet ambassador in Buenos Aires to request his government's veto to an inevitable British resolution after the invasion. The Russians listened with interest, as did the Chinese when the same request was made of them, but when the showdown came in New York they surprised the Argentines by abstaining from the Security Council vote, allowing passage of a resolution that demanded the immediate withdrawal of all Argentine troops. So rather than face a British government that was unable to mobilize sanctions against Argentina, Galtieri suddenly faced a belligerent Prime Minister Thatcher who claimed that justice was on her side.[51]

Third World nations were supposed to become another source of support for Argentina, if only because they were expected to celebrate a blow being struck against a colonial power by a fellow underdog. But they too failed to live up to expectations. While some praised the Argentine effort, very few did so enthusiastically. Most had never been very fond of a once affluent, Europeanized Argentina whose citizens often displayed a superiority complex when visiting other Third World nations. Nor were they impressed that its military government was cozying up to the United States and helping it fight against liberation movements in Central America. Not even the Organization of American States did what the Argentines wanted. Instead its members held back, paying lip service to Argentina's cause but not approving of its invasion. So two weeks after they had taken the islands, the best that the Argentines could get was U.N. Resolution 502 which called for the withdrawal of troops from both sides.[52]

While diplomats labored in vain, the British fleet headed south, regrouping and refueling at Ascension Island with supplies provided secretly by the United States. The British submarine *Spartan* arrived on station off Port Stanley, the islands' capital, on April 12 to begin to set up an exclusionary zone around them and block Argentine efforts to supply their troops by sea from the mainland. On April 25 the British landed some distance to the east at South Georgia, swiftly overwhelming a meager Argentine garrison there. Then on May 1 a Vulcan bomber flown from Ascension struck the airport in Port Stanley, as did guns fired from ships, as well as Sea Harrier jet fighters. It was then that the British pulled off what would become the most controversial incident of the war. The next day, at the orders of the British cabinet in London, the nuclear submarine *Conqueror* torpedoed the Argentine cruiser *General Belgrano* just outside the exclusionary zone as it was heading back into port on orders of the Argentine command. The *Belgrano* sank swiftly in the freezing waters, taking 368 Argentine sailors with it. The tragedy shocked Argentina and the rest of the world and gave Galtieri an excuse for not pulling out until the British met his terms.[53] But it did force the Argentine fleet to stay in port for the rest of the war as Thatcher and her commanders wanted. Not until after the war did she admit that the *Belgrano* actually had been outside the exclusionary zone, just as the Argentines had contended. But even then she claimed that the attack was justified because the British believed that the ship was giving navigational assistance to aircraft that were sent from shore to attack the British fleet.[54]

For the next twenty-five days the battle was fought offshore, in the air, and at sea. The British fleet was quite vulnerable to attacks from the air, but its distance from the mainland restricted the Argentine air force to only a single attack on each trip. Still, the Argentine pilots hit hard, sinking the destroyer *Sheffield* on May 4, the *Antelope* on May 24, and the *Coventry* and *Atlantic Conveyer* transports on May 25, often with radar-guided, sea-skimming Exocet missiles launched from Super

Etendard fighters. The British were fortunate that the Argentines had only a few Exocets in their arsenal; had there been many more the fleet might have been devastated long before the invasion had begun. In the air war both sides fought intensely and the Argentines paid the most for their efforts, losing seventy Skyhawk, Mirage, and Dagger fighter planes, while the British sacrificed only ten Harriers since most of them could defend themselves effectively with American-made AIM-9L heat-seeking Sidewinder air-to-air missiles.

Diplomacy was tried one last time just before the British forces landed at San Carlos Bay on May 21. But when U.N. Secretary General Javier Pérez de Cuellar asked Thatcher on May 19 to delay the invasion and give him more time to persuade the Argentines to pull out, she refused and announced in the House of Commons amid great cheers that British forces were about to recover the Falklands. Actually, Galtieri was just as uncooperative with the secretary general, insisting as before that the British agree to discuss the sovereignty issue first. But it was all moot on May 20 when the British cabinet authorized Rear Admiral John Woodward to go ashore and get the job done.[55]

Galtieri never has explained why he refused to bargain when given what was obviously his last chance to negotiate. Perhaps he was convinced by then that Admiral Woodward was coming ashore regardless of what Argentina offered at the bargaining table, seeing that Thatcher seemed to want revenge more than peace negotiations. Or maybe he was afraid to appear a coward, knowing that if he did his military colleagues would never accept it. Whichever it was, he could not get out of what had become a no-win situation: if he brought the troops home without much to show for the original invasion, he would look a fool for having sent them on April 2; but if he left them they were certain to be humiliated in battle by a stronger force.

The British landed at San Carlos Bay on the opposite side of East Falkland island from Port Stanley where most of the Argentine troops were concentrated. Not anticipating their coming ashore there, the Argentines were caught off guard, unable to marshal their forces for a swift counterattack against a very vulnerable advance force. And fortunately for the British, cloud cover made detection of the invasion by air impossible at its inception, depriving the Argentine air force of a chance to strike before the expedition could set up minimal air defenses on shore. When they attacked on the second day the Argentine pilots fought bravely and inflicted damage on the invaders, but the latter's firepower proved too much for the Argentine flyers whose losses were heavy. Quickly the British set up a base and sent expeditionary forces inland, attacking first at Goose Green a few miles away. The battle lasted nearly a day as the Argentines fought tenaciously, but they were no match for the very professional British paratroopers, 450 of whom secured the surrender of 1,200 Argentines after killing 50 of them and losing 17 themselves.[56]

In the end the Argentines' fortress mentality and British skill at warfare dictated the latter's swift victory. Authorities in Buenos Aires made no effort to improve their troops' chances once the British landed, leaving Major General Mario Benjamín Menéndez and his soldiers to draw together around Port Stanley in the hope that they could somehow hold off the rapidly approaching British forces.[57] Many Argentine soldiers fought hard, but few were pleased with the conduct of their commanders who became notorious for their arrogance and cruel treatment of their men. Horror stories of food shortages and inappropriate clothing for the bitterly cold weather become common, as were complaints of low morale in the final days. As one Argentine soldier summarized it:

> After some hours watching the English troops preparing for battle the picture became clear. Helicopters took them from the front to San Carlos or Darwin to eat or be treated by doctors, or to get anything else they needed. We, in contrast, were stuck at the same places all the time, freezing and hungry. We had spent sixty days on the islands and they only fifteen or twenty. We were fed up with the place and could not take it anymore. Some of us had lost feeling in our feet to frostbite. But the English had incredible outfits and impermeable boots. The difference was just too much.[58]

Public disillusionment with Galtieri soon followed the defeat, especially when people finally recognized that he had lied to them about the war's progress right until the end. Argentines were told, for example, that the British had been immobilized at San Carlos and "were awaiting their Dunkirk." And frequently anonymous military sources were quoted in the press and on radio and television dismissing reports of a large British landing, insisting that only five hundred had come ashore, a number that was no match for Argentine forces. Some local newspapers did publish British accounts and contrasted them with Argentine ones, but only the most skeptical discounted the accuracy of what they were being told by their own government. That is why the loss came as such a shock when it finally occurred twenty-four days after the San Carlos landing. While the rest of the world watched and waited for the inevitable British triumph (most of them more confident of victory than the British commanders were, given their vulnerability to air attack), Argentine citizens believed that their Malvinas fortress was well defended. Defeat was not comprehended when it occurred, but the realization of what had happened soon set in, filling everyone with depression that swiftly turned into rage against the armed forces.

Nearly all of the 11,313 Argentine troops were herded onto ships and sent home. When they arrived the public was kept away, as if hiding them would make the debacle more bearable. But soldiers soon told their stories to the press, and within a couple of months the entire country came together as never before in its hostility toward a military government that had taken them from celebration to an embarrassing defeat, killing over 700 young men in the process.[59]

The Argentine armed forces were disgraced not just because they lost but also because the three services had cooperated so ineffectively in the fighting. While the army, navy, and air force had planned and implemented the invasion in unison, thereafter their collaboration ceased. They agreed on nothing: communications, codes, strategy, or tactics. It was as if each had fought its own war, the navy staying in port after the *Belgrano* was sunk, the air force attacking when it felt able, and the army commanders disagreeing among themselves about how to fight on the islands. No doubt this was due in part to their not expecting a war to occur. They had really convinced themselves that after the invasion everyone else would force the British to negotiate seriously with them rather than launch an invasion. But it was also due to the perennial inability of the Argentine armed forces to work together on anything. Politically the army always tries to dominate and the smaller navy and air force resist as best they can. To make matters worse, war against a foreign enemy was not something they had practiced together in over a hundred years.

In addition, it is now obvious just how much Galtieri had underestimated Thatcher's resolve and Reagan's commitment to his old ally, as well as how he ignored the reluctance of neighboring countries to become directly involved, especially the sake of an Argentina that previously had exhibited little affection for other South Amercians. Moreover, the Argentine armed forces knew little about diplomacy, and this showed when Galtieri left himself no peaceful way out by invading. Once on the islands he had to either fight or leave if the British did not agree to his terms. They refused, and since he would not admit defeat and pull out, he had to fight. In a rare admission General Menéndez later confessed all of this when he was asked to assess the whole affair. Testifying before the military's own Rattenbach Commission in 1983 he mused: "My final impression . . . well . . . I guess it is that we really did not know how to negotiate with the flexibility necessary to avoid the kind of defeat that became inevitable at the hands of an enemy stronger than ourselves."[60]

A Verdict on Military Authoritarians

Political failure has been a way of life for the Argentine armed forces. The Videla-Viola-Galtieri debacle was only the latest example. In 1930 Uriburu was forced by his friends in the upper class to give up his corporatist adventure before it had really begun; Aramburu gave way to Arturo Frondizi in 1958, a politician whom he did not trust, and none of the armed forces were pleased to see Arturo Illia replace them in 1963. Most frustrating, after Onganía's unsuccessful "revolution" they even had to watch Juan Perón return and see terrorism rage.

Their failure, it seemed, was inherent in their assignment and the public's ambivalence toward it. They always began by achieving their most immediate objectives only to be forced to give up before they reached their ultimate ones. Taking over in times of crisis, they asserted their authority, closing political parties and legislatures and intervening against labor unions. Then they would go to work on the economy, more often than not imposing austerity to deal with high inflation and other disorders, determined to maintain the integrity of the capitalist economy and promote its development with a combination of incentives to the private sector and investments by the public one. Within a couple of years some progress would be made and the military's triumph celebrated, especially in the international business community.

The military's initial achievements were always short-lived, however. New economic problems would arise and their political reforms aborted before they had really started. To cope with such failures they would either cling to their authoritarianism, exercising repression to deter opponents, or they would just give up and allow new elections that returned to office the very politicians whom they had intended to expel from the nation's politics.

Authoritarian government not only incited opposition among the politicians and labor leaders that it abused, but it also alienated a middle class that wanted its liberties returned after order had been restored. Even entrepreneurs would turn against the officers who were trying to assist them by suppressing labor. They did not complain much at first, but when economic recovery cost them more than they wanted to pay, they would criticize the armed forces and demand more favorable treatment. And when that happened, no promises by the junta to hold firm to its original plan were enough to prevent entrepreneurs from abusing their economic policies.

Officers like Onganía and Videla dreamed of launching a new form of politics, something in which civilians were supposed to participate after they developed a greater desire to obey authority. It was as if they wanted Argentines to submerge their class differences and competing interests in order to please authorities they did not really respect. The armed forces never learned that they could not expect the conformity they so desperately craved when they did so little to build effective new political institutions that could handle the conflicts that plagued Argentine society.

A well-ingrained habit of dissension and rivalry among the three services and among army commanders also debilitated juntas when they tried to lead the nation. Conflicts among officers could be hidden from public view for a time, but they always reappeared when presidential succession became an issue. Actually, the problem would begin with the appointment of each junta's first president. Officers disagreed less over the choice of officer than over how much authority to give him, some preferring to let the new president govern the nation while they tended to conventional military business; while others, fearful of losing control over their presidential colleague, demanded that authority be kept collegial, reserving substantial power for the three service commanders in the junta. The arrangement was never very neat, no matter how much the junta wanted to appear united behind the president.

Another problem arose whenever officers went through their usual promotions and rotations. New commanders in the army would seldom come from the same faction, and the higher the appointments the more the factions competed with one another for power. In military government nothing was automatic, neither continuity nor disruption; rather, the military junta and its president had to deal with far more conflict beneath them than they wanted, and it always increased from one year to the next. Their responses were often self-destructive, however. For example, when officers removed Onganía in 1970 after waging a battle with him over policy, military commanders began to dispute among themselves, leaving the new president, General Roberto Levingston, without a solid base of support to sustain his command. Less than a year later General Alejandro Lanusse replaced him and led the way back to elections. Similarly, controversy between the navy and army over the choice of General Roberto Viola to succeed Videla in 1981, and his policies once in office, weakened his presidency and led to General Leopoldo Galtieri's replacing him less than a year later, in what once again marked the beginning of the end of military rule. Over and over again, the armed forces became their worst enemy.

Their task was not made any easier, of course, by how little confidence the public had in their ability to improve anything. People expected juntas to impose order on society and repair the economy, but not to make any real progress toward political reform. They never believed that generals had the intellectual or organizational capacity to create new institutions that would work for very long. Unlike in Brazil where civilian politicians resigned themselves to spending many years working with the ruling officers toward the design of new political rules that accommodated military preferences, the Argentines believed that sooner or later the armed forces would fail and politics would return to "normal." When General Alejandro Lanusse called elections in 1973, for example, he wanted to form a new political movement, joining conservatives and moderates behind his candidacy or that of another officer, but it fizzled well before taking off for lack of support by politicians. Nor did the Argentine people want to elect military presidents. They just wanted to get on with their own business unmolested by anyone—military or civilian.

Notes

1. *New York Times,* April 27, 1985, p. 3. Although a coup was not imminent and Alfonsín, no doubt was using the threat of one to mobilize support for a government that was in danger of losing its popularity, the fact that he would resort to such warnings after pretending for two years that he had the armed forces under control is an indication of how real the possibility has become once again.

2. Torcuarto S. Di Tella, "Reflections on the Argentine Crisis: Are We at the End of an Epoch?" Occasional Paper Series, no. 3 (Washington, D.C.: American Enterprise Institute, January 1982), pp. 10–11.

3. Alain Rouquie, "Hegemonia militar, estado y dominación social," in *Argentina Hoy,* ed. Alain Rouquie (Mexico City: Siglo XXI, 1982), pp. 26–27.

4. Robert Potash, "The Impact of Professionalism on the 20th Century Argentine Military," University of Massachusetts Program in Latin American Studies Occasional Paper, no. 3, 1977. Also see Alain Rouquie, *Poder militar y sociedad política en la Argentina, Vol. I, hasta 1943* (Buenos Aires: EMECE, 1978), pp. 89–100.

5. Rouquie, *Poder militar y sociedad política,* pp. 101–104.

6. Robert Potash, *The Army and Politics in Argentina: 1928 to 1945* (Stanford: Stanford University Press, 1969), p. 11.

7. On the 1930 coup and Uriburu's rise and fall, see ibid., ch. 2.

8. Ruben M. Perina, *Onganía, Levingston, Lanusse: Los militares en la política argentina* (Buenos Aires: Belgrano, 1983), pp. 48–49.

9. Adrian J. English, *Armed Forces of Latin America* (London: Jane's 1984), p. 65.

10. Perina, *Onganía, Levingston, Lanusse,* pp. 50–53. Also Potash, *The Army and Politics in Argentina 1945–1962,* ch. 1.

11. On Perón's tactics and his rivals' concessions to him in late 1945, see Felix Luna, *El 45* (Buenos Aires: Sudamericana, 1971).

12. Bejamín Menéndez was also the father of Major General Mario Benjamín Menéndez, the officer whom President Galtieri appointed as governor of the Malvinas Islands after the invasion in 1982 and, therefore, the person who surrendered to the British much as his father had done to the Azules twenty years before.

13. The Azul-Colorado conflict is summarized in Luis Gregorich, *La república perdida* (Buenos Aires: Sudamericana-Planeta, 1983), pp. 118–119; and Alain Rouquie, *Poder militar y sociedad política en la Argentina, Vol. II* (Buenos Aires: EMECE, 1982), pp. 359–361.

14. Guillermo O'Donnell, *El estado burocrático autoritario* (Buenos Aires: Belgrano, 1982), pp. 85–87.

15. For a discussion of the dispute among scholars over the causes of bureaucratic authoritarianism, see Michael Wallerstein, "The Collapse of Democracy in Brazil," *Latin American Review* 15, no. 3 (1980): 3–43.

16. The inventor of this explanation was Argentine political scientist Guillermo O'Donnell, who elaborates on it in several works, beginning with *Modernization and Bureaucratic-Authoritarianism: Studies in South American Politics* (Berkeley: Institute of International Studies, University of California, 1973). Also see David Collier, ed., *The New Authoritarianism in Latin America* (Princeton: Princeton University Press, 1979).

17. In his more recent study of the Onganía regime O'Donnell confirms the variety of motives that led to the coup. See O'Donnell, *El estado burocrático autoritario.*

18. Alfred Stepan, *The Military in Politics: Changing Patterns in Brazil* (Princeton: Princeton University Press, 1971).

19. Gregorich, *La república perdida,* p. 143.

20. General Golbery do Couto e Silva, *Geopolítica do Brasil* (Rio: José Olympio, 1967), p. 9, quoted in José Comblin, *The Church and the National Security State* (Maryknoll, N.Y.: Orbis, 1979), p. 90.

21. On the debates within the army that preceded the coup, see O'Donnell, *El estado burocrático autoritario,* pp. 85–103.

22. Quoted in Comblin, *The Church and the National Security State,* p. 76.

23. Wayne Smith, "The Return of Peronism" in Frederick C. Turner and Jose E. Miguens, *Peron and the Reshaping of Argentina,* (Pittsburgh: University of Pittsburgh Press, 1983), p. 98.

24. O'Donnell, *El estado burocrático autoritario,* p. 95.

25. On the "stage theory," see Gary W. Wynia, *Argentina in the Postwar Era: Politics and Economic Policy-Making in a Divided Society* (Albuquerque: University of New Mexico Press, 1978), p. 172–176.

26. Wynia, *Argentina in the Postwar Era,* chs. 6; O'Donnell, *El estado burocrático autoritario,* chs. 4–5.

27. Daniel Villar, *El Cordobazo* (Buenos Aires: La Historia Popular, 1971).

28. See Felix Luna, *Golpes militares y salidas electorales* (Buenos Aires: Sudamericana, 1983), ch. 12.

29. The military's thinking and the documents it issued to explain itself are presented in Marcelo Cavarozzi, *Autoritarismo y democracia: (1955–1983)* (Buenos Aires: Centro Editor de America Latina, 1983).

30. Gustavo Druetta, "Guerra, política y sociedad en la ideologia de la corporación militar argentina," *Critica y utopia* 10/11 (1983): 127–128.

31. Ibid., p. 131.

32. This interpretation of events draws heavily on the findings of the Sabato Commission, which President Raul Alfonsín appointed to investigate the disappearances and which reported its findings to him in October 1984.

33. Jorge Schvarzer, *Martínez de Hoz: La lógica política de la política económica* (Buenos Aires: Centro de Investigaciones Sociales Sobre el Estado y la Administración, 1983), p. 34.

34. Marcelo Cavarozzi, "Argentina at the Crossroads: Pathways and Obstacles to Democratization at the Present Political Conjuncture," Woodrow Wilson Latin America Center Working Paper, no. 115, 1982, p. 3.

35. The implications of tariff policy are examined in Adolfo Canitrot, *Teoría y práctica del liberalismo y apertura económica en la Argentina: 1976–1981,* 3, no. 10 (Buenos Aires: CEDES, 1980).

36. Ibid.

37. Schvarzer, *Martínez de Hoz,* p. 37.

38. This summary relies heavily on Guido Di Tella, "La Argentina económica," *Criterio* (Navidad 1982): 761.

39. Between January 1977 and June 1982, twenty-six banks and seventy-eight finance companies went bankrupt. For more detail see Ernesto V. Feldman, "La crisis financiera argentina: 1980–1982," *Desarrollo económico* 23, no. 91 (October–December 1983): 449–455. Also see Jan Peter Wogart, "Combining Price Stabilization with Trade and Financial Liberalization Policies: The Argentine Experience, 1976–1981," *Journal of Interamerican Studies and World Affairs* 25 no. 4 (November 1983): 468 ff.

40. *Latin American Regional Report: Southern Cone,* March 6, 1981, p. 6.

41. Canitrot, *Teoría y práctica del liberalismo y apertura económica en la Argentina: 1976–1981,* pp. 61–65.

42. Wogart, "Combining Price Stabilization with Trade and Financial Liberalization Policies," pp. 462–465.

43. Ibid.

44. William P. Glade, "Latin America: Options and Nonoptions in Contemporary Development Strategy," *American Enterprise Institute Foreign Policy and Defense Review* 5, no. 3 (Winter 1985): 13.

45. The Argentine troops were ordered to hold their fire in order to avoid the kind of provocation they feared would come from their killing islanders and the marines who defended the islands. They really believed that the British would take a kinder view of the whole thing if bloodshed were avoided.

46. Fritz L. Hoffmann and Olga Mingo Hoffman, *Sovereignty in Dispute: The Falklands/Malvinas, 1493–1982* (Boulder, Colo.: Westview Press, 1984), chs. 2–4.

47. Desmond Rice and Arthur Gavshon, *The Sinking of the Belgrano* (London: Secker & Warburg, 1984), pp. 4–6.

48. Guillermo Makin, "Argentine Approaches to the Falklands/Malvinas: Was the Resort to Violence Foreseeable?" *International Affairs* 59, no. 3 (Summer 1983): 291.

49. General Galtieri, Foreign Minister Costa Mendez, and Admiral Anaya defended their decisions before what became known as the Rattenbach Commission, a military investigative body that held secret hearings in 1983. Excepts from their testimonies were published in *Gente* magazine, December 8, 1983.

50. This interpretation draws heavily on testimony by Galtieri and Anaya before the Rattenbach Commission, ibid.

51. O. R. Cardoso, R. Kirschbaum, and E. Van Der Kooy, *Malvinas: la trama secreta* (Buenos Aires: Sudamericana-Planeta, 1983), pp. 120–123. These are three reporters from the newspaper *Clarín* who prepared the book after conducting interviews in London and Washington, D.C., as well as Buenos Aires.

52. Max Hastings and Simon Jenkins, *The Battle for the Falklands* (New York: Norton, 1983), pp. 139–148.

53. For more details on the British decision to sink the *Belgrano* see Rice et al., *The Sinking of the Belgrano.* The authors argue that Prime Minister Thatcher and her cabinet had made up their minds to evict the Argentines from the islands militarily, and even

though the *Belgrano* was outside the exclusionary zone declared by the British, they decided to attack it and begin the war. Two days after the *Belgrano* was sunk the Argentine air force sank the British destroyer HMS *Sheffield* with an Exocet missile, killing twenty-one sailors.

54. Ibid.

55. *New York Times,* May 24, 1982, p. 7.

56. The battle is described in detail by Hastings et al., *The Battle for the Falklands,* pp. 233–253.

57. See Menéndez' testimony before the Rattenbach Commission in *Gente,* December 8, 1983.

58. Daniel Kon, *Los chicos de la guerra* (Buenos Aires: Editorial Galerna, 1982), p. 37. Also see Nicolas Kasanzew, *Malvinas: a sangre y fuego* (Buenos Aires: Editorial Abril, 1982); and Carlos M. Turolo (h), *Asi lucharon* (Buenos Aires: Editorial Sudamericana, 1982). Many collections of war stories telling of gallantry as well as suffering were published immediately after soldiers were discharged, and in 1984 *Los chicos de la guerra* was made into powerful and popular antiwar film.

59. On Argentine coverage of the war, see *New York Times,* May 24, 1982, p. 7.

60. *Gente,* December 8, 1983, p. 82. Also see book version of the entire report: *Informe Rattenbach: El drama de Malvinas* (Buenos Aires: Ediciones Espartaco, 1988).

5

The Radicals Rebound

The Radical party was not supposed to win the 1983 presidential election, but thanks to Raul Alfonsín and the nation's fatigue, it did. Long a dissident in his own party, Alfonsín pulled the upset of his generation by defeating Peronist Italo Luder with 52 percent of the popular vote to Luder's 40 percent. A decade before the numbers had been reversed, with Perón winning in a landslide and Radical Ricardo Balbín receiving only 24 percent. But suddenly, after being relegated to what seemed permanent minority status, the Radicals were back, enjoying majority support for the first time since 1928.

Although Perón's death in 1974 certainly helped the Radicals, it was not the sole cause of the Peronists' defeat. The Peronists still had the CGT to draw upon, and union leaders worked hard to rally the masses for another battle, winning, in fact, a plurality of seats in the Senate and second place in the Chamber of Deputies. What Argentines rejected in 1983 was not the Peronist party per se, but the idea of another Peronist president. The memory of Isabel Perón's disaster in 1976 was fresh, as was fear of living through another cycle of Peronist and military rulers. Most people wanted a respite from militarism, and the unspectacular Alfonsín, known more for integrity than charisma, seemed to offer the best possibility for achieving it. He could not save the nation from its worst vices; no one could. But committed as he was to old-fashioned democratic government, he could become a vehicle for restoring badly needed civility to national life.

Alfonsín was more popular than the Radical party was in 1983, but he was very much a Radical, the new leader of one of the nation's oldest parties and, since World War II, its second largest. By attracting more voters than any Radical had done since 1928 and carrying several gubernatorial candidates on his coattails, he gave Radicalism new life, saving it, for the moment at least, from permanent residence among the anti-Peronist minority. But it was still *the* Radical party, a modest, closely knit community of democratic politicians who were convinced that they were morally superior to their rivals. They had suffered occasional persecution, repeated electoral defeats, and destructive divisions within their own ranks, but they were once again eager to demonstrate their love for old-fashioned constitutional government.

Radical Origins

The name "Radical" seems a misnomer today, for Alfonsín's platform resembled nothing more extreme than an Argentine version of European social democracy. But at its inception almost a century ago the party was radical, at least it seemed so to the oligarchs, who had no intention of sharing their control over the nation with others. Argentina pretended to operate as a constitutional democracy during the last half of the nineteenth century, but it never came close to being one for any but the 10 percent of the population that was allowed to vote. The people who founded the Radical party wanted this changed through political not social reform. Most of them came from the same class as those who ruled the country but were excluded from the inner circles of government and resented it. Desperate to make their way in, they tried every tactic imaginable, from petition to violent insurrection, but a quarter-century would pass before they were given what they wanted.

Argentine oligarchs were a powerful lot, who contested with each other for the nation's economic bounty while coexisting politically. They had fought among themselves for almost fifty years before coming to terms and creating a lasting political order in the 1850s. Thereafter their competition was confined to the marketplace, where land and labor were acquired and incredible wealth accumulated. It was never as neat as it seems in retrospect, for their enterprise was always a vulnerable one, dependent on markets and investors from abroad. Economic crises brought dissension within their ranks, as some among them used their power to advance themselves under the worst of conditions at the expense of colleagues who were less well positioned. Typical was the depression that struck in 1889, the result of one under way in Europe at the time. When its pain was felt, it was not the country's small and vulnerable proletariat that protested, but the merchants and less-favored cattlemen who watched as the ruling *porteño* elite and their British backers prospered while everyone else paid dearly for the crisis. It was in the midst of such discontent that the Radical party was born on September 1, 1889, when a few men calling themselves the Unión Cívica del la Juventud (Civic Union of Youth) organized a public protest to demand greater influence over the government's handling of such infirmities via honest elections and real representation. Two years later, on July 2, 1891, the movement's founders relabeled their creation the Unión Cívica Radical, the name the party retains today. Highly moralistic in their rhetoric and unprecedented in their dedication to the accomplishment of a single objective—free elections—they called on the largely disenfranchised Argentine middle class to join them in their effort to force their way in. Revolutionary they were not, except in their belief in universal manhood suffrage. But their cause was a popular one in this rapidly urbanizing country of disenfranchised immigrants, and the Radicals milked it for all that it was worth.[1]

Their stubborn campaign is instructive for what it says about political rivalry and the measures that were required to dislodge incumbents at the time. It is also a reminder of how democrats had to sacrifice their principles in order to acquire political power. Three times the Radicals resorted to conspiracy and popular insurrection only to be defeated by the authorities each time. But they continued just the same until the ruling oligarchs finally saw fit to let them in twenty-four years after their struggle had started.

Their quest began with a try at elections in 1892. Instead of selecting of one of their own to lead the ticket, they nominated retired army general Bartolome Mitre, hoping to outfox the conservative incumbents by making it difficult for them to oppose the popular old general. But it was they who were tricked, as right under their noses the incumbents stole Mitre from them, persuading him to merge his ticket with theirs, leaving the Radicals out in the cold. The incident left them in confusion, some deciding to stay with Mitre in the hope of getting a foot in the door while most of their colleagues angrily boycotted the election in protest. Dividing and conquering oppositions is a favorite tactic of political elites everywhere, and in Argentina the Radicals would become its victims often in the years ahead.

Frustration grew and the Radicals' patience declined swiftly after their election debacle, leading some to resort to violence in 1893. With the aid of a few sympathetic military officers they tried to launch a revolt, only to be defeated rather easily. Undaunted, they resorted to force again in 1897 and 1904, only to meet the same dismal fate. Yet by taking on the oligarchy directly they won the support of many in the country's middle and lower classes who gradually accepted the Radical cause as their own. No one was bothered by the apparent contradiction between their advocacy of democracy and their fomenting violent insurrections, for they knew that theirs was hardly the kind of liberal society in which the ruling class conceded reforms without putting up a fight.[2]

Yet, concessions did eventually come, two and one-half decades and three insurrections after the Radicals' quest had begun, when in 1912 conservative president Roque Saez Peña pushed passage of electoral reforms that guaranteed for the first time a secret ballot and universal manhood suffrage (women did not receive the right to vote until the Peronists put it in their constitution in 1949). Why a ruling elite gives ground politically to its democratic opponents is seldom apparent, and historians are of different opinions in Saez Peña's case. Concern about the mobilization of the immigrant proletariat by socialists in the labor movement may have convinced him that Radicals were preferable as the government's inevitable opponent. A working class loyal to moderate Radicals who were content with the economic status quo posed less of a threat than did a proletarian party inspired by visions of radical re-distributions of property. This explanation, though quite plausible, gives more credit for foresight and cunning to the old guard than they prob-ably deserve. As likely was their conviction that they could dispose of the noisy Radicals by defeating them in an honest election. Con-servatives believed that the Radicals' popularity was due more to clever exploitation of their victimization than it was to what they had to offer the nation as prospective rulers. It was not hard for them to imagine that when faced with a choice between Radicals and conservatives, most Argentines would stick with what they knew best. Incumbents, es-pecially those who have ruled for more than a half-century, tend to make such assumptions until their unanticipated defeat forces them to think otherwise. Paternalists at heart, oligarchs believe that their people ap-preciate the direction they have given them and will reward them accordingly. No doubt that was the case in Argentina in 1916 when, to their surprise and regret, the incumbents watched as the Radicals triumphed easily in the presidential elections, leaving only the Senate for the conservatives to control.[3]

The Raul Alfonsín of 1916 was Hipólito Yrigoyen, the slayer of an opposition that was supposed to be impossible to defeat. Having been the party's leader for twenty years he was the natural candidate for president. He proclaimed a belief in democracy but since 1896 had ruled over the party like an autocrat intolerant of dissent. His politics was less that of the twentieth-century democrat than of a "nineteenth-century caudillo in modern dress," as his biographers have often noted, a man who was dour and aloof, self-righteous and stubborn, and without many redeeming virtues other than his loyalty to those devoted to him.[4] He seldom spoke in public to anyone, preferring instead to deal in private with friends and foes alike, much like the clandestine conspir-ator whose followers waited in rapture for notice of his next move. It was the kind of behavior that would inevitably divide the party, but it also set a standard that his successors would try to imitate, making this party of democracy heavily dependent on the leadership of one or two strong persons.

The oligarchy had little to fear from Yrigoyen initially, for though they had taken their government from them, he had no intention of evicting them from the *pampas* as well. He understood his nation's export economy and what made the country prosper and was not about to upset it in any significant way. The Radicals wanted their piece of the pie, but that never required their baking a new one to get it. As nationalists they gave the government more control over the nation's resources, as when they created a government petroleum company, and they filled the bureaucracy with their constituents, but they imposed few regulations on an economy they accepted as the country's only legitimate means to development. They did not ignore the working class entirely, since much of Yrigoyen's support had come from it, setting higher standards for working conditions in factories, adopting an eight-hour workday, and putting limits on child employment. But their sense of social justice never included toleration of proletarian militancy. And if there had been any doubts about how far they would go to preserve the power structure of which they were now a small part, they were ended during the infamous Semana Trágica in 1919, when strikes provoked Yrigoyen's sending the police in to pound on the culprits and bring them into line.[5]

The Radicals wanted to become the nation's permanent majority party, and they appeared to be on their way to doing so in the 1920s. It was a good time for the country economically; the oligarchy and the middle class prospered, and the Radicals, with their strident nationalism and neutralism during and after World War I, gave Argentines a new pride in their embryonic nationhood. But they never quite made it, becoming victims of their own internal divisions, Yrigoyen's obstinacy and feebleness of mind, and the oligarchy's refusal to trust the Radicals' leading the country from a crisis in which the wealthy had the most to lose.

That someone like Yrigoyen would sow the seeds of division within his own party was predictable. It began with the choice of his successor to the presidency in 1922. Marcelo de T. Alvear was Yrigoyen's candidate, but he brushed away his mentor immediately after his election, accepting leadership of the "antipersonalists" in the party, who, as their name suggests, had grown weary of the party's domination by Yrigoyen. They were more urbane than Yrigoyen's crowd and wanted a president that fit more into the twentieth than the nineteenth century. That is why they backed the more pragmatic and less populist Alvear, a man who was never embarrassed by his upper-class origins and one whose presidency more resembled that of a constitutional monarch than a middle-class politician.[6] There was little Yrigoyen could do to rein in Alvear during his presidency, so he waited and struck back by running for the presidency again in 1928. A battle for the nomination ensued with the seventy-six-year-old Yrigoyen the easy victor; frustrated, the antipersonalists defected to the opposition, supporting Yrigoyen's conservative opponent at the polls, but it was hardly enough to halt the old patriarch's populist campaign, which collected him 57 percent of the vote.

It was all downhill thereafter, however. To begin with, Yrigoyen's crusade for personal vindication alienated what few friends he had among the oligarchy, people who had worked with the Radicals and kept members of their own class at bay during the 1920s. Then, after one of the most prosperous years ever in 1928, the depression struck, catching by surprise the reclusive old president, who showed little inclination to do anything about his collapsing economy or for its victims. Policy decisions had to be made but few were, and the longer he waited the more the public turned away from him, becoming easy prey for an opposition that warned of disaster. In concert, oligarchs and antipersonalist Radicals persuaded fascist-admiring José Uriburu to end it all with a coup on September 6, 1930, terminating the country's fourteen-year experiment in constitutional democracy.

Yrigoyen died three years later, a rejected man. But that has not prevented his successors in the Radical party from elevating him to heroic stature in their memories, much as the Peronists do with Juan and Evita, though most Radicals would deny being party to such myth-making. To them he is the founding father whose dedication to the fight against rich authoritarians became a fundamental Radical objective. No party meeting begins anymore without paying homage to the "spirit and purpose" given Radicalism by Yrigoyen and his cohorts. It is symptomatic of a sentimentalism that the politically liberal Radicals do not really want to shake.

But whatever the use of legend, the impact of Yrigoyen is undeniable, as even his opponents noted at his death:

> Few men have exercised as vast an influence in our political, economic and spiritual life in the last fifty years. His achievements are as memorable as the great epidemics. . . . The old curse of superstitious caudillism is a fatality of our Indo-Hispanic inheritance. It reproduces and will continue to reproduce itself for many years in notable ways. But it will never again repeat in a form as complex, grand, and perfect.[7]

One can only speculate about what would have become of Radicalism had Yrigoyen not divided it when he returned to the presidency in 1928 and then mismanaged the nation's greatest economic crisis. He might have chosen a younger and wiser successor, who could have taken the party and the country through the depression without provoking a coup. Alternatively, however, the antipersonalists might have prevailed, making the party more conservative and less popular with its lower-middle- and working-class membership and losing its majority in the process. But most likely Radicalism was doomed by the country's power structure and by the oligarchy's unwillingness to trust any party but its own to protect its interests in a time of such obvious crisis. Whatever might have been the case, the depression quite definitely brought the destruction of the Radical experiment in democratic government and the disappearance of the Radical majority. For the next half-century it would seem that the party's chance had come and forever gone.

Radicals in Opposition

With Yrigoyen in jail after the coup and his party seemingly broken, the oligarchy replaced fascist Uriburu with the less ambitious Agustín Justo in the hope of gaining some legitimacy for the new order. As a popularity test, gubernatorial elections were called in Buenos Aires province not long after the coup, with the oligarchy hoping that a new realism would drive most people to lend their support to the regime. But these hopes were to be disappointed. Just as they had done back in 1916, the Radicals rallied the opponents of authoritarianism and roundly defeated the government's candidates, making a mockery of its claim of legitimacy. Getting the message, Justo and his upper-class backers decided to give up their quest for popularity and get on with engineering the nation's economic recovery. With the collaboration of several antipersonalist Radicals who preferred power over principle, they rigged subsequent elections, allowing other parties only some seats in what became a rubber-stamp legislature.[8]

Their subjugation left the rest of the Radicals with old but familiar choices. They could abstain from participating in the new political charade and protest democracy's abuse by authorities, as they had done before 1916, or they could accept the military-backed conservative government as a necessary fact of life and play the role of loyal but subservient opponent that it demanded of them. Not surprisingly, they chose abstention, hammering away at the government's unpopularity in hopes of forcing its retreat. In 1931 they were joined by Alvear, who chose to abandon his antipersonalist followers, realizing that with Yrigoyen jailed he had a chance to retake control over the largest wing of the party. His return was not celebrated, but he was rewarded with the leadership post, nevertheless.

Radical protests had little effection the ruling Concordancia alliance of conservatives and antipersonalists who devoted their authority
to keeping everyone in line while they dealt with the troubled economy.
But they were never comfortable with popular opposition and persisted
in their attempts to co-opt Radicals into the regime. In 1935 they
promised Alvear that they would hold free elections in the early 1940s if
he would lend his blessing to elections in 1937, offering his own candidacy in a contest that everyone knew would be rigged for the Concordancia candidate. Always ambitious and now tired of exclusion,
Alvear went for the bait, trying as best he could to lead his party back to
the polls. To complete the show, the government chose as its candidate
Roberto Ortiz, himself a Radical who had signed up with the Concordancia in 1931 along with other antipersonalists. His service as
Justo's finance minister between 1935 and 1937 had proved his re-
liability and loyalty. In the tightly controlled presidential election, he was
rewarded with 54 percent of the vote, with only 40 percent allowed to go
to Alvear. The episode left the Radical party more divided than ever.
Many of its younger members left the party to protest Alvear's opportunism and to demand the formation of a new Radical party that would
be truer to Yrigoyen's original commitment to popular democratic government.[9]

The nation's political farce did give authorities some latitude for
dealing with its economic recovery. But the politics practiced inflicted
permanent damage on the country, making a mockery of the oligarchy's
pretense to civility and reinforcing already rampant cynicism about the
purposes that democratic institutions really served. By turning the clock
back and abusing the Radicals into colluding in the maintenance of a
fraudulent political process after 1937, they halted progress toward the
integration of the middle class and the masses into the national power
structure. What they achieved instead was the division of society into a
politically alienated mass and a ruling class whose paternalism never
extended very deeply below its own ranks. It could not help but invite a
challenge from below that would be as belligerent as it was desperate.
That it would turn out to be so unrevolutionary when it came a decade
later was due more to Perón's sharing their fear of the Marxist left than
it was to anything they had done to make accommodation easier
through their actions in the 1930s.

The 1930s was not a total loss for the Radical party, however. When
Alvear agreed to participate in the 1937 elections youthful protestors
in the party formed the Fuerza de Orientación Radical de la Joven
Argentina (FORJA), an idea factory that advocated a more militant
nationalism and greater state involvement in the country's industrialization, starting with the nationalization of all natural resources and public

utilities and the breaking up of all foreign oligopolies. They were frustrated not just with the oligarchy and its abuses of authority and party leaders and their self-defeating opportunism, but also with the nation's rush to restore its reliance on Britain for trade and capital as revealed in the humiliating concessions that Britain extracted from Argentina in the Roca-Runciman agreement in 1933. The FORJA people convinced themselves that Argentina's malaise stemmed from foreign exploitation of its immense wealth and that its progress would come only after its dependence on foreigners was ended. It was a popular argument and remains so today. Argentines rely on their nationalism to explain a great deal to themselves, and the more difficult conditions are for them, the more appealing the notion of foreign exploitation becomes. The young Radicals thought they had an issue that would rejuvenate their party, but they were ignored by Alvear and his aged colleagues. Instead it was young military officers who found such ideas attractive and incorporated them into their own agendas after they removed the oligarchs in 1943. Not surprisingly, several from the FORJA crowd turned up in the Peronist party when it was organized two years later.[10]

Alvear died in 1942 at the age of seventy-three, leaving the Radicals without a dominant personality to lead them for the first time since their creation. Moreover, it marked the end of nearly a half-century in which this party of democracy had been run by just two persons, Yrigoyen and Alvear. It survived them thanks to its solid infrastructure of grass-roots committees and provincial organizations and Alvear's cronies retaining substantial control at the top. It was also sustained by its participation in congressional elections after 1937, for despite being outfoxed in the presidential contest, they were allowed to add seats in Congress, winning a majority of those contested in 1940. To his credit Ortiz refrained from tampering with Congress while he was president, giving the Radicals a sense of rising up once again, albeit slowly and under the watchful eye of authorities who were not yet ready to turn the entire government over to them.

The Radicals' resurrection took a turn for the worse after 1940, though the fault was not theirs this time. Illness forced Ortiz to relinquish the presidency to his vice president, the very conservative Ramón Castillo, who had never shared his faith in tutelary democracy. Later when the time came to announce candidates for elections in 1944, he made it known that his choice was a fellow conservative, the reactionary provincial oligarch Robustiano Patrón Costas, whom Castillo intended to assure election using all of the authority he had. Bitterly disappointed, the Radicals had little choice but to look for help elsewhere, as conservatives had done when discontent with Yrigoyen peaked in 1930, military intervention being the obvious choice to rid the nation of Castillo and start over. There is no evidence that they conspired with officers to stage a coup, but they did not have to since nationalists within the military were already prepared to take matters into their own hands. When they did, no complaints were heard from Radical circles; instead they set their sights immediately on preparing for what the Radicals hoped would be the restoration of constitutional democracy and an easy victory for them in new elections.

Thanks to the oligarchy's monopolization of power and the repression of movements on the extreme left (moderate socialists were allowed to function and occupy seats in Congress), no other popular party had developed the support needed to defeat the Radicals. That is why when elections were called by the military for early in 1946, the Radicals were convinced that victory would come easily, so much so that they refused help from army officers who offered to write the election rules to favor them. And when Juan Perón, still unsure of his base in mid-1945, proposed to join forces with them, with him leading the ticket, they refused outright. Not until the outpouring of working-class support for Perón on October 17 did they begin to comprehend how popular their real competitor had become, and in last-minute desperation they turned to conservatives and socialists for help, creating an electoral alliance aimed at stopping the Peronist surge. But they were too late. After fifteen years on the outside looking in, the Radicals would spend twelve more watching while Perón stole the agenda of their most progressive members and blocked their access to power even more effectively than the oligarchy had.[11]

A New Era: Two Radicals Instead of One

A casual glance at events between Perón's election in 1946 and Raul Alfonsín's in 1983 reveals why the Radicals were so euphoric about Alfonsín's triumph. Winners always celebrate victory, to be sure, but 1983 was very special, being the first time ever that a Radical had defeated a Peronist in a free presidential election. Getting there had not been easy. The quest began in 1955, when the military sent Perón into exile and promised to restore constitutional democracy to the country. The Radicals endorsed the coup and played an active part in the military's preparation of the new rules of electoral competition. Aramburu was determined to destroy the Peronist movement by purging labor of its leadership and banning all other Peronist organizations, freeing the rank and file to express their preferences through another party, such as the Radicals. Convinced that Perón had stolen the working class from them, Radicals found it hard to question Aramburu's motives or to do anything but celebrate his punishing Peronists. They believed that it gave them a chance to woo the Argentine masses back to the party that most of their parents had supported in 1928.

But life is not that simple in Argentina, and wishing an end to Peronism did little to eliminate it. Well before election day it was obvious that a working class that had watched under duress while the Radicals collaborated with the military in the elimination of the Peronist party was not about to thank them for their liberation by voting Radical. Whoever won in 1958 would do so with the knowledge that the nation's majority had effectively been excluded from their selection. Recognition of this fact confronted the Radicals with an unpleasant dilemma. If the Radicals won an election that excluded the Peronists and led to working-class protests against the election itself, the Radicals would not secure anything resembling the popular legitimacy that they needed to govern a very divided nation. Yet if they appealed to the Peronists with promises to legalize their party after the election, they invited the wrath of the armed forces and, most likely, defeat by the still-popular Peronists at the next election. There was no satisfactory solution and the Radicals knew it.

When they went to their convention in 1957 they had to make two decisions: one regarding how they would deal with the Peronists who were excluded from the election, and the other on the choice of presidential candidate. They solved both by splitting into two Radical parties whose presidential candidates took opposite positions on Peronism. Before the convention had progressed very far, one faction lined up behind Arturo Frondizi and called itself the Unión Cívica Radical Intransigente (UCRI), while the other chose Ricardo Balbín and his Unión Cívica Radical del Pueblo (UCRP). Balbín and Frondizi were once good friends who had collaborated in an assault on the party leadership after its defeat by the Peronists in 1946, turning their reformist Movimiento Intransigente Radical into the dominant force within the party. They were rewarded with Balbín's nomination for the presidency and Frondizi's for the vice presidency in the 1951 elections won by Perón. When elections were called again in 1958 Frondizi insisted that it was his turn to lead the ticket but Balbín refused to go along with it. So when Frondizi attracted enough delegates to win the nomination, Balbín boycotted the convention and organized one of his own with nearly half of the party in attendance a few weeks later.[12]

The two factions were separated as much by matters of strategy as they were by personalities. Balbín accepted the military's exclusion of the Peronists, convinced that it was justified by the Peronists' anti-democratic behavior. Until democracy was restored and its ethics practiced by everyone, allowing Peronist participation would be self-defeating for democrats. Frondizi, in contrast, believed that with or without Perón to lead it, the Peronist movement was there to stay, too large a part of the electorate to be excluded entirely. No president could rule for long over an alienated majority. He also knew that with Peronist support he would be unbeatable, so in January 1958, a few months before the election, he sent close friend Rogelio Frigerio to Caracas, where he negotiated an agreement with the exiled Perón in which Frondizi promised to legalize Peronist organizations after his inauguration in exchange for Perón's endorsement. It worked just as planned on election day: with substantial Peronist support Frondizi came out on top just short of a majority while Balbín received only 29 percent.[13]

Frondizi was full of surprises after his inauguration. A notorious nationalist prior to his nomination, he was forced by rising inflation and a balance-of-payments crisis to invite the help of the International Monetary Fund, which brought recommendations for tough austerity measures with its financial aid. But that was not all. As he prepared for the election Frondizi became convinced that something new was essential to launch the Argentine economy into more rapid growth after a decade of stagnation. Heavily influenced by confidant and businessman Frigerio, Frondizi concluded that populism had run its course, creating a large consumer goods industry whose imports of capital goods and basic supplies exhausted the nation's export earnings far too rapidly. Its only option was to build its own capital goods industry, displacing imports just as consumer goods industries had done a decade before. Argentina needed more iron, steel, and petrochemical industries, and Frondizi was determined to see them built even if it took multinational corporations to get the job done.[14]

It was a bit strange, the president who had sought an alliance with the Peronists selecting policies that were certain to alienate the working class and its nationalist cheerleaders. But Frondizi had little choice in the matter once in office. The Argentine economy was in trouble, and it needed substantial new investment to re-ignite growth. Yet, that which is so obvious to the economist is seldom reasonable to the partisan who thinks that he is adversely affected by new policies. Frondizi was attacked from all sides during his four-year tenure, by a labor movement that felt itself betrayed, by rivals in the UCRP who accused him of abandoning the Radical platform, and by conservatives who resented a foreign policy of nonalignment whose most offensive gesture was Frondizi's welcoming Che Guevara on his visit home in August 1961. But Frondizi's real battle was always with the armed forces, who had lost what little trust they had in him when he made his pact with Perón.

In normal democracies political parties participate within a single political system, competing with other parties for control over the government. Not so in Argentina: after 1955 it had two political systems, one in which political parties competed for the right to direct the government; and a second one in which the Peronists and the military were locked in a battle that spilled onto everyone else. Frondizi was an obvious case in point. He had used the Peronists for political advantage and they him, but the conspiracy left him at the mercy of a suspicious military. No president before or since has suffered more rumors of coups, many of which ended in attempts that were abortive. The last straw was Frondizi's keeping a promise to allow the Peronists to participate in elections during his tenure. When he did so in 1964, they scored impressive victories in gubernatorial elections in the most populated provinces, something the armed forces were not yet ready to tolerate. Within a few days they moved in and Frondizi moved out, first to prison, where he was held until the ruling junta could sort things out.

When new elections were called for July 1963 and the Peronist party was again excluded, victory went to the UCRP. This time, however, Balbín stepped aside, allowing provincial physician Arturo Illia to head the ticket in an attempt to attract some of Balbín's enemies back into the Radical party. It was a strange election in many ways. Until just before the election it was not certain whether the military would allow the Peronists to participate or not. When they chose to exclude them, causing Peronists to promise abstention, they improved the chances of conservatives who backed the candidacy of retired General Pedro Aramburu. Though not the favorite of everyone in the armed forces, Aramburu seemed to offer Argentines the opportunity to select someone who stood a better chance than any Radical did of withstanding pressures from the armed forces. But with twenty-eight other presidential candidates to contest with, Illia won with just 25 percent of the vote. It was an auspicious beginning for the quiet, grandfatherly new president whose small plurality invited complaints of illegitimacy throughout his tenure.

Illia refused to act like a president who was supported by only a fourth of the electorate. Faithful to his belief in constitutional democracy almost to a fault, he governed the nation as if he had a real mandate, hoping that steady and unspectacular leadership would calm his people and teach them the virtues of political liberty. His economic policies were nationalist in spirit but hardly extreme, his respect for civil liberty consistently enforced, and his tolerance for the opposition greater than Argentines had ever known. Yet, neither such noble virtues nor bumper crops and a booming recovery proved enough to prevent the powerful forces in society from undermining this latest try at democracy.

The armed forces were the least prepared to tolerate democracy. They had fought among themselves during 1962 over its desirability in Argentina, and in 1963 the winners of the dispute proceeded to hold elections, hoping that a new party led by General Pedro Aramburu would triumph. But their gamble failed and they were left with Illia, another of the politicians for whom they had nothing but disdain. Soon after the new president's inauguration the officers who had defended constitutional government in 1962 were heard complaining privately that they had made a mistake, one that became even more obvious as they watched the new president attacked by the CGT and its *plan de lucha* that was aimed at immobilizing the Radical government. Illia tried to calm his union adversaries by raising their wages, something the Radicals also hoped would pacify the masses and even win a few to their side, but the protests were more political than economic and did not end until 1,400 factory "occupations" later when Illia had fallen.[15]

Illia did not help his relations with the armed forces when he committed himself to an open political process that allowed every party a chance to participate, including the Peronists. No doubt he was enticed by the thought of defeating the Peronists at the polls as much as he was by simple democratic principle. The temptation to do battle with the Peronists in honest elections comes naturally to democrats like the Radicals, who insist on believing that if the masses came to know them many would prefer their honesty and integrity to the corruption and bullying of their Peronist bosses. It did not seem to matter that Yrigoyen was remembered by the working class more for his repression of them than his paternalism or that to the masses the Radicals had become a minority party of shopkeepers, dentists, and schoolteachers rather than the populists that they pretended to be. But what else could the Radicals do? They wanted to govern and knew that they could not do it for very long if the majority remained Peronist.

The Radicals went into congressional elections in March 1965 hoping for a good showing and they got one, but the Peronists did even better, topping the UCRP's 28 percent with 30 percent of their own. Not all seats were up so Illia retained a plurality in Congress, but their entrance into the legislative process gave the Peronists another point of attack from which to harass the president. Unlike in 1962 the armed forces reacted calmly at first, letting the Peronists take their seats and allowing Illia to deal with them. But their passivity could not disguise further unhappiness with the situation that led to their planning Illia's removal a year later.

Still, the need for a military coup never seemed less obvious than in 1966. No single event or crisis provoked it. Nor was the economy in deep trouble. On the contrary, the national product had grown by almost 20 percent in two years and inflation had risen only from 24 to 29 percent, hardly anything to cause concern in Argentina. Moreover, people were enjoying more liberty than they had in decades, and despite CGT militancy, most were exercising it judiciously. So why a coup?

It pays to recall that militaries do not behave like machines that explode only when their engines become overheated. They had ideas about how their societies should be governed just as everyone else does. They also react to their own expectations for the country and the failure of incumbents to meet them. In 1966 the nation was not accomplishing as much as they thought it could, and it was easy to blame democratic politics and its waste of energy for the country's plight. Officers dreamed of a powerful Argentina that was prosperous at home and prominent abroad, and they were convinced that it would never be theirs as long as Radicals and Peronists were slugging it out, distracting citizens from their real duties to the nation. They, like so many Argentines, were prisoners of the country's glorious past and frustrated with its conflict-ridden present; it was easy to believe that greatness awaited them just around a corner which they coud turn if only people with conviction and determination took charge and led them there. If they needed encouragement, the country's foreign and domestic bankers and industrialists offered it with their complaints about the nation's political retardation and promises of abundance once a politics-free investment climate was achieved. Moreover, they only had to look next door for the model they needed: the Brazilian armed forces had seized the initiative and were hard at work stabilizing their economy in the name of modernization, meeting little resistance from the politicians whom they had deposed. It seemed just the thing for officers who had grown weary of *planes de lucha* and procrastinating presidents.[16]

The 1966 coup was not, however, just the work of military officers and businessmen out to protect their respective interests. Labor leaders were just as eager to see Illia toppled as the military was. They did not conspire directly with them but did all they could to encourage a coup by undermining Illia's authority at every turn, quite aware of where their efforts would lead. Peronists have always been a bit schizophrenic about the armed forces, having been created by a military government only to be repressed by General Aramburu and his successors. But their persecution had never caused them to abandon hope of drawing the military back to their side, and there were always a few nationalistic colonels around who encouraged them to believe that it could be done. Trying for it was certainly tempting since a combination of the military and the masses guaranteed the Peronists a powerful state to direct. So as remote as the possibility seemed in 1966, the prize was too big to ignore when the time came to place a few bets.[17]

The fact that capital and labor would combine to destroy one of Argentina's more democratic regimes says much about the nature of Argentine politics and reliance on authoritarian methods to achieve narrow partisan ends. It also says something about how little confidence Argentines have in democracy itself. Few people are willing to bet on democracy working whenever it is tried; instead, within a year of a government's election it becomes popular to predict its demise and leave its defense to those who run it. Conventional wisdom teaches that even if one does not work for its termination many others will, so little is gained from planning on its survival. Instead, one just watches from a distance while someone else puts the constitution into storage. That is how it seemed on June 30, 1966, when a few officers entered Illia's office and informed him that they had been ordered by their commander-in-chief to remove him. Not one to suffer insult lightly, he threw them out, insisting that he was the commander-in-chief and had given no such order. Taken by surprise they departed to consult, and then sent in the police to arrest the president and escort him from the Casa Rosada.[18]

The Radicals spent the next decade and a half reassessing their role in politics, never accepting their irrelevance even though it appeared that they were doomed to permanent minority status. Their party was closed by the military in 1966, forcing them to cling to the friendships they had made during decades of politics. They took on the appearance of a kind of fraternal organization that was kept alive by the habits of small-town, petit bourgeois career politicians whose love of legality and fondness for each other prevented their disappearance as a political community. Radicals had always enjoyed a collegiality that was unusual in Argentine politics, sustained by their devotion to doing everything in committees, from plotting future political strategies to sharing the latest gossip. In contrast to Peronists, who take their energy from mass demonstrations and demagogic rhetoric, Radicals can be downright boring in their endless meetings and consultations. It does not make for spectacular or even exciting governance, for nothing ever seems to get settled and presidents obligated to involve dozens of party stalwarts in their decisions give the appearance of never really deciding anything. It also makes them easy targets for opponents who demand instant solutions to every problem. Nonetheless, Radicals carry on, self-righteous in their convictions of moral superiority in an undemocratic society and confident in their capacity to withstand all forms of persecution.

Their tenacity paid off, and in 1973 when the military called new elections they were ready and waiting. But as in 1946 General Juan Perón got in their way again, this time by leading a campaign for his return that attracted half of the electorate to his stand-in candidate. Ricardo Balbín insisted on being the Radical nominee only to be embarrassed by attracting less of the vote than Illia had a decade before. An "old school" politician who, like Yrigoyen and Alvear before him, never recognized that his day had passed, Balbín alienated the younger members of his party, many of whom, like their predecessors in the 1930s, used the party's youth organization, the Juventud Radical, to lead an assault on his leadership. They complained of his ideological moderation and unwillingness to challenge the Peronists head-on, a failure that made the Radicals look irrelevant to the country's politics and helpless in competition with Peronism. To make matters worse Balbín just patted them on the head and ignored their pleas with characteristic unconcern.

In their challenge to Balbín the Juventud were joined by a youthful grandfather named Raul Alfonsín, a lawyer and career politician who had never been admitted to the party's leadership because of a well-known independence of spirit that bred distrust among an old guard that demanded complete loyalty to the committee. In 1973 he formed the Movement of Renovation and Change in order to organize a campaign for the party's presidential nomination. It was a bold move, but Balbín survived it easily, leaving Alfonsín to settle for a seat in the Senate during the next three years. But it was the beginning of what would become a long and stubborn effort to become the party's leader, one that took longer than anyone expected and overcame great odds through skillful campaigning and substantial good fortune.[19]

Alfonsín went on the attack after Balbín's nomination, accusing him of having retarded the party's adjustment to a new age, one that demanded a bold new social democratic platform. When Isabel Perón moved to the right in 1975 in her battle with defiant labor unions, Alfonsín urged his party to move to her left and make a serious effort to attract lower-class voters away from Peronism, which, he pointed out, was the only way it could become a majority party once again. But the more he and his colleagues tried to push Radicalism to the left, the more Balbín resisted them, leaving things much as they were when the military stepped in and closed all parties again in 1976. With the party back to reliance on the personal ties of its members for its sustenance,

Alfonsín busied himself defending the human rights of victims of the military police state while at the same time laying the foundation for his next try for the party's presidential nomination should the opportunity ever arise again.

His first objective was to fashion an ideological stance that separated him from both Balbín and the Peronists. Innovation was his theme, though not at the cost of a complete break with the past. Thus, he criticized populist economics as obsolete and too costly to a country that could no longer afford high inflation and overbureaucratization. However, the free-market principles of Martínez de Hoz and his colleagues were equally inappropriate, if only for their excessive simplicity and insensitivity to diversity within the country's economy. What was needed was something he called "integrated" economic development, a solution which offered a little something for everyone: improved wages for workers; real investment opportunities for the private sector; and reform of the public sector aimed at reducing waste and increasing its efficiency. Hardly radical ideas, even in Argentina, but as Alfonsín saw it, they offered a more realistic and, he hoped, more popular solution than those that had been tried previously.[20]

He also portrayed himself as the democrat that Argentina needed after nearly two decades of military and Peronist rule, criticizing them both as birds of the same autocratic feather. To spread his message he published the mandatory book of diagnoses and solutions, a 244-page paperback filled with high principles, economic prescriptions, and aspirations for the future titled *La cuestión argentina*. In it he offered a few new ideas, but at its core it was a very Radical statement, filled with the kind of moralism that had characterized party thinking since its founding nearly a century before. Like his predecessors he wanted everyone to know that

> Radicalism is before anything a moral requisite. It was an ethic before an ideology. Better put, its ideas were developed from a moral conception that obligated it to fight to solve the problems of the dispossessed and raise highest the banner of human dignity and respect for essential rights. . . . Because it is an ethic, it cannot be put anywhere along a continuum from left to right. It does not represent any sector exclusively but can defend the concrete interest of any sector when it fits with the Radical morality. In other words Radicalism is neither left nor right nor just interested in the plight of the middle class as some would have you believe.[21]

Was this an example of dedication to the highest principles or just the propaganda of a politician pursuing a multiclass following? It was a little of both in Alfonsín's case, since he wanted to distinguish Radicals from everyone else, reminding a country that had grown weary of tyranny that Radicals were still the nation's most dedicated political liberals, and also to tell the working class that he, too, was different from the rest, ready to listen to their pleas in ways that more partisan Radicals never had.

But it was nothing but verbiage as long as Alfonsín was the rene-gade and not the leader of the Radical party. He had to gain the party's nomination before the next election, and to accomplish that, he had to get by his old nemesis, Ricardo Balbín. Without knowing when the election would be held, he quietly went to work laying the foundation of his campaign with the help of a small collection of people who were loyal to him and his advocacy of political renovation. Some were fellow dissidents within the Radical party, others young academics who thought they had found a progressive democrat who could defy the odds against his election. Together they worked on establishing Alfonsín's credibility within and outside the country, portraying him as a fresh alternative to his many older and discredited rivals.

His first break came when the seventy-seven-year-old Balbín died in September 1981, a year before Alfonsín announced his candidacy. Balbín's departure did not guarantee Alfonsín anything; there were still many others in the party who were determined to hold on to their positions by preventing his candidacy. But it did deny his opponents the leader they had relied on for the past twenty years, one who was tough and skilled at outmaneuvering his opponents. Moreover, it lifted the confidence of his supporters within the party, who were encouraged to know that the contest would be easier than anticipated.

The military also contributed to his good fortune. In an effort to weaken the control of Peronist bosses over the rank and file, the outgo-ing officers required that the delegates to presidential nominating con-ventions be selected in provincial primaries hastily called during the first half of 1983. This was exactly what Alfonsín needed, for it gave him the opportunity to use the grass-roots following that he had accumu-lated almost unnoticed during the previous three years to take on the candidate of the party establishment. Where his rival would depend on lifelong party members to secure endorsement, Alfonsín took advantage of the military's unsolicited assistance to recruit thousands of new members to the party.[22]

There was, of course, no certainty that elections would ever be held when he began his effort in the late 1970s. But such uncertainty has never stopped Argentine politicians, past or present, from pursuing public office. Their world is one neither of continuity nor of revolution-ary change but of political cycles whose regularity they have come to take for granted. Obviously, it is also in the interest of party politicians to believe that the effects of military interventions will one day be reversed; that is what keeps them going in difficult times and prepares them for a counterattack when they are given a chance to launch it.

They sensed an opportunity for change when General Viola replaced Videla in March 1981. He inherited a deep recession and declining confidence in the military's management of the economy, especially among businessmen, who found themselves with huge debts and high interest rates and far too many bankruptcies. Jumping in, the Radicals and Peronists organized a multiparty coalition that petitioned Viola to schedule elections within two or three years. He refused, of course, but that did not discourage them. Still, it was not the protests of civilian politicians but defeat in the Malvinas War that ended the life of the military government. With its self-confidence temporarily shattered and recriminations within and among the three services tearing the new junta apart, the armed forces had to pull out and call elections. Another experiment in military authoritarianism had ended, only this time it came down with a bigger crash than ever before.

1983: A Very Special Election

The number of people who registered as Radicals when the books were opened again at the end of 1982 surprised even Alfonsín. The party was totally unprepared for its sudden popularity, as were the Peronists, who looked on in amazement. What it meant could not be determined for another ten months, however, since both parties had to go through a succession of provincial primaries and conventions that would select candidates for nearly every office in the land, and then hold national elections in October. As the process went through each phase, Alfonsín implemented his opportunistic campaign strategy, starting with an attempt to attract previously apathetic middle- and upper-middle-class voters who feared the Peronists' return to the Casa Rosada. It was a long shot but it was the only one he had. Better yet, it worked. In one primary after another he was victorious, the momentum building until June 18, when he trounced rival Fernando de la Rua in the Buenos Aires provincial primary, always the stronghold of the party leadership. With a majority of the delegates securely under his control, he entered the convention in July already triumphant.

Success in the primaries taught Alfonsín what the Argentine middle class wanted in their politicians in the 1980s, most notably an ability to stand up to Peronists and the military whenever called upon to do so. Wrapping himself in the Radical banner was necessary for Alfonsín to keep the party's regulars behind him, but being a Radical did not help him with the rest of the electorate. Rather, for them he had to be the man whom they could put in charge of the country for five years. To accommodate them, he used television to attack the armed forces and their crimes and to denounce Peronists for their corruption and intolerance. Almost overnight this quiet, mild-mannered politician, known more for rumpled suits strewn with cigarette ashes than for anything resembling charisma, was transformed by his television appearances into a poised and deeply committed slayer of well-known dragons.[23] It was obviously what middle-class Argentines wanted to see. As one journalist remarked at the time:

> When I went in to see Alfonsín, he was holding his thirteenth grandchild in his arms. He was the same warm, decent man, the same convinced democrat, the same stickler for the law. But as Argentines discovered as they watched his campaign, something had happened to him. He had become the person who seemed able to save Argentina. The transformation he personifies is little short of miraculous.[24]

From the day of his nomination it became obvious that his chances depended as much on what the Peronists did as on his own efforts. The majority was theirs if they could keep it together, but this could no longer be taken for granted, given the loss of their supreme leader and their sad performance in the mid-1970s. They had always functioned better as a loosely organized mass movement whose labor leaders and white-collar politicians carried out Perón's directives than as a modern political party with sophisticated campaign organizations. Thus they were quite unprepared when primary elections were suddenly called. Previously, they had drawn their support from union members and the small-town poor, who had allowed Perón and CGT secretaries to choose candidates for them. Now, however, they were expected to register individual members and hold provincial primaries to elect delegates who would pick senatorial, congressional, and presidential candidates. It was not the Peronist way of doing things, and that is exactly why the armed forces did it.

Old habits die slowly, and the Peronists were not about to be democratized overnight, however. Well-known party bosses led most provincial delegations that went to the convention prepared to contest with one another over the nomination. In the past Perón would have made the critical choices, but now they had to manage without an authority to determine how their differences would be settled. There were "verticalists" who wanted exiled Isabel Perón to return home to pick a candidate for them, imitating her late husband as closely as possible, as well as "antiverticalists" who preferred to take their chances with back room bargaining over the nomination. Isabel may have favored the former, but she never said so, repeatedly refusing to exercise what authority she had. That is why when the national convention was held in early September it was wracked by confusion and quickly fell into a state of near chaos as rival factions challenged each other's credentials, postponing candidate selections for several days. Eventually the disputes were resolved and they turned to nominations, and before the week was out they had chosen ex-Senator Italo Luder to lead the ticket.

Luder was no Perón. A taciturn bourgeois lawyer, he made it to the top less on popularity than on his skill at sneaking up on his rivals within the party. Starting with a slight plurality among the delegates, he stayed aloof of the scuffling at the beginning, leaving the other candidates to knock each other off, which they proceeded to do. At the start, each of the two wings of the CGT favored a different candidate, the CGT-Azopardo backing Angel Robledo, while labor leader Lorenzo Miguel's CGT-Brasil went with Antonio Cafiero. But Azopardo dropped Robledo when it became obvious that he had little support among the rank and file, and Brasil leaders eventually shifted over to Luder after they became convinced that Cafiero could not get the nomination. To expedite the nomination Cafiero agreed to back Luder in exchange for the latter's supporting Cafiero for the governorship of Buenos Aires province, always a Peronist stronghold because most of its population came from the working-class suburbs that surrounded the nation's capital. That left the nomination to Luder, the patient compromise candidate who had quickly become everyone's second choice. It helped that Luder made it all seem quite reasonable, portraying himself as representative of a new, buttoned-down Peronist leadership that wanted to work with everyone to make the country a more democratic place. Bourgeois respectability, not blue-collar militancy, was the new look that he offered the movement, even if it was not quite ready for it.[25]

But no presidential candidate could unite the disparate and quarreling collection of politicians and labor leaders who called themselves Peronists in 1983. The best that Luder could hope for was their staying together long enough to mobilize mass support for the ticket. It would not be easy, however, since the rivalries that had torn apart the convention continued afterward. The biggest problem was posed by the antics of Buenos Aires provincial party leader Herminio Iglesias, a neofascist ward boss who refused to allow Cafiero the nomination for governor. Iglesias represented an old-fashioned Peronism and did not apologize for it, the kind that thrived on shouting insults at its opponents (he loved to call Alfonsín a bastard and a worm), and believed that democracy was whatever the *descamisados* and their orators said it was.[26] Luder could not shut him up and suffered for it throughout the campaign, his new image being tarnished every time Iglesias stood up and reminded everyone that Peronism had not matured after all. As election day approached Luder found himself boring crowds and Iglesias exciting them; at the last minute he panicked at the thought of losing and joined in the name calling, futilely trying to become a demagogue without the instinct for it. But that was all right with Alfonsín, for the more nasty Luder became, the more he played into the Radicals' hands, since fear of Peronism was the best thing they had going for them.[27]

Alfonsín could have treated the Peronists as respectable rivals in a democratic contest, trying to make the nation think it was choosing between two equally legitimate parties. Doing so might have strengthened democracy by making the contest resemble those of most other constitutional regimes, but it risked giving the respectability to the Peronists that they needed to win. That is why he chose to launch an attack on Peronism aimed at reminding non-Peronist voters what a menace Peronism really was. Unless conservatives and moderates from other parties voted for him to prevent the Peronists from doing what they did in 1973, the Radicals would remain a minority party. With that in mind he hit the Peronists hard, reminding the nation that his election was the only thing that stood in the way of their return.

The strategy was devious and brilliant. His attacks on the Peronists began on April 25, 1983, three months before he received the nomination, when he claimed that Peronist leaders had reached an agreement with military officers that promised absolution for all of the crimes they had committed in their antiterrorist campaign in exchange for the military's tolerating the formation of a Peronist government after the party won the election. Alfonsín never proved that such a plot had actually been hatched, but its plausibility allowed him to exploit it to the fullest.[28] The press was delighted to have the story, and they kept it alive until the election, just as he hoped they would, constantly reminding people that their armed forces were still plotting against them. It also gave Alfonsín the chance to portray himself as the human rights activist demanding justice while his Peronist opponents were doing what they could to obstruct its achievement. He was not, he claimed, trying to revive the old Peronist/anti-Peronist division in society, but merely living up to his pledge "always to say exactly what I think." Alfonsín the moralist thrived on defending political integrity against assaults on it, real or imagined, by unscrupulous Peronist bosses and their very unpopular military conconspirators. Of course, the Peronists denied the whole thing, but their doing so did little to change the minds of people who wanted to believe it.[29]

At the root of Alfonsín's handling of the Peronists was his determination to take advantage of their internal divisions not only to win the election but also to weaken their control over the working class permanently. In 1983 the Radicals still believed that Peronist strength in elections derived primarily from union control over the masses, a control that could be broken now that Perón was no longer there to keep it operating. By taking advantage of dissent and division within the movement using the power of government to draw workers away from Peronist union leaders, they intended to reorganize the electorate and expand the mass base of the Radical party simultaneously. Succeeding always seemed a little farfetched, even to most Radicals, but they had to try since even modest success was necessary to end Peronist domination in elections. So rather than write off the working class entirely, Alfonsín tried hard to appeal to workers who watched his campaign on television but avoided Peronist rallies, promising them real liberty and higher wages in return for their taking a chance on him. It was the line he and his wing of the party had been developing since they began their attack on Balbín in 1973, and now he was putting it to the test.[30]

What for the Radicals was a choice between good and evil never became so simple for most of the electorate. Confidence in the Radicals was not much greater than it was in the Peronists, especially among the middle and upper classes, for whom the election began as an unfortunate choice between suboptimal alternatives, neither of which promised the nation strong leadership. Frondizi and Illia were remembered less for their overthrow by the armed forces than for their weakness as leaders. No matter that they were not entirely at fault for their performance; many of the same forces were present in 1983, and it was not certain that a Radical could deal any better with a Peronist opposition, a disastrous economy, and the armed forces than his predecessors had. It was not uncommon to find executives from large corporations who even admitted a preference for Peronists over Radicals, not becuase of any affection for Peronism but because they had always found it so difficult to deal with the rigid legalism and intense partisanship practiced by Radicals. In contrast the Peronists were always ready to "make deals." But, of course, executives had very few votes and, despite their wealth, little control over elections.

As election day approached most polls gave the Peronists a slight edge, in itself a surprise since until then their victory was believed inevitable. The key to their defeat would be Alfonsín's support among people who normally voted for one of the country's several minor parties on the left and right and his attracting some votes from people in the lower middle class who were not ready to be governed again by a Peronist president. October 30, 1983, when the votes were counted, the country was shocked, the Peronists embarrassed, and the Radicals elated to discover that 52 percent of an electorate had chosen Raul Alfonsín as their president. Commercials portraying Peronists as models of civic responsibility had obviously not been enough to deny the effect of the likes of Herminio Iglesias and his compatriots or to overcome memories of terrorism and economic chaos in 1976. The Peronists were not ready to govern the country in 1983 and many of them knew it. And until they were it would be the Radicals who did, thanks to the electorate's caution when it was given another opportunity to make democracy work.

As the vote was studied, it became clear how well Alfonsín had done in areas where he was not expected to triumph, like the suburbs around Buenos Aires, where the working class should have carried Luder to victory. Clearly he had attracted the vast majority of upper and middle classes to his side, but he had also penetrated working-class districts deeply enough to gain the votes of their more affluent residents. Nationally Luder won only seven of twenty-four provinces, nearly all of them the nation's poorest and most lightly populated: Tucuman, Jujuy, Chaco, Formosa, La Rioja, Santa Cruz, Santiago del Estero. A working-class vote for Alfonsín was not necessarily a vote against Peronism, however. Many of those who had abandoned Luder did not forsake their party, but split their tickets and sent Peronists to Congress, giving them a slight plurality in the Senate, 21 seats to the Radicals' 18, and second place in the Chamber of Deputies with 111 seats to the Radicals' 131-seat majority.

No one who wanted Argentina to learn to govern itself democratically could have hoped for a better result under the circumstances. Constitutional democracies are composed of majorities and minorities, elected officials who govern and loyal opponents who work with and against them according to rules respected by both. Argentines have never found it easy to practice politics in that manner, but they gave themselves a chance to try in 1983. To begin with they forced a new role on the Peronists. By taking their majority away from them in a free election Alfonsín denied them for the first time their credible claim of being the nation's only legitimate majority party. Since 1955 they had nurtured themselves by attacking the legitimacy of all Radical and military governments, but now the complaint had no basis in reality. No longer could they say that the Radicals "deserved" to be evicted because they had cheated the majority out of its right to rule the nation in a fraudulent election, as Frondizi and Illia had done; now the Radicals were the majority, giving the Peronists no real choice but to play the part of the loyal opposition if they wanted to attract a majority of the electorate back to their side. Equally important was the fact that the Peronists managed to hold on to substantial power in the legislature. They had not been excluded by their defeat but were able to block legislation and support or harass the president, putting a Peronist mark on his programs. Rather than alienating them from the process, the election had kept them within it, giving them an essential role to play and a chance to regain majority support as a reward for their success in the opposition. It was the strongest incentive yet to cooperation.

It was a powerful prescription for tutorials in democratic politics, though as always, one without any guarantee of success. But it did give democrats their best chance ever. It would be a very difficult test to pass, as everyone knew all too well. Political power is not easily confined to processes prescribed by law, nor is authority recognized because it is given to one person by a majority of the electorate. Moreover, the contest was not simply one involving Radicals, Peronists, and the politicians of minor parties. Equally critical to Alfonsín's survival was his treatment of a very sick economy and the way businessmen, farmers, laborers, and the armed forces responded to his cures.

Notes

1. Marcelo Luis Acuña, *De Frondizi a Alfonsín: La tradición política del radicalismo/1* (Buenos Aires: Centro Editor de America Latina, 1984), p. 24.

2. For details on what is obviously a more complicated period of political intrigue than presented here, see Roberto Etchepareborda, *Yrigoyen* (Buenos Aires: Centro Editor de America Latina, 1983), chs. 1–7.

3. These and other speculations about Saez Peña's motives are discussed in Acuña, *De Frondizi a Alfonsín*, p. 29.

4. Mark Falcoff, "Political Developments," in *Prologue to Peron: Argentina in Depression and War, 1930–1943*, ed. Mark Falcoff and Ronald Dokart (Berkeley: University of California Press, 1975), p. 42.

5. Etchepareborda, *Yrigoyen*, pp. 188–193.

6. Ibid.

7. From the periodical *La Fonda*, July 4, 1933, as quoted in Gerardo López Alonso, *Cincuenta años de historia argentina, 1930–1980* (Buenos Aires: Belgrano, 1982), p. 35.

8. Luis Gregorich, *La república perdida* (Buenos Aires: Sudamericana-Planeta, 1983), pp. 34–35.

9. Acuña, *De Frondizi a Alfonsín*, pp. 47–49.

10. Ibid., pp. 50–51.

11. For a detailed account of Radical preparations for their greatest electoral disappointment ever, see Francisco Hipólito Uzal, "La encrucijada radical de 1946," *Todo es historia*, no. 201 (January 1984): 8–40.

12. Miguel Angel Scenna, "El radicalismo: Noventa años de historia," *Todo es historia*, no. 170 (July 1981): 30–31. Also see Acuña, *De Frondizi a Alfonsín*, ch. 1.

13. On the *pacto* arranged between Frondizi and Perón, see Ramón Prieto, *El pacto: Ocho años de la política argentina* (Buenos Aires: En Marcha, 1963).

14. Gary W. Wynia, *Argentina in the Postwar Era* (Albuquerque: University of New Mexico Press, 1972), ch. 4. Also see Marcelo Cavarozzi, *Autoritarismo y democracia (1955–1983)* (Buenos Aires: Centro Editor de America Latina, 1983), pp. 13–35.

15. Guillermo O'Donnell, *El estado burocrático* (Buenos Aires: Belgrano, 1982), p. 76.

16. Ibid., pp. 65–84.

17. Ibid.

18. The story is told by Geraldo López Alonso in *Cincuenta años de historia argentina*, pp. 220–221.

19. Acuña, *De Frondizi a Alfonsín*, pp. 204–207.

20. Ibid., pp. 222–223.

21. Raul Alfonsín, *La cuestión argentina* (Buenos Aires: Propuesta Argentina, 1981), p. 191.

22. *Buenos Aires Herald,* July 24, 1983, p. 3.

23. An interesting little book was recently published on advertising by all candidates in the 1983 campaign by Alberto Borrini, titled *Como se hace un presidente* (Buenos Aires: El Cronista Comercial, 1984).

24. Robert Cox, "Argentina's Democratic Miracle," *The New Republic*, March 19, 1984, p. 22. Cox had watched Alfonsín's rise while he was editor of the daily *Buenos Aires Herald*, a post which he was forced to abandon in 1979 when the military threatened his life because he had refused to refrain from criticizing them.

25. *Buenos Aires Herald,* September 11, 1983, p. 3.

26. Ibid., October 16, 1983, p. 3.

27. Ibid., October 30, 1983, p. 3.

28. Alfonsín listed labor union leaders Lorenzo Miguel, Herminio Iglesias, Diego Ibanez, and Rogelio Papaleo as the Peronist culprits in the plot and generals Cristino Nicolaides, head of the army, Jorge Suárez Nelson, and Juan Carlos Trimarco as their collaborators at a news conference on May 2. See *Buenos Aires Herald,* May 8, 1983, p. 3.

29. In an interview Alfonsín stated: "I did not want to infest the campaign with the Peronist–anti-Peronist dichotomy, but work for the cause of national unity. I knew that if I revealed the plot they would accuse me of reviving the old antagonism that we need to overcome. . . . [But] . . . I was obligated to do it because my golden rule in politics is intellectual honesty, that is, to say exactly what I think." *SOMOS*, May 6, 1983, pp. 6–13.

30. Ibid., May 6, 1983, interview with Alfonsín and interview in *Siete dias* 15, no. 830, p. 16.

6

An Economy at Bay

Raul Alfonsín inherited an economy in real trouble. The source of great pride before 1930, it had become the cause of much despair, steeped in recession, astronomical inflation, and record foreign debts, with real per capita income actually less than it was fifteen years before. That 30 million people who were nearly self-sufficient in petroleum, blessed with an abundance of food, and without a large rural proletariat should have fallen on such hard times is surprising but not impossible to explain.[1]

After World War II Argentina was supposed to "take off" into sustained growth and mass consumption, making it a regional power as affluent as the industrial nations of Western Europe. But its flight was a short one. Perón's subsidization of private industry proved costly and inefficient, nationalized enterprises and new social programs very expensive, and the confiscation of profits from grain exports damaging to farm production. And most of the investments made before and after 1955 were inefficient—the result of volatile and often inconsistent policies, import substitution, and high and variable inflation, forcing governments to impose severe austerity measures time and again that caused negative growth in 1952, 1959, and 1962–63. Some stability was achieved between 1964 and 1974 with the addition of heavier industry and an increase in crop production, encouraging people to hope that the era of "stop-go" cycles had ended, but such optimism proved unfounded. After a high of 8.5 percent in 1969, growth rates fell again, down to only 3.1 percent in 1972. And then in 1976 the economy went into a tailspin as inflation soared to 600 percent. The armed forces took over and tried to stabilize and "liberalize" the economy simultaneously, but in the end they too failed, especially in their attempts to trim the public sector deficits that had become a major source of the country's economic difficulties after 1973, financed as they were by an accumulating external debt and inflation-inducing monetary expansion. While countries like Brazil were doubling the dollar value of their exports between 1977 and 1981, the Argentine military could increase theirs by no more than 60 percent, a particular embarrassment since raising the level of exports had been one of their primary objectives.[2] By 1979 the Argentine share of the Latin American GNP, which had been 24 percent in 1950, had fallen to only 13.2 percent because countries like Brazil and Mexico had grown so much faster during the interim.[3] It only became worse when the country was hit by the world recession in 1981 and 1982 followed by the Malvinas War, which cut it off for a period from European financial markets (see Table 6.1).

**6.1 National Product Annual Growth Rates, by Sector,
1979–84 (at 1970 prices)**

Year	Per Capita GNP	Agriculture	Industry	Commerce
1979	5.0	3.5	10.2	11.0
1980	−0.8	−6.7	−3.8	5.6
1981	−7.9	2.4	−16.0	−6.8
1982	−6.9	6.4	−4.7	−18.3
1983	1.2	0.8	9.9	3.6
1984*	0.9	3.5	3.8	3.3

Source: *Clarin*, economic supp., November 4, 1984, p. 7.
*Estimates for 1984.

When democracy was tried again in 1983, the new government inherited 400 percent inflation, accelerating capital flight, and a foreign debt that had risen from $18.8 billion in 1978 to $48.4 billion in 1984, far more than the country could pay on schedule. It was the latest phase in an incredible history that had seen prices rise in great bursts, the annual rate of inflation peaking in 1976 at nearly 700 percent, then falling below 100 percent in 1980, only to rise to 1,000 in mid-1985.[4]

Argentines adapted to inflation and stagnation by investing less in their economy. Financial wheeling and dealing, not long-term productive investment, absorbed increasing amounts of national capital; so did investing abroad, so much so that officials estimated that 20 percent of the capital owned by Argentines was outside the country in 1985. It resembled a badly managed casino in which profit depended more on cunning and good fortune than on productivity as everyone hustled to anticipate price increases and currency devaluations.

Unless one experiences hyperinflation, it is hard to appreciate what it does to the saver and investor. The worst thing that one can do is nothing, holding onto pesos while inflation reduces their value by 15 to 20 percent monthly. Instead you spend them as fast as you can either for goods you can consume or for commodities that will retain value, like gold or dollars. Normal savings accounts are unprofitable since the interest paid usually lags behind inflation. For example, if you had deposited 100 pesos in an account in an Argentine bank at the beginning of 1984, their value would have increased to 257 pesos by October of that year because interest rates averaged 15.5 percent monthly during those nine months. Yet you were poorer than you had been in January since prices rose 20 percent a month during the same period, netting you 30 percent less in buying power. The only way that one can profit from such conditions is by moving money quickly from one commodity to another, trying to buy and sell at just the right moments. As one banker mused,

> A smart investor is constantly shifting his capital from place to place to ride the price increases. . . . He goes from the dollar to the stock market, the next day he sells the stocks and buys bricks, and the week after that he sells the bricks and lends in the intercompany loan market at 22 percent interest. Then he collects his loan in a month and goes back to the dollar. It all goes in a big circle, faster and faster. If you sleep ten hours, you lose.[5]

Everyone tries to cope, most often by delaying the payment of bills. But stores and industries anticipate such maneuvers and post prices high enough to compensate them for such delays, accelerating inflation as they do. People with money to invest and goods to sell often lose despite their best efforts in money markets, but they are not inflation's principal victims. It is the wage earner who suffers the most; without credit cards to delay payments or extra income to invest he can do little but watch his real income fall. He may fight for higher wages, but when inflation is as rampant as it was in Argentina in 1984 and 1985 even indexed wages could not really keep up. Worse still, the situation always becomes more painful before it gets better. Sooner or later authorities will decide to wage war against inflation, and when they do, real wages will fall. If their crusade works, nearly everyone will be better off eventually, but if it fails, as it often does, the wage earner will end up poorer than before. Labor leaders and the rank and file know this, and that is why they are so reluctant to cooperate with officials who promise them lower prices tomorrow in return for their accepting austerity today.

This is no way to run an economy, as every Argentine knows, but doing something about it is a monumental task. When Alfonsín looked about him in 1984 he saw much to worry about and a great deal that was beyond his power to cure. But there was no reason to give up on it, as he well knew, for alongside its many ills were some rather impressive achievements and great strengths on which to draw in order to pull the country through it all. Topping the list was a rural economy that had finally decided to become part of the modern world.

Beef and Grain

Being a commodity exporter remains an embarrassment to urbane Argentines, who think of the countryside as a vast space still populated by oligarchs and tenant farmers whom the country's modernization has left far behind. But were it not for farmers increasing their product substantially during the past two decades, the country would be in much worse shape than it is today.

North American farmers know what is happening on the *pampas* and are studying its effects with concern. What they see are the results of Argentina's second agricultural revolution. Cereal exports, which averaged around 12 million tons in the 1930s before falling to 5 million in the 1940s and 1950s, recovered and stabilized at around 8.5 million annually from 1962 to 1976. But then, almost unnoticed anywhere but in world commodity markets, Argentine grain production rose steadily to a 14 million ton average, reaching a peak in 1983 of 22 million tons, almost triple what it had been two decades before. At long last, it seemed, Argentine farmers were on their way to achieving what U.S. and Canadian farmers had accomplished forty years ago, namely putting technology to work to augment production significantly. Three advances accounted for most of the increase: the introduction of higher-yielding varieties, including hybrids; increased use of plant-protecting chemicals, such as fungicides, insecticides, and herbicides; and continued mechanization. They were also helped some by the U.S. government when it imposed an embargo on sales of grain to the Soviet Union in 1979, allowing Argentina to increase its share of the world grain and soybean market from 5.8 percent in 1979 to 11 percent in 1984, which, though substantially less than the U.S. share of 52 percent, marked an almost 100 percent increase.[6]

There was nothing easy or inevitable about the Argentine achievement. Sixty years ago its agricultural product grew at rates similar to those in the United States and Canada, but then it fell far behind, as farmers eschewed the technological innovations that transformed North American farming. Contentment with cheap and easy modes of production contributed to their inertia, but so did Juan Perón's redistribution of income from agriculture to industry. From then onward farmers were burdened by a host of policies that increased the cost of farm inputs and depressed domestic prices. Food prices were kept down to placate urban consumers, tariffs were placed on imported farm equipment to protect domestic industry, and commodity exports were taxed because they were a convenient source of revenue. Inevitably, import duties and export taxes produced major distortions in the ratio between the farmer's input costs and commodity prices, making innovation unprofitable even to the most ambitious farmers. Only when government policies were reformed and world prices rose high enough to make using higher-yielding varieties of grain profitable during the 1970s did production finally take off.[7]

Mechanization also became essential to growth after the depopulation of the countryside in the 1940s, when thousands went to the cities, where industry and government offered rural laborers and tenant farmers higher income. On the *pampas* alone the rural work force declined by 52 percent between 1947 and 1960. With less labor to draw upon, landowners initially fell back on cattle raising, leaving grain primarily to the tenants who remained.[8] Simultaneously, however, the land tenure structure began to change, the number of owner-operators increasing from 36 percent in 1947 to 74 percent by 1974, and the proportion of tenants and sharecroppers dropping by half, from 24 to 13 percent. Many things contributed to the shift in ownership, though much of the credit belongs to the freezing of land rents by populist governments after World War II, the longest episode lasting during the Peronist decade. Landowners occasionally found it more economical to sell pieces to tenants than pay rising taxes in a time of frozen rents.[9] None of this transformed the *pampas* into a province of egalitarian farmers since 5 percent of the landowners continued to hold nearly half of the land, but it did increase the number of middle-size farmers, who saw an advantage in modernizing crop production rather than relying primarily on cattle raising.

Beef remains a major export, but it was surpassed by cereals in the 1970s and now brings only a third as much income to the country. The quality of Argentine beef is renowned, the Aberdeen Angus making up 80 percent of its stock, but that does not make selling it abroad any easier these days. The annual slaughter fell from 2 million to 1 million head during the 1940s, then rose to 3 million head in the 1960s, only to suffer the loss of its principal markets when Great Britain banned beef imports in 1964 and the European Common Market nations did likewise in the early 1970s in order to protect their own cattle industries. Argentine production fell back to 2 million in the mid-1970s, then rose again to 3 million at the end of the decade. However, Argentines consume between 80 and 90 percent of it, the rest going to a variety of markets in the Third World where they must compete with Brazilian as well as European exports. Consequently today they export 500,000 tons annually, about the same amount as they did in 1940.[10]

It is not hard to find *estancias* devoted entirely to cattle raising today, but the "typical" enterprise is a mixed operation. Some are quite large but many are "medium-size" farms (500–2,500 acres), their number having grown along with the increase in ownership and the consolidation of smaller units. It is usually owned and operated by a family or a manager working for a family living in a nearby town. They have some cattle, essential because they serve as "quasi-money" from which the owner can draw cash through sales whenever it is needed. Crop rotation is also common, with shifts from something like corn and flax one year to wheat the second and then all three the third. It is their reluctance to specialize in one crop that distinguishes most Argentine farmers from their U.S. and Canadian peers. Always preoccupied with unscheduled changes in government as well as fluctuations in world prices, the Argentine farmer is quite cautious and, therefore, always more interested in minimizing risk than in maximizing gain.

Argentine farmers complain a great deal about the disadvantages they suffer from the perpetuation of policies that keep prices of their inputs high and returns on their commodities lower than they prefer. Despite occasional government efforts to remove such obstacles, many remain. Worse still, in an economy like Argentina's the internal terms of trade for commodities continue to rise and fall wildly; for example, it took twice as much wheat to buy a harvester in 1980 as it had five years before, making it hard for farmers to plan long-term capital investments.[11] The country's need to pay its enormous foreign debt with dollars earned by commodity exports gives the rural sector some leverage over policy, but hardly enough to prevail against competing urban interests. Moreover, populists in the Peronist and Radical parties were unconvinced that the lowering of export taxes would increase production enough to induce increases in exports that would eventually raise revenues. Government revenue needs are too immediate to allow for the testing of such "supply-side" logic. In the meantime, the country has no choice but to hope that despite the handicaps they suffer its farmers will continue to supply the food they love to eat and the dollars they like to spend.

Marketing has also changed during the last half-century. Fifty years ago only a few firms dominated the grain market, the largest being the Bunge & Born Company, which handled nearly half, and the Louis Dreyfus Corporation, which marketed a third of the grain exported in 1930. They and a few other large grain traders continue to dominate trade in the private sector as they do worldwide. But the depression forced the government to become involved in trading in order to protect farmers, and then Perón created a public corporation through which most grain had to pass. Ever since, the government has gone in and out of the market depending on the economic philosophy of those in office, the Peronists increasing the state's share of trade to 52.9 percent in 1975, while their market-oriented military successors reduced it to only 5.6 percent in 1979.[12]

In contrast to the grain trade, foreigners have all but abandoned the meat-packing industry that was once their monopoly. British and U.S. firms began operating in Argentina in the 1880s. The British, worried about contamination from unhealthy imported livestock, required slaughter abroad before shipping. Foreign packers seized the opportunity, buying and expanding plants devoted previously to local production, three of them owned by North American corporations and two by British ones. Within only two decades they had cornered 90 percent of the beef export trade, the Armour and Wilson companies alone controlling 60 percent of it. They became notorious for rigging prices against cattlemen and playing them off against each other to weaken their opposition to such practices. It continued against little effective resistance until the 1930s, when the depression induced government intervention into the market and concessions to cattlemen who demanded the creation of a semipublic corporation that was guaranteed 11 percent of the British market by authorities. The meat packers' control over the market was never the same again, but in the end it was not Perón who sent them home—he never did nationalize them—but inevitable changes in the industry itself after 1950.[13]

When World War II broke out Argentines were consuming just a little more than half of the beef they produced, but Perón saw to it that the working class received more, and by 1955 there was only 14 percent of the annual slaughter left for export. Changes in technology struck the final blow. Ways were found to prepare meat in small cuts fit for shipping directly to markets, giving advantages to those who adopted the new technology. Conversion proved too costly for the antiquated foreign firms, so when several dozen local entrepreneurs built smaller and more efficient plants, they took over much of the market, forcing the foreigners to close down and go away.[14]

In the United States people occasionally wonder why the Argentines, even when governed by reactionary military regimes, sell so many commodities to the Soviets. The reason is quite obvious, at least to any Argentine: they have no other choice. As if pulled by an invisible hand, they have been forced to move slowly but steadily from west to east to find markets, from Great Britain before the war to Italy and Spain after it, and then, when their access to the Continent was cut off by a decision of the Common Market in 1974, to Eastern Europe and the Soviet Union, the biggest step coming when the United States boycotted the Soviet market in 1979. Guided entirely by economic self-interest, Argentina's anticommunist military rulers stubbornly ignored U.S. requests that they participate in the boycott, preferring instead to capture a desperately needed new market. Consequently by 1981 almost 80 percent of the country's exported wheat was going to the Soviet Union, bringing the country $3 billion in return, and dividing the nation's total exports into almost three equal parts, one-third going to the Soviet Union, another to Europe, and the remaining third to the rest of the Americas, including the United States.[15] It is quite different when it comes to imports, however. Nearly 70 percent of what Argentina imports is raw products for industrial use and 17 percent capital goods, but only 2.4 percent of it came from the Soviet Union and Eastern Europe in 1984. The United States and Canada supplied 36 percent, Western Europe 29 percent, and the rest of Latin America 21 percent. The Soviets are insisting on more sales in Argentina, but so far little has changed.[16]

What the Argentines have learned from all of this is that they cannot, as they once did, rely only on other capitalist nations for trade. Nor can they count entirely on the socialist ones, for there is nothing to prevent the Soviets from buying large volumes from the Americans again. In other words, they know that their position in the world economy is quite vulnerable, making it essential that they remain flexible and aggressive within the world market. What they do with their grain, beef, and other exports in the future will have less to do with political ideology than with their need to keep commodities flowing fast enough to pay their enormous foreign debts.

What Became of the Industrial Revolution?

Agriculture earns desperately needed foreign exchange, but it is industry and commerce that generate the employment that keeps Argentines consuming. Unfortunately, industry has fallen on hard times lately, the sector's growth actually being negative three of the past five years (see Table 6.1, p. 136). Industrialists do not invest as much as they once did simply because they and their potential stockholders are convinced that there are more profitable things to do with their money than back industry in an economy as depressed as Argentina's.

They started running into trouble in the mid-1970s when the

Peronists governed. Production, hours worked, and employment fell, rose again after Videla took over, and then declined precipitously in 1979, languishing in recession for the next three years. Worst hit was the industrial work force, whose size fell by an incredible 30 percent between 1975 and 1982. Record numbers of medium and small firms went bankrupt, and several large ones merged with multinationals. Martínez de Hoz was not unhappy with all of this, of course, since he had wanted to shrink the industrial work force and improve productivity through plant modernization, but his cleansing of industry did not generate the new era of industrial growth that he had promised. Instead, authorities found themselves in the mid-1980s with an economy plagued by declining investment.

On the surface its industry does not look all that different from what one finds in the other industrializing Latin American countries. It developed gradually, rising to about 20 percent of the GDP by the time of the 1930 depression and then surpassing agriculture as a contributor to the national product in 1939. It continued to grow during and after the war, encouraged by government import substitution policies that protected national firms against competition from less expensive imports. The last big push came in the early 1960s, when multinational firms were invited to build plants in Argentina to produce basic goods like petrochemicals, vehicles, and machinery. Despite interruptions by occasional recessions, the industrial product grew by an annual average rate of 5.7 percent between 1950 and 1965, when it contributed nearly twice as much to the national product as did agriculture.[17]

As in most capitalist economies, a few large corporations dominate in most Argentine industries. Just 2 percent of the firms operating in Argentina employ 49 percent of the industrial work force and generate 65 percent of the industrial product. Their employees, nearly all of whom belong to labor organizations, earn, on the average, 50 percent more in wages than the employees of smaller firms.[18] Control over large industry is divided between foreign and nationally owned firms, the former dominating in the automotive, electronics, and chemical industries, with a share in petrochemicals, while national firms operate in the steel industry, building materials, packaged food, as well as chemicals and textiles. Of the largest 100 industrial enterprises ranked by sales in 1981, 41 were foreign owned.[19] Government enterprises are less well represented in manufacturing, being confined more to transportation and utilities, except for heavy participation in oil, steel, machinery, and weapons.[20]

Foreign investment has always played a prominent role in the country's industrialization, though initially a much greater one in the construction of the transportation and communications infrastructure and in banking than in industry. But investments in industry did accompany agricultural development at the turn of the century, and the flow remained steady until the depression struck in 1929, most of it English in origin, though Americans began competing with the British in the industrial sector after World War I. After a long pause brought on by Perón's hostility toward foreigners as well as uncertainty about where he was taking the country, foreigners came back in the early 1960s. This time most of them were North American multinationals invited by Radical president Arturo Frondizi to assist with the construction of more basic industries. By 1976 the U.S.-based firms owned 40 percent of what foreigners had invested in industry, most of it going to manufacturing, especially automobiles, rubber products, machinery, chemicals, and electronics. Switzerland was a surprising second with 12.2 percent concentrated in utilities, transportation equipment, chemicals, and food products. Great Britain was third with 7.7 percent, the Netherlands next with 6.2, and France and West Germany with 5.8 percent each. Japan, which is a heavy investor in Brazil, has shied away from less stable Argentina, supplying only 0.4 percent of the nation's foreign investment.[21]

What is most striking about foreign involvement is not the amount of it—though nationalists claim that there is far too much—but how much less Argentina has received than other industrializing nations in the region like Brazil and Mexico. The latter have attracted 35 and 30 percent, respectively, of all the foreign investment made in Latin America during the last two decades, while Argentina received only 3 percent of it. As a result, total foreign investment in Argentina by 1983 was just $5.8 billion, compared to $24.6 billion in Brazil and $13.6 billion in Mexico.[22] Quite obviously, its economic instability made it less inviting, as did its government's frequent shifts in foreign investment policy, making entrance easy only to put extensive restrictions on it whenever it grew.

The most recent effort to extend hospitality to multinational firms was launched by Martínez de Hoz and the military in 1976. Commitments to invest nearly $3 billion were made, though some of them were canceled when recession hit in 1980; not surprisingly, 53 percent of it came from U.S.-based corporations, 12 percent from Italian ones, and 6.5 percent each from France and West Germany. This time it was spread over several sectors, with 19.7 percent going to mining, 17.8 percent to gas and petroleum production, 14 percent to automobiles, and 13.4 percent to banking. Investment in mining and fuel production was encouraged by the military, and banking also was promoted by a reduction of restrictions on foreign bankers; the financial sector remained largely in national hands, nevertheless, the government's banks holding 50 percent of all deposits, private national banks 35 percent, and foreigners 15 percent (the Bank of Boston ranked sixth and Citibank twelfth among the fifteen largest holders of deposits).[23]

The issue of foreign investment remains a very controversial one. Nationalism is strong and, as before, is often expressed as resentment of foreign capitalists and calls for their eviction. Some economists, however, claim that the country has no other reasonable alternative. The government is already overextended financially and is in no condition to create many more industrial enterprises on its own, and Argentine capitalists continue to fail to reinvest what the country needs. Moreover, if it is modern technology that industry needs in order to increase its productivity, multinationals can supply some of it. As much as they resent their country's dependence on foreign capital, Argentines are hard put to suggest effective alternatives to it. Even Peronists and Radicals admitted as much in their platforms in the 1983 election.

Big businesses are not the only kind that exist, of course. To a large degree the country remains a land of small enterprises. There are, for example, around 120,000 manufacturers, or 90 percent of the nation's total, which employ fewer than twenty-five persons. Small industries are common during the first stages of development, but in Argentina they have hung on in large numbers. There is a risk to it, naturally, since they are so vulnerable to inflation, credit squeezes, recessions, and other common features of the Argentine economy. But their total number stays about the same as people start over after bankruptcy or the sale of their firms, and new ones keep appearing.

Populists like the Peronists and Radicals have always defended small business, trying hard to protect it with high tariffs, subsidized interest rates, and stimulants to consumption. Economic liberals, in contrast, tried to withdraw protection in the late 1970s, driving some firms out of business deliberately. Nevertheless, Argentine entrepreneurs are a resilient lot, evidencing a spirit of enterprise begun by immigrants a century ago.

Nothing seems more essential in the days ahead than clear signals sent from government through its macroeconomic policies. They must be consistent and reliable. That was how they were advertised under the recent military regime, but they never came very close to the ideal. Eliminating price controls, increasing credit availability, and controlling unions were supposed to stimulate growth, but when accompanied by an inefficient financial sector that expanded without supervision and by enormous variations in relative prices, interest rates, and real effective exchange rates that reduced the time horizon and decision-making ability of industrialists, they had little effect.[24] Moreover, no matter who rules Argentina, be he Peronist, Radical, or someone else, he will have to find some way to promote the export of many more industrial products. With a domestic market too small to sustain sufficient growth, Argentines must manufacture for sale abroad, as difficult as it is against stiff competition from neighbors and the countries in the Far East. It does export 800 percent more now than it did twenty-five years ago, but total world exports have grown three times that during the same period. Only 22 percent of what it exports comes from industry, far too little if manufacturing is to grow again and employment return to previous levels. It will not be easy. Other nations are putting up trade barriers to protect their own industries, and consumption was reduced by recession in the early 1980s and is now recovering slowly. But if there is one thing that economists of both the Peronist and Radical parties can now agree upon, it is the need to sell what Argentina manufactures in as many parts of the world as possible.[25]

The State Entrepreneur

Few people have kind words for the government bureaucracy anymore. Even Radical and Peronist economists, once dedicated defenders of public enterprise, have resorted to blaming the nation's woes on government waste and inefficiency. Yet, neither has shown much capacity for taming the beast. Details of its actual size are never published, but we do know that there are seventeen major, nonfinancial government corporations, thirty military factories and mixed-equity enterprises, and around one hundred smaller ones like hotels, airlines, and television stations. Provincial and municipal governments own another eighty-nine enterprises.[26] An estimated 343,000 people are employed in the thirteen largest corporations (111,000 of them on the railways), or the equivalent of about 22 percent of the nation's industrial work force. Estimates of total public employees at all levels indicate that about 1.6 million persons are working in the public sector.[27]

In 1922 the Radicals created what has become the wealthiest of the public corporations, the petroleum-producing Yacimientos Petroleros Fiscales (YPF), which refines 70 percent of the crude that is processed within the country, the rest going to multinationals Esso and Shell, which refine 12 percent each. Most utilities were publicly owned as well, including nearly all gas, electricity, and telecommunications companies as well as the national railway and airline. The weight of the state was felt everywhere, most notably in its paying for half of all construction activity in the country and two-thirds of all investment in durable equipment purchased annually. It was all very expensive and the deficits of enterprises like the railways were notorious, causing the central government to spend about 5 percent of the domestic product to cover public enterprise losses.[28]

It is not hard to understand why Argentines complain so much about government enterprise, the quality of services, and persistent deficits: whether it deserves reprobation or not, the state is the perfect scapegoat. Nevertheless, it is a reality that few people are willing to change. As in all capitalist countries the nation's entrepreneurs curse it for its inefficiencies and high costs but rely heavily on its purchase of their products and services. Military officers claim to want inflation reduced, though never at the cost of cutting their portions of the budget or the financing of their enterprises. Thousands of public employees have made careers operating enterprises and delivering services and are organized to defend their power and privileges. And political parties, regardless of their platforms, are always torn between a fondness for the resources public office allows them to share with their constituents and their economists' advice to trim federal budgets. To an even greater degree than in other capitalist economies everyone relies too much on the Argentine state to make serious changes in it.

The Peronists are blamed for all of this coming about, but its growth began before Perón. Strong government was essential in Argentina just to put the nation back together after regional rivalries had torn it apart in the early nineteenth century. Originally authorities restricted themselves to clearing the way for the nation's private entrepreneurs, doing only what was necessary to assure the flow of grain and meat to European markets. Yet demands for greater state participation in the economy accompanied economic development, and by the turn of the century tenant farmers were demanding intervention into the land market on their behalf, cattlemen protection against meat packers, and labor unions state enforcement of collective bargaining.

The Radicals were the first to listen. Their reliance on thousands of grass-roots constituency organizations as well as their nationalism made them receptive to arguments for a more active government. They expanded public education, made the government responsible for the exploration and extraction of petroleum, and promulgated labor legislation sanctioning the eight-hour workday and the forty-eight-hour week. Hardly extreme measures by contemporary standards, but they marked a change for Argentina that brought with it new opportunities for patronage which in turn made citizens more dependent on the state for their well-being. Not only job seekers but also entrepreneurs in need of friends in high places began looking to government for assistance.

But, ironically, it was the oligarchy that really put the government into the marketplace when they dealt with the effects of the 1929 depression by regulating the beef and grain trade. Necessity dictated a more activist state. Later it took little imagination for Perón to use existing boards and commissions to buy and sell commodities whose profits he confiscated to finance the expansion of public enterprises. His nationalism, along with the enormous gold reserves that were accumulated during the war years when imports from Europe were halted, allowed his purchase of the nation's railways from the British and other utilities from foreign stockholders, and it permitted the construction of a merchant fleet, the expansion of government petroleum and coal companies, and the building of an iron and steel complex for the armed forces. Each measure generated hundreds of jobs, which Perón eagerly filled in order to absorb the labor surplus created by rural to urban migration during the war years. It also allowed him to play favorites, increasing the already partisan character of the Argentine state. Thanks to him and the Radicals before, it became the home of the middle and lower classes, giving them resources to compensate minimally for the disadvantages imposed on them by the oligarchy.

Not surprisingly, the Argentine government continually must increase its revenues to pay its bills. Total public expenditures equaled 34 percent of the GDP in 1970, rose to 39 percent in 1975, and then to an incredible 50 percent in 1983. Some of the growth was caused by military rearmaments, but by far the largest share was taken by the servicing of a rapidly growing debt, rising from 5.6 percent of the budget in 1974 to 37.1 percent in 1982 while consuming the equivalent of 15 percent of the gross domestic product. The central government was responsible for most of it, though state enterprises accounted for a third, and municipal and provincial governments nearly one-fourth. Deficits are common among state enterprises not only because of their well-known inefficiencies but also because authorities are reluctant to price public services high enough to cover their costs. Consequently, they leave themselves no choice but to borrow or raise revenues some other way.[29]

Deficits also result from the Argentines' refusal to pay their taxes. Tax evasion, in the words of a noted Argentine economist, "has become a sport for us, evidenced by the fact that at parties we praise the biggest evader as if he were a hero of some kind, ignoring how such behavior increases what the rest of us have to pay."[30] Today officials estimate that revenues equal to as much as 23 percent of the GDP are lost annually to tax evasion (about $4 billion in 1984).[31] Everyone does it, from the wage earner to the store owner to large corporations, though it is easier for the latter to get away with it than it is for the wage earners whom they employ. Lawyers, doctors, and dentists document very little of their income, and firms are notorious for underestimating their sales and foreign exchange dealings. As a result, income taxes generate no more than 6 percent of the government's income.[32]

Tax laws do exist but the system must rely very heavily on regressive sources of revenues to overcome the incapacity for efficient income tax collection. Most comes from excise taxes (principally on fuels), tariffs on imports, export taxes on agricultural commodities, a value-added sales tax, and social security taxes. The total intake fluctuates with the volume of exports and imports and the rate of inflation, ranging from highs of nearly 30 percent of the GDP to lows of 17 percent during the past decade, making tax revenues an unreliable source of finance. Equally indicative of its unreliability is the fact that total tax collections ranged from 75 percent of public expenditures in 1980 to just 46 percent two years later, largely due to the economy's lack of growth that year.[33] Such sudden changes in government income always occur when economies move from recession to growth and vice versa. But even if the Argentine economy begins growing again, it will have a long way to go before it has a tax system that is both equitable and effective. The problem is in part a technical one of law enforcement, but it is also very political since so many people are determined to use what influence they have to avoid paying for their share of public services. It does not help, of course, that the low quality of much of what they get for their money is not very conducive to their feeling any obligation to pay.

Poverty in Argentina?

As if inflation and recession were not already enough of a burden, Argentines have recently added poverty to their list of misfortunes. The poor have always been with them, but in smaller number than in neighboring countries, and many of them had migrated to Argentina from Paraguay and Chile. But when the economy went into a tailspin in the 1970s many more joined their ranks, nearly all of them Argentine to the core.

Authorities finally got around to taking a systematic look at the matter just a couple of years ago and assigned the staff of the national statistics institute to go over the 1980 census to see what they could find. They began by creating an index for measuring poverty made up of five indicators—children between six and twelve not in school; more than three persons to a room; precarious housing structures; unsafe water; living on a subsistence wage—and then used it to study their data. What they discovered was shocking, even to people who knew that poverty was on the rise. An estimated 22.3 percent of the nation's households was "poor," compared to only 8 percent in 1970. The proportion was much higher in rural areas—41.9 percent—than in cities with over 50,000 inhabitants—17.4 percent—as one might suspect, but that did not make the national total any more tolerable.[34] They also discovered that Argentines were less literate than they were supposed to be: nearly 27 percent were functional illiterates, among them almost a fourth of the people who lived in the Greater Buenos Aires area. In the northern provinces an estimated 54 percent of the population was functionally illiterate, a shocking figure for even the poorest parts of the country.[35]

The number and diversity of items used in the index undoubtedly exaggerated the severity of the problem somewhat; it is not uncommon for some people in remote towns to have bad water even though they earn more than the subsistence wage; moreover, even those below the subsistence wage usually find enough cheap food to keep from starving. But poverty is there and it is growing as the visitor to the northern provinces and to slums on the edges of the largest cities discovers. And despite recent government efforts to bring food to the most impoverished, prospects for poverty's reduction are not good given the austerity measures that authorities have been forced to impose on the public sector. Austerity increases unemployment and reduces real income for a time, making it probable that the number of poor will increase in the years ahead; and even should Argentina recover from its current plight in a decade or so, its poorest will be the last to benefit from the recovery.

Economic Interests, Politics, and Policy

The sources of some of Argentina's economic problems are deep and structural and without simple solutions, stemming from export and financial dependence, a bloated populist state, and heavily protected industries. A world capitalist economy that once sustained Argentina ceased doing so a long time ago. But something more than economic structure has inhibited progress toward the successful treatment of the nation's economic ills. People with concrete interests to protect also got in the way, some of them politicians and military officers, but others cattlemen, farmers, industrialists, foreign investors, and labor leaders, who are quite adept at defending their interests against policies that threaten them.

Argentines love to complain about villains. In fact, conspiracy theories abound, most arguing that *oligarquías* and *patrias financieras* (financial fatherlands) conspire to exploit everyone else. They are said to be very rich and often in collusion with foreigners, who delight in pillaging the national patrimony. Given the country's history of foreign penetration, the appeal of such notions is obvious. Businessmen do "wheel and deal," often at some cost to the nation, and they feed the corruption of officials, both civilian and military. Yet most of what authorities do to solve economic problems is not the result of perverse conspiracies but the consequence of endless struggle between government officials and well-known, organized and semi-organized private interests, just as it is in other capitalist countries. Landowners do not dictate the nation's course any longer, nor do industrialists or labor leaders, yet each is powerful enough to subvert most anything he wishes if he is willing to accept the political costs for doing so.[36]

The wealthy are not hard to find, but that does not mean that they "run" the country. They only occasionally unite long enough to do battle with the proletariat; more often they function as a collection of separate economic interests who have much to contest for among themselves as well as to protect from other social classes. Diversification came with industrialization, and no amount of investment by cattlemen in industry or by industrialists in land has prevented substantial plurality among them. The largest corporations do influence policy, but they act separately as much as they do together.

Divisions also exist between people involved in one phase of production and those devoted to another. Take the rural sector, for example. Originally the richest cattlemen on the *pampas* were represented by the Argentine Rural Society (SRA), created in 1866. It was truly elitist at first, limiting membership to 2,500 cattlemen well into the 1930s. It was also powerful in politics, supplying half of all cabinet ministers who served between 1910 and 1943. But rich cattlemen were not the only ones in the countryside who spoke out in defense of the sector. In 1912 poorer tenant farmers organized the Agrarian Federation (FAA), a much larger organization than the Rural Society that contested with it over issues of land rents and tenant rights and championed the cause of progressive land redistribution. In 1932 both organizations were joined by another, the Confederation of Rural Associations of Buenos Aires and La Pampa (CARBAP), formed by cattle breeders who sought greater influence over policy affecting their relationship with cattle fatteners and meat packers. The three organizations and the people they represented were not implacable enemies, but they clashed often over policy, the first two on issues that separated the rich from the poor and the second two over narrow matters that separated breeders from fatteners. With the transformation of many tenants into middle-class farmers after World War II, class differences in the rural sector were reduced substantially, making sectoral unity on policy issues easier to achieve. Nevertheless, disagreements persist because of fundamental differences between the rich cattlemen who fatten herds on extensive holdings and invest much of their profits in industry and high finance and the full-time farmers, whose profits depend almost entirely on what they earn from the land, much like their peers in North America. The latter feel discriminated against by populist governments who want to channel their surplus to consumers and industrialists and mistreated by military governments who do not compensate them sufficiently for their past losses despite promises to do so. They are not subsidized nearly as much as farmers in the United States and Western Europe are and resent it, claiming victimization by leaders devoted to pacifying urban society at their expense.[37]

Industrialists went into politics separately from cattlemen. A few hundred manufacturers formed the Industrial Union (UIA) in 1889 to advocate more favorable treatment of industry by governments that did not welcome it because of the threat it posed to British trading partners who supplied most of the country's consumer and capital goods. Even the Radicals were not enthusiastic about protecting domestic industry in the 1920s, though they did defend it from organized labor. During the 1930s the UIA received some of the subsidization it wanted, though less because of its political clout than because of the conservative government's decision to promote local enterprise with a Keynesian-style recovery program after the 1929 depression. Perón divided industrialists from one another, some preferring populist subsidization and others happier to go it alone. Among the former were many small, native-owned firms, several of them from cities in the interior of the country. During Perón's first presidency they formed an organization called the General Economic Confederation (CGE), which he invited to represent all industry in consultations with the government as industry's counterpart to labor's CGT. The military closed the CGE in 1955, but it was legalized again by Arturo Frondizi and allowed to represent the more nationalist wing of Argentine business, achieving its hiatus when its leader José Gelbard designed Perón's "social pact" in 1973 and served as economy minister in the Peronist government during its first eighteen months.[38]

Until the 1970s the UIA represented most of the country's largest firms, including multinational ones, leaving the vast majority of medium and small ones to the CGE. UIA and CGE leaders disagreed on many economic issues, the UIA being the more conservative of the two, especially on fiscal and monetary policy and relations with labor, and the CGE favoring a state paternalism characteristic of populist economics involving government subsidization of business and collusion between government, business, and labor in the design of policy. When he returned in 1973, Perón forced the two organizations to merge, ostensibly to help with his social pact, but it was little more than window dressing. In 1976 the military shut them both down in its efforts to restructure political participation, only to legalize the UIA again in 1983.

Industrialists would be the last to claim that they dictate economic policy. And they would be right. Many firms are powerful, and the mere fact of industrialization has made industry essential to the economy's development, bringing with it influence over policy. But industries do not benefit equally from all policies, and some even suffer from them, as happened often in the previous decade. It is also important to recall how dependent industry is on the government for its business. Though conservative industrialists can be heard complaining of the state's size and power, most industrialists rely on government purchases for a substantial portion of their incomes. Like industrialists everywhere, they are quite selective in what they want the government to do and not to do. They all want lower taxes, fewer regulations, and less government inefficiency, but as individuals they rely too heavily on the public sector to allow it to shrink very far. Businessmen love to complain of the government's favoring consumers and laborers, but let someone take away negative interest rates, import tariffs, and the government's purchase of goods, as Martínez de Hoz tried to do, and they are among the first to cry foul.

The relationship between the rural and industrial sectors is an important but hazy one. Some of the wealthy are involved in both and in finance as well. Their exact number has never been documented, but many connections are obvious. That does not mean, however, that today agriculture and industry are supervised by the same directorates; each sector is too large and too diverse to be linked so easily. Rather it means that some people are much more able than others to move resources from sector to sector to take advantage of the vicissitudes of the economy.

Where does this leave foreign capital? Its participation in national development is important and it too has a large stake in government policy. Ford, Renault, and Mercedes-Benz rule the automotive industry; Firestone, Pirelli, and Goodrich supply tires; and Esso (Exxon) and Shell share petroleum retailing with the government's YPF. But the multinationals are not organized to dictate policy, aware as they are of the unpopularity of their appearing to manipulate authorities. Instead, they employ skilled Argentine executives who help them bargain with officials in unobtrusive ways. Nothing comes to them automatically anymore, but they are favored by the country's capital shortages and do exploit it. At the same time, economic instability makes operating in Argentina less attractive than in countries like Brazil and Mexico. In short, multinationals deal with authorities like everyone else does in Argentina, doing so as quietly as possible, seeking advantages where they can get them, sometimes in coincidence with national industry and at others in conflict with it.

Not to be overlooked is what some call the "state bourgeoisie." These are the people who staff government agencies and corporations, the military among them, and work to aggrandize their enterprises just as private capitalists do. They should be easier to control than private business but they seldom are. Their employees are well organized, either by the military or labor unions, and are well schooled in subverting presidential programs they oppose, able to draw support from clients on short notice. As in other Latin American countries where the state is equally large and heavily involved in the production of goods, they operate their largest enterprises in a subsidized, capitalist manner, much as many of the private firms do. If there is a structure to the economy, it is one that blends public and private enterprises in the exploitation of the nation's resources.

Finally there is organized labor, as influential in politics as any sector of the bourgeoisie. We learned in Chapter 3 that the Argentine labor movement is the most durable and independent of all that exist in Latin America. Those who lead the largest factions of the General Confederation of Labor represent the working class whether its members want representation or not, and in their own way they have become part of the nation's ruling "establishment," able to prevent any government from sustaining its programs for very long without their cooperation. It is this achievement and its exploitation by labor leaders that has earned them the envy and enmity of the country's economically impotent political left and the resentment of the middle and upper classes.

Such a diversity of interests is not unusual in capitalist economies, of course, so why is it important to understanding the trouble that Argentine authorities have in dealing with the country's economic woes? The answer rests not in their number or diversity, but in the way they have lined up into two opposing camps that have done so much to stop one another during the past quarter century. As in politics, each side takes its turn in government, only to relinquish the Ministry of Economy to the other before its job is done.

The National Debate

The same two issues have captured Argentine attention for the past forty years. One is the distribution of income and the other is economic growth. The annual reports of ministers and the financial sections of leading newspapers discuss little else.[39] It is the priority given to one or the other that sets Argentines apart from each other. On one side sit the "populists," a coalition joining organized labor, the state bourgeoisie, and the more nationalistic entrepreneurs of the CGE variety who put highest priority on income redistribution of a progressive variety. On the other is an "internationalist" coalition involving some combination of multinational firms, large local manufacturers, and the wealthier cattlemen, who are convinced that deliberate efforts to redistribute income "progressively" deter real growth and are the cause of the nation's primary development problems currently. The populists are more numerous, while internationalists hold immense economic power because of the nation's dependence on commodity exports and large manufacturers for its sustenance. But theirs is not just a simple class struggle between capitalists and proletarians. Capitalist mentalities dominate both coalitions, populists favoring some form of nationalistic, progressive redistribution of wealth and internationalists a more regressive one, at least for the short haul. In the former, for example, many industrialists and labor leaders share a devotion to high tariff protection and government subsidization of industry since both were nurtured on it by Perón. The national origins of a firm have less to do with its policy preferences than does the manner of its nurturing. That is why firms like the Ford Motor Company that grew up in Argentina under tariff protection will defend the status quo much more than foreign and national manufacturers who never depended on it. In other words, membership in either coalition is determined more by the particular economic self-interest of each manufacturer, farmer, labor leader, and government bureaucrat than it is by grand designs about how Argentina should be governed. Politics is a means to very concrete ends, the populists believing in the fruits of instant economic gratification and the internationalists confident that they have more to gain from domination over their competitors through the exercise of their advantages in freer markets, nationally and internationally.

How influential each coalition is at any particular moment depends a great deal on the country's economic condition at the time. It is during times of growth that the populists' wage increases, business subsidies, and public welfare programs are most affordable. But inevitably, populist measures lead to higher inflation, declines in private investment, and a bursting of the expansionary balloon. It is then that the internationalist coalition reasserts itself, telling authorities how to put everything back together again. Theirs is an income-regressive, investment strategy rather than a distributionist one, emphasizing the use of conservative fiscal and monetary policies to create conditions that make investment and production more profitable and long-term growth more sustainable. They are notorious for decrying the calamities caused by populism and demanding that the nation atone for its gluttonous ways by tightening its belt and disciplining its behavior.

But whatever their claims to truth and justice, neither coalition has solved Argentina's fundamental growth problem. Perón sought to redistribute income from the upper class to the working class, from agriculture to industry, and from foreign investors to the Argentine state in 1946. It lasted for five years, then droughts, the exhaustion of gold reserves, and balance-of-payments problems forced him to slow down and impose austerity measures to compensate for populist excesses. But faith in populism never died, and when they came back in 1973 the Peronists wanted to start all over again. Unfortunately high inflation prohibited their adopting all of the same expansionary measures this time, so they turned to the *pacto* for securing agreements between management and labor with a mixed package of wage restraint and fiscal and credit expansion. Yet, again inflation rose and within two years they were forced to impose another austerity program, provoking enough working-class opposition to undermine Isabel Perón's authority.

Is it impossible for populist economics to succeed in Argentina? The Peronists have done little to convince one otherwise: each time they tried they overheated the economy or were undermined by international adversities not of their making. Populism suffers from inherent weaknesses that will always undermine it unless fundamental changes in it are made. It redistributes some wealth, though never as much real income as it pretends, and it expands economic activity temporarily, but it never extracts enough resources to pay its own bills. Peronists seem content to take revenues that are readily available rather than make fundamental changes in income and property taxation. They rely far more on income from exports than they should. Inevitably they must borrow money or expand the monetary supply to pay their bills, measures which eventually accelerate inflation. Populist economics has relied on the government's skimming income off the top of the economy rather than really redistributing wealth and property from the rich to either the state or to the poor. It is a kind of "rip-off" strategy for progressive purposes that makes many people happy for a few years but is never enough to sustain its redistributions or to keep the populist coalition satisfied.

The internationalist strategy has not done much better, even though it is the more radical of the two. Populism created a state that exercised substantial influence over the economy and tried, when conditions permitted, to placate the lower class, elevate bureaucrats, and promote national industry. The advocates of the internationalist strategy, in contrast, sought to destroy the populist state, replacing it with a market economy in which everyone competed more and was subsidized less. Changing the status quo is a radical endeavor in Argentina, especially when it involves restoring the economy to many of its nineteenth-century ways. Like any "revolution" it can be carried out only through the exercise of immense authority against those who resist it. If Marxists require a Leninist state to crush counterrevolutionaries, Argentine internationalists must rely on the power of the armed forces to deal with their adversaries.

At first glance the military might seem to have what it takes to stamp out populism. But they repeatedly failed, as we learned in Chapter 4. Populists survive them every time because they know they have the power to do so, most of it coming from the labor movement and its ability to resist complete subjugation by austerity-minded internationalists. Argentine authorities simply cannot sustain the kind of repression against the masses that succeeded in Brazil, Chile, and Uruguay. Again and again military presidents learn to their regret that unless they find some way to incorporate labor into their design and implementation of policy, they cannot rebuild their country.

A State That Does Not Work

Argentina is in trouble not only because the people we label populists and internationalists differ over how their economy should operate. Its problem is as much institutional as ideological, stemming largely from its failure to develop the means for resolving the conflicts they create. The Argentine state is big and powerful, but it is more successful at preserving the interests of its bureaucratic machinery than it is in resolving the disputes of society's combative members.

Politics everywhere is the result of social relations reflecting a balance of forces in given situations. What individual agents do is determined by their own motives and relations with others as well as by the constraints imposed on them by structures that no one agent or set of agents can easily change. In societies possessing several competitive and well-organized interests, deliberate efforts are made to create structures that constrain the competition, bringing a form of order that is acceptable to the participants. Most common in modern capitalist societies is either a kind of pseudo-democracy known as pluralism or a more centrally coordinated form of politics commonly referred to as corporatism. Either one can do the job of organizing politics in a manner that supports the exercise of enough authority to keep the complex society operating, as the history of the pluralistic United States and neocorporatist democracies of Northern Europe demonstrate. Unfortunately, Argentina has found it impossible to live by the rules of either in recent times.[40]

Pluralist politics places the state at the service of the electorate while giving it enough autonomy to act as arbiter among competing interests. Government decisions may be influenced by some interests more than others, but none will actually control it completely, at least not for long periods. The "common good" is not defined centrally, but emerges from the resolution of disputes. The good of society is determined, in other words, by the accumulation of settlements among competitors. Pluralism never works as neatly in practice as it does in theory, but its approximation offers a convenient means of coexistence in the liberal democratic society.

When elections were held and a constitutional government was chosen in 1983, Argentina once again took on a pluralist veneer as interest groups rushed to Congress and the government's ministries to make their partisan cases before the authorities. However, such appearances are deceiving, for no president, not even Raul Alfonsín in 1983, enjoyed enough authority to arbitrate disputes among interests whose leaders persistently refuse to be bound by settlements they dislike. Some presidents, of course, most notably those in uniform, show little interest in mediation, but even they find it hard to settle class and economic conflicts without repressing them, albeit temporarily. The result is a society that has little confidence in the ability of its would-be authorities to regulate much of anything that really matters.

But what about corporatism? If anything seemed necessary in a country as troubled by conflict as Argentina, it was the creation of a set of institutions that brought separate interests together where they could be closely supervised by the government "for the good of all." In this manner the state can exercise the authority needed to define and enforce a national agenda on the country. Disputes, if they arise at all, could be handled decisively and resistance quickly overcome by a powerful executive backed by all of the interests that have a stake in preventing any one of them from operating according to its own rules. That is exactly the kind of arrangement that Perón claimed he was creating when he flirted with corporatism during his first presidency and allowed his stand-in Hector Campora to supervise the *pacto social* in 1973. But Perón's corporatism turned out to be window dressing for his autocratic manipulation of everyone else.

Corporatism eludes Argentines for the same reason that pluralism does, namely, a public distrust of those who operate the nation's weak and partisan state apparatus. For corporatism to work the state must be accepted as independent of most interests and much stronger than all of them put together. But the Argentine state is neither, as we have seen repeatedly.

So what does this leave them with? A rather paradoxical condition, actually, in which a large and powerful state bureaucracy is headed by presidents whose authority over society lacks sufficient legitimacy for them to govern effectively. In other words, successive governments have increased the importance of public enterprise and government regulation without concomitantly institutionalizing a political process whose basic rules everyone comes to accept. This is why the state looks incredibly powerful but really is very weak. It is always quite powerful in its patronage, regulation, economic subsidization, and investments, creating for itself clienteles that are deeply involved in its activities regardless of who occupies the presidency. In fact, it is the reliance of these constitutents on the government for subsidies that makes it so difficult for presidents to reduce its size. But political authority over society does not follow automatically from such state power. It is quite separable in Argentine minds, as their noncompliance with political authorities continues to show. While they work closely with the organs of the state, they continue to defy authorities when they can get away with it.

This arrangement is not without its benefits, though "consolations" might be a more appropriate term. For all of its waste and inefficiency, economic strangulation, and resistance to reform, the government does sustain a great portion of the society through bad times. That is one reason why Argentina does not self-destruct as a political society: too much of it has been bureaucratized (at a high price admittedly) to collapse under the pressure of a permanent political legitimacy crisis. It is not a very satisfactory arrangement, to be sure, but it does allow the nation to operate when so much of it is always breaking down.

It was into this that Raul Alfonsín confidently walked with the presidential sash around his neck in December 1983. As a lifelong Radical, he retained a faith in government and a characteristic dedication to converting others to his civic religion. But as a politician unaccustomed to directing a country steeped in economic crisis, he would soon discover that he had much to learn about leading people who shared neither his trust of public authority nor his optimism about the nation's future.

Notes

1. *Clarín*, economic supp., October 28, 1984, p. 8.
2. Ibid., October 7, 1984, p. 9.
3. Brazil's share of the regional GNP rose from 21.7 to 34.1 percent during the same period. See Livio Guillermo Kuhl, *Una política industrial para la Argentina* (Buenos Aires: Club de Estudio, 1983), p. 566.
4. Guido Di Tella, "The Economic Policies of Argentina's Labour-Based Government, 1972–1976," Woodrow Wilson Center Latin American Program Working Paper, no. 47 (1981): 3–7.
5. Quoted in *The Washington Post National Weekly Edition,* October 8, 1984, p. 22.
6. *Wall Street Journal,* November 11, 1984, p. 1; and World Bank, *Economic Memorandum on Argentina,* June 1984, pp. 126–138.
7. World Bank, *Economic Memorandum on Argentina*, pp. 148–150. It has taken two to three times more wheat to buy the same amount of nitrogen in Argentina as it has in the United States during the past decade, for example.
8. This is the thesis of Jorge Federico Sabato, *La pampa prodiga: Claves de una frustración* (Buenos Aires: CIESA, 1980).
9. Osvaldo Barsky, Horacio Ciafardini, and Carlos Alberto Cristia, "Producción y tecnología en la región pampeana," *Primera historia integral* 28 (1980): 184.
10. Consejo Técnico de Inversiones, *Anuario-1983,* p. 334.
11. Jan Peter Wogart, "Combining Price Stabilization with Trade and Financial Liberalization Policies: The Argentine Experience, 1976–1981," *Journal of Inter-American and World Affairs* 25, no 4 (November 1983): 458.
12. Private shares in the marketing of wheat in 1979–80 were divided as follows: Bunge Born 10.5 percent, Andre 8.8, Cargill 14.1, Continental 8.0, Louis Dreyfus 3.0, others 13.4. Naciones Unidas, Estudios e informes de la Cepal, *Empresas transnacionales en la industría de alimentos: el caso argentino* (Santiago, 1983), pt. 2, p. 38.
13. Ibid., pp. 42–45.
14. Ibid.
15. Flacso Santiago, *America Latina–Union Sovietica* 1, no. 1 (November–December 1983): 8.
16. *Clarín*, economic supp., February 10, 1985, p. 10.
17. Argentina's industrial growth rate was slightly less than Brazil's (6.1 percent) and Mexico's (8.9) during the same period. See Adolfo Dorfman, *Cincuenta años de industrialización en la Argentina: 1930–1980* (Buenos Aires: Solar, 1983), pp. 106, 576.
18. Consejo Técnico de Investigaciones, *La estructura de los mercados en Argentina– 1979* (Buenos Aires: CTI, 1979), p. 17. Only 319 industrial firms employed more than 500

people, and another 1,986 employed between 100 and 500; added together they were 2 percent of the total firms and employed 49 percent of the industrial work force.

19. Jorge Schvarzer, "Cambios en el liderazgo industrial argentino en el periodo de Martínez de Hoz," *Desarrollo económico* 23, no. 91 (October–December 1983): 418–512. The largest foreign firms by sales rankings were: Esso (2); Ford (4); Massalin Particulares (5); Renault (6); Shell (7); IBM (13); Mercedes-Benz (17); Volkswagen (22); Refineria de Maiz (25); Lever (27).

20. Dorfman, *Cincuenta años de industrialización en la Argentina*, pp. 390–392.

21. Kuhl, *Una política industrial para la Argentina*, pp. 508–527.

22. *Clarín*, economic supp., December 23, 1984, p. 5; and *Finance and Development* (March 1984): 33.

23. Latin American Linguistic Service, *Foreign Investment in Argentina: An Updated Handbook of Legislation and Statutes*, April 22, 1983, pp. 85–87; and *Mercado*, May 17, 1984, pp. 34–42. The largest public banks are the Banco Nacional de Desarrollo (1), Banco de la Nación (2), Banco de la Provincia de Buenos Aires (3), Banco Hipotecario Nacional (9), Banco de la Ciudad de Buenos Aires (10). Two American banks are in the top ten, both of them having been in Argentina for decades: Citibank (7), Banco de Boston (8).

24. World Bank, *Economic Memorandum on Argentina*, p. 162.

25. A detailed examination of Argentina's potential for industrial export development is made in Kuhl, *Una política industrial para la Argentina*.

26. Consejo Empresario Argentina, *Las empresas públicas en la economía argentina* (Buenos Aires: FIEL, 1976).

27. *Clarín*, economic supp., January 6, 1985, p. 9.

28. Kuhl, *Una política industrial para la Argentina*, pp. 194–205. Government industries in the top 100 industries in the country ranked by sales are: YPF—petroleum (1); Somisa—steel (8); Afne—shipyard (15); Fabricaciones Militares—weapons, machinery, chemicals (24); Siam—machinery (40); Petroquemica Mosconi—petrochemicals (48); Ing. La Esperanza—sugar (73); Giol—beverages (88). See Schvarzer, "Cambios en el liderazgo industrial argentino en el periodo de Martínez de Hoz," pp. 418–421.

29. World Bank, *Economic Memorandum on Argentina*, pp. 32–104. The World Bank study is the most complete to date on the financing of the Argentine public sector.

30. Juan Carlos de Pablo, *Mercado*, December 22, 1983, p. 53.

31. *Clarín*, July 26, 1984, p. 26.

32. World Bank, *Economic Memorandum on Argentina*, p. 99.

33. Ibid., pp. 96–121.

34. *Clarín*, international ed., November 19–25, 1984, p. 10; and *Clarín*, economic supp., January 13, 1985, pp. 6–10.

35. *Clarín*, international ed., September 3–9, 1984, p. 10; and *Latin America Weekly Report*, May 25, 1984, p. 8.

36. Alain Rouquie offers a summary of different perspectives on the Argentine power structure in his essay, "Hegemonía militar, estado, y dominación social," *Argentina, hoy* (Buenos Aires: Siglo Veintiuno, 1982), pp. 35–41.

37. See Gary W. Wynia, *Argentina in the Postwar Era* (Albuquerque: University of New Mexico Press, 1978), pp. 23 ff.

38. Ibid., pp. 56 ff.

39. I am indebted to Professor Javier Villanueva and his students, who reached this conclusion about the persistence of the same two issues after examining ministerial documents from 1970 to 1982. He reports their findings in "Doce años de política económica en la Argentina—1970–1982." Unpublished paper, July 1983.

40. An enormous literature was written in the 1960s and 1970s about pluralism and corporatism in capitalist systems, pointing to the conditions that caused politics to move in either direction. A good place to start is with Andrew Shonfield, *Modern Capitalism: The Changing Balance of Public and Private Power* (New York: Oxford University Press, 1967); and Phillipe Schmitter, "Still the Century of Corporatism," *Review of Politics* 35 (1974): 85–131.

7

The Rise and Fall of Raul Alfonsín

Democracy has never come easily for Argentines and it was no different in 1983. While most people enthusiastically celebrated their new freedom, they also knew that they lived in a nation where the people who had tortured and killed over 8,000 of them still walked their streets freely. Consequently, they not only expected their new authorities to revive an economy deeply in debt and badly damaged by the nation's isolation during the Malvinas War, but they also wanted them to punish those responsible for such brutality. It was no meager task, especially when many in the armed forces believed that they had committed no crimes.

Even more fundamental was the need of the Argentines to rediscover how democratic government actually worked. No constitution would decide for them exactly where to draw a line between the government's authority and the rights of its citizens, nor could it determine exactly how "representation" and "participation" would be practiced democratically. In a nation where presidents had always tried to reign supreme, and where influence over them was seldom exercised by a national legislature or by provincial governments, adjustments were necessary for liberal democracy to function. People knew this, but they also knew that they still disagreed over exactly how to practice democracy.

To lead them they selected Raul Alfonsín, the consummate politician, not the democratic miracle-worker. He ignored polls when they did not look good and praised them when they did. He did favors for his family and friends when they called on him and he never felt guilty about it. Yet through it all, he did understand that it was the Argentine voter who would determine his ultimate fate. And that was no small achievement.

Defeating the Peronists in 1983 and demolishing their claim to being the nation's only real majority party was thrilling for Alfonsín. Yet it was not enough, for like most Radicals, he also could not suppress his desire to turn the Peronists into a permanent minority. He wanted to believe that the working class longed for its liberation from the unscrupulous labor leaders who had commanded them for so long, and he presumed that by changing labor laws to allow more worker control over union leadership, he could ruin the Peronists' political base. With more freedom, his thinking went, the rank and file would give their support to many different parties, including the Radicals.

Radical party politicians were encouraged by the divisions that plagued the CGT when the new democracy began. The largest of the CGT factions, known as the "62," was headed by metallurgical workers' chief Lorenzo Miguel and was supported by nearly 40 percent of the member unions; the "25" faction was backed by 26 percent, and the "15" faction by about 23 percent. To work a compromise they had selected Saúl Ubaldini as their new secretary general, a little-known leader of the beer workers who came from the smallest faction. Reuniting the CGT was not easy, however, since Miguel wanted to reconstruct a traditional "verticalist" command structure that was tightly directed by a few people at the top while the "25" resisted, demanding that unions open themselves up more to the rank and file. Such division only encouraged Alfonsín to believe that the time was right to disrupt the CGT.

The First Round

Alfonsín began by trying to force the unions to allow free elections and proportional representation within their organizations. As it stood, dissidents within many unions were repressed without any chance to influence what their leaders did. By giving them better representation, Alfonsín hoped to help them build enough support to dislodge their entrenched Peronist leaders. Since in a democracy new legislation was required to do this, he sent a reform bill to Congress immediately after he took office, expecting its swift passage by a narrow vote. To his surprise the Peronists drew together in panic and, with the help of a couple of provincial parties, they turned their plurality in the Senate into a majority and blocked the bill's passage. As quickly as Alfonsín had tried to liberate the labor movement, it had just as quickly stood up and defeated him.

The other part of the strategy involved denying the labor movement control over the *obras sociales* funds that were created from contributions by workers and employers ostensibly for the purpose of health care and other welfare projects. They formed a huge trough of savings and it was no secret that the Peronists had paid their campaign bills with the funds, contrary to Radical wishes. The armed forces had "intervened" the funds in 1976, putting them under the supervision of the federal bureaucracy, but when democracy was restored the Peronists demanded them back. Alfonsín refused, offering instead a joint, public-private, arrangement that would assure government supervision of their uses. Keeping the funds out of political campaigns was essential to the Radicals' efforts to limit the power of Peronism at the polls, and Alfonsín made no secret of it. But an impasse developed, for after having lost his labor reform bill in the Senate, he feared the same fate for the *obras sociales* reform, so the issue was left unresolved during his first two years.

Peronist power in Congress facilitated their resistance to the new government. It should be recalled that despite his impressive victory, Alfonsín never really controlled the Congress. He started with a majority in the Chamber of Deputies—131 of its 254 seats—but half of the Chamber's members had to stand for reelection every two years.[1] And the Radicals were weaker in the Senate with eighteen seats to the Peronists' twenty-one; moreover, the Senate's forty-six members were all appointed by provincial legislatures (two per province), one third of them every three years. And no one expected the Radicals would control enough provincial legislatures to assure them a majority in the national Senate. That is why ruling by decrees rather than legislation would become very tempting even to someone as democratic as Alfonsín.

Within a year Alfonsín knew that his dream of attracting the Peronist rank and file to the Radical party was just that, a dream. Fundamental differences between the two parties hindered the Radicals' cultivation of working-class support far more than they cared to admit. The Radical party was a party led by middle-class professionals who believed that politics was done in committees, carefully, deliberately, and collectively. The Peronists, in contrast, were more concerned with substantive ends than with procedural means. They came from all sectors of society, and their leaders were driven by a desire to use governmental power to deliver the goods to their kind of people, most of whom expected to be served by strong and belligerent politicians. They had little patience with the kind of deliberations that occupied so much of the Radicals' time. Nor did they find appeals to principle all that attractive. Incrementalism, the most characteristic mode of Radical behavior, requires more patience than the Peronists possessed. This is one reason why the two parties often appear to be talking right past each other. Another is the Radicals' self-righteousness in pretending that because they believed that their way of doing politics was morally superior to the Peronists' ways, they did not have to defer to them, something the Peronists found offensive.

Looking Abroad

Alfonsín next tried to restore pride at home by taking some initiatives abroad. The Radical party had always been nationalistic, and often doctrinaire, and while in principle Alfonsín was no different, he knew that Argentina could not afford to go its own way any more after its debacle in war and in view of its enormous foreign debts. Consequently, he decided to prove that he could be as reasonable as anyone else if dealt with fairly by allies and adversaries.

His opening move came promptly during a dispute with Chile over three little islands in the Beagle Channel, one that had nearly brought the two countries to war in 1978. At issue were not just the islands but also some fundamental principles of foreign relations. Argentines were not accustomed to yielding territory that they believed was theirs nor in giving the appearance of compromising with foreign nations. World War II had freed them from British domination, and Perón had tried to increase the country's "independence" in every way possible. Independence means many different things but to Argentine populists it meant defiance of other nations, especially the industrial ones in Europe and North America. It also included a renewed commitment to territoriality and the notion that national power was derived in part from land and its defense. Before Alfonsín became president critics of such notions claimed they were counterproductive because they mistook territorial independence for real power. What Argentines needed to understand, critics insisted, was their involvement in an interdependent world that rewarded a nation more for cooperation than for combat. Bargaining was the method, not the "either/or" ultimatums that had drawn the country into war with Great Britain. In short, Argentina did not need the Beagle Channel Islands as much as it needed peace with Chile.[2]

In October 1984 the Vatican supplied Alfonsín with a proposal that it had developed during five years of mediating the dispute. It assigned the islands to Chile while allowing Argentina to keep the eastern entrance to the Straits of Magellan. Chile was also allowed some access to the Atlantic but denied juridical claims over it, and both countries were asked to agree to abstain from warfare in the area and to create a binational commission devoted to achieving the economic integration of the region.

Ratification came easily in Pinochet's Chile but its prospects were not good in Argentina where nationalists mounted a campaign against Chilean possession of the islands. Alfonsín's suggestion that Argentina accept the treaty seemed to give his opponents the issue that they had been looking for to assault his popularity before the end of his first year. But just as the debate got under way, he surprised them by calling a plebiscite that allowed the Argentine public to express its opinion on the subject without binding the senators who planned to vote on the treaty a few weeks later. It was a gamble that paid off handsomely, for on November 25 nearly 73 percent of the eligible voters turned out and 77 percent of them approved ratification.[3] Alfonsín's victory not only put his critics on the defensive but it also gave senators the courage they needed to ratify the treaty. It was close enough as it was, passing after intense debate by a vote of 23 to 22 with one abstention on March 14, 1985.

Similar progress was not made with the Malvinas/Falklands issue, however. Technically Argentina and Britain remained at war in 1985 since Argentina had not declared the conflict over. Nevertheless contacts with the British were made and discussions were held briefly in Switzerland in July 1984, but Foreign Minister Dante Caputo returned home when the British refused to discuss the sovereignty issue until Argentina declared an end to the war. In fact, there was no chance of compromise no matter what the Argentines did since the Thatcher government apparently had decided that by starting the war Argentina had sacrificed its right to govern the islands. Though some opposition members in the British Parliament expressed an interest in talking with Alfonsín about some kind of "leaseback" arrangement in which Argentina would be given sovereignty over the islands on the condition that they lease them to the Falklands Company or the British government, Thatcher would have none of it.[4]

There was one more issue that Alfonsín could not evade because it worried his potential allies more than it did Argentine citizens. Nuclear power produced electricity in Argentina, but since Perón's time the Argentines had been accused of developing it for military purposes even though they always denied it. Now foreigners were demanding that the Argentines reassure them of their peaceful intentions.

Actually, Perón had never accomplished much with his nuclear policies and Argentina never developed a nuclear weapon. Still, it had created an indigenous research capacity and, with the help of foreign technology, its own nuclear power industry. Everything was supervised by a presidentially appointed Nuclear Commission whose director was an admiral through most of its history. Under its tutelage the country began processing native uranium in 1953 and it built its first reactor in

1958, adding three more research reactors by 1967. In 1968 it started work on its first nuclear power plant, Atucha I, located just up-river from Buenos Aires, using West Germany technology, and completed the heavy-water/natural uranium 320-megawatt facility in 1974. A second power plant with twice Atucha's capacity was completed with Italian and Canadian technology at Embalse, Córdoba, in 1983, and a third one, Atucha II, was slated for operation in the early 1990s, though economic problems severely slowed its completion. Most impressive, however, was the variety of facilities that operated in the country, among them two uranium mining sites, four mills, an industrial-scale heavy-water plant, a plutonium plant, and eight reactors used primarily for research.[5]

Nothing indicated how far Argentina had come better than its announcement just before Alfonsín's inauguration that it had completed construction of its own uranium enrichment plant (one that uses the gaseous-diffusion method). Work on it had been kept secret and nuclear authorities around the world were caught totally by surprise. The new plant, located in southern Argentina at Pilcaniyeu, could, in principle at least, provide the capability to enrich uranium to weapons-grade levels, though Argentines denied that such an objective was ever their intention. Instead, it was explained, the plant had been built to compensate for the U.S. government's cutoff of enriched uranium for the country's nuclear reactors in 1978; Argentina needed to assure itself a supply for use in radioisotopes in medicine and agriculture, as well as for fuel for the reactors that it had begun selling to other Latin American nations for their research programs.[6]

Alfonsín inherited all of this, convinced that Argentina had as much right as anyone to advance the peaceful use of nuclear energy. Yet he was aware that his country had never signed the most important international nuclear nonproliferation treaties like the 1967 Inter-American Treaty of Tlatelolco aimed at prohibiting nuclear weapons in Latin America and the Nuclear Nonproliferation Treaty of 1968. In their defense Argentines had always argued that the treaties were discriminatory since they asked nations like Argentina not to build weapons while allowing nations with nuclear weapons to keep them. If weapons development was to be prevented, the Argentines argued, every nation in the world should stop building them.

Alfonsín did assert his control over the Nuclear Commission by replacing its director, Admiral Carlos Castro Cordero. But that still left him with an impressive little industry. As one foreign study noted at the time:

... there is little question that Argentina today has the general scientific and industrial infrastructure necessary for the development of nuclear weapons. Indeed, Argentine officials have said as much since the mid-1970s, when the nation's nuclear specialists first separated small amounts of plutonium. At present, however, the nation lacks facilities—enrichment and reprocessing plants—for the production of the nuclear weapons materials in significant quantities, although both types of plants are under development.[7]

Nearly every Argentine was proud of this, but Alfonsín spoke for them when he reassured anyone who asked that he had no intention of creating weapons. At the same time, he used the issue to project Argentina into discussions of nuclear questions all over the world. No one really expected that Argentina would make any difference in what the United States, France, or the Soviet Union actually did, but that never stopped Alfonsín from seeking attention for Argentina's position on disarmament. It was a small prize in today's world, but was the best that he could get.

The Price of Justice

A defender of human rights during the dark days of military repression, Alfonsín knew that he was expected to act swiftly in prosecuting hundreds of officers involved in the *Proceso* (1976–83). Nevertheless, despite the clamor for action, he moved cautiously, convinced that a direct assault on the armed forces might provoke military retaliation. He opted for investigations that were intended to diffuse the rancor while laying the foundation for later prosecutions.

He benefited initially from the military's preoccupation with its internal problems in the wake of the war. They had fallen into disarray after their humiliating defeat in the Malvinas. Confusion and popular disgrace gave them no alternative but to call elections in 1983, and when they did their weakness became a source of the new president's strength. He set out to make it clear that he wanted a line of command that descended from the president through his civilian defense minister to the joint chiefs and then to the service chiefs. His purpose was to deprive the latter of what had become virtual autonomy in military matters. When the commander of the army ignored one of his first orders, Alfonsín dismissed him for insubordination without hesitation, making it clear that he would not tolerate defiance. Moreover, during the next six months he sent into retirement all but three of the fifty-three generals who remained from the prewar administrations.[8]

Most officers bitterly resented their subjugation to total civilian control, believing that it had always been their responsibility to defend their nation from its own citizens as well as from its foreign enemies. To their way of thinking, they, and not a constitution written by civilians, had the final word on matters of internal and external defense, broadly defined. And to do that they could not allow total civilian control over their institutions. While they could play by the democratic rules in some things, they still wanted to reserve for themselves the right to make independent judgments and act accordingly.

Alfonsín knew this but he also realized from the outset that much more than presidential control of the armed forces was demanded of him by the electorate. The *Proceso* had ended, but it had left behind thousands of missing civilians whom the military had never accounted for. The public wanted officers judged and, when found guilty of crime, punished appropriately. Moreover, democratic government required the rule of law over military force, and it was left to the new president to make the system work.

The departing junta members had tried to settle the issue for him before they left the government by decreeing that no soldier bore any responsibility for what he had been ordered to do, and no one but God could stand in judgment of those who had given the orders. But when the public reacted with hostility to this "Final Document," the departing junta tried a different approach just five weeks before the October elections, this time granting amnesty to all members of the armed forces and the guerrillas they had fought. It was a desperate political move that no one celebrated, including many officers who believed that since they had committed no crimes, amnesty was an insult.

Peronist candidate Italo Luder agreed to respect the amnesty decree if he were elected president, but Alfonsín did not. Nevertheless, President Alfonsín was careful to communicate that he did not intend to put every officer on trial. Instead he distinguished three groups among them: those who had given the orders during the *Proceso*, those who obeyed them, and those who had exceeded them, making it clear that he would insist on prosecution of the first and third groups, but not the second. He was equally cautious after his inauguration when in his first act he only ordered that the nine members of the first three juntas be prosecuted in civilian courts. After that he asked Congress to ratify a plan that would declare the military's self-amnesty null and void, but permit military rather than civilian prosecution of junior officers as long as the military completed the task within six months. If they did not, the cases would be transferred to civilian courts. While Congress agreed, it also amended the bill to permit civilian trial of any officer who had committed "atrocious and aberrant acts," that is, torture and execution, a major change that would complicate Alfonsín's task in the months that followed.

Simultaneously Alfonsín appointed a twelve-member civilian commission that was to determine once and for all the fate of those who had disappeared. Chaired by novelist Ernesto Sabato, it took testimony from 5,792 witnesses during nine months before submitting its 350-page report and 50,000 pages of evidence to the president in September 1984. Its findings, which confirmed what the country's eight human-rights groups had been saying for years, documented the disappearance of 8,800 people, many of them tortured in one of 280 secret prisons. It also named 1,200 police and military personnel who had participated directly in the secret operations, most of them still in uniform and some routinely promoted by the president and the legislature just before the report was issued.[9]

In October 1984 the nine officers who had ruled the nation in three juntas between 1976 to 1982 were brought to trial. The trials were conducted orally and publicly, the first federal trials ever so conducted in a legal system that relies almost entirely on written testimony for adjudication. They began swiftly, and during the next five months the Argentine public heard testimony from victims and their relatives as well as from members of the armed forces, while human-rights groups agitated for the severest punishment.[10]

In their defense the officers' attorneys argued that their clients had begun their "war" under orders issued by President Isabel Perón in 1975 and after that had merely completed the assignment under their own government. Civilians, not military officers, were responsible for what they had done, they contended. The weakness of such a defense soon became apparent, however, as military witnesses admitted to having been part of a deliberate "holy war" against a "godless communism" that they would fight all over again were the need to arise.[11]

On December 9, 1985, the judges handed down their verdicts and gave life imprisonment to General Videla and Admiral Massera, seventeen years to General Viola, eight to Admiral Lambruschini and four-and-a-half years to General Agosti. The remaining four officers who were members of the last junta that began in 1980 were absolved. The Supreme Court confirmed the judgment the following year but reduced Viola's sentence to sixteen-and-a-half years, and Agosti's to three years and nine months.[12]

As the new law allowed, the twenty retired officers who formed the Supreme Council of the Armed Forces began their investigations of other officers while civilians watched and waited. Council members interviewed people for almost five months, then, without prior warning, they stopped and informed the president that they had found no one guilty. In their judgment Argentine officers at all ranks had fought a war to save the country, doing what was essential to win it and, therefore, none were guilty of military crimes. Nothing could have been more unwelcome to Alfonsín who had relied on military justice to reduce the public pressure that was building for swift conviction and retribution. From then on little of what happened was anticipated.

Alfonsín confronted something for which the obvious judicial solution was incompatible with the practical political one. If Argentina were a normal democracy, criminals in the rest of the armed forces would also have been convicted and jailed, and then replaced by a new generation of officers. But Argentina was not "normal"; it was experimenting with a democracy that could easily be destroyed by frightened soldiers. The president did not want to jail over a thousand officers because they were responsible for what the Sabato Commission called "the most savage tragedy in our history." It was naïve to expect that the Argentine armed forces would submit to justice without fighting back, as Alfonsín knew too well. His dilemma was an insoluble one, for as long as he did little or nothing to bring them to justice, several thousand well-trained, experienced, and unscrupulous torturers and murderers equipped with vast amounts of weapons would remain at large, beyond the control of constitutional authorities. But his only practical political choice, albeit a sad one, was to ignore most of the offenders, hoping that time and dedication to democratic processes by everyone would reduce the usefulness of such characters to the rest of society.[13]

With public pressure on the courts to prosecute more officers growing in 1986, and Alfonsín unwilling to let it go very far, he won congressional approval of his *Punto Final* (Last Stop) law on December 24, 1986. It allowed the future trial only of cases that judges could prepare within sixty days after the law was passed. The sixty days included the Christmas and New Year holidays and January, which is the country's normal vacation month. Alfonsín hoped that this would keep the total number of cases pending prosecution to less than a hundred. But judges in several provinces canceled their vacations and when the sixty days had passed, four hundred officers had been charged.[14]

This had devastating repercussions for Alfonsín soon thereafter. It began during the week of Easter 1987 when army Lieutenant-Colonel Aldo Rico and a group of commandos, who called themselves the *carapintadas* (painted faces), seized an army base near the city of Buenos Aires and dared the rest of the army to evict them.[15] They knew that other units would not strike back because most officers welcomed Rico's demand that Alfonsín end all trials and liberate Videla and his colleagues. Alfonsín went to the occupied base, negotiated with Rico, and returned to the capital to announce that Rico and his troops had given up. But what most civilians did not realize until later was that the settlement came at a high price to the government. Six weeks after the rebellion Alfonsín submitted new legislation to Congress, called the Due Obedience Law, which stated that no officer would go on trial for something that he had done when he was a lieutenant colonel or of lower rank. The bill passed easily, leaving just two hundred officers for possible trial. A few months later the Supreme Court reduced that number to only forty-one.

In fact, Alfonsín had done what he had originally intended to do with his Punto Final legislation: limit the number of trials in order to put the entire matter behind him and his government as quickly as possible after prosecuting the junta members. But his being forced to do this by military protest weakened him as president. Though no military coup was ever intended, it was a reminder that no matter how popular the democratic Alfonsín had been in 1983, he had found no way to get enough control over the armed forces to prevent their using guns to force presidential and congressional retreat on the most crucial issues.[16]

Officers also bitterly resented Alfonsín for reducing their budgets drastically and cutting the military conscription in half. As they saw it, it was not the reorganization of the armed forces that he sought, but its total destruction in the crudest of ways. No matter how much he denied such charges, they would never forgive him. Officers were also bitter about what they regarded as the unjustified conviction of junta members and the public's desire for more trials. Some officers, especially the younger ones, were also unhappy with their own senior commanders who, in the wake of the humiliating Malvinas defeat, had failed to modernize their own forces for fear of losing their commands to more innovative officers.

Rico's success cost Alfonsín far more than it seemed immediately after he returned to the Casa Rosada by helicopter from his meeting with Rico and claimed a victory for democracy. The president who was supposed to wield authority over the nation actually had very little. Alfonsín became vulnerable and thereafter his Peronist opponents seized on the experience to portray him as something other than the leader that he had claimed to be.[17]

Moreover, Rico's was not the only army revolt. In December 1988 some army units rebelled again, this time led by Colonel Mohammed Ali

Seineldin. After seizing a base near Buenos Aires and demanding that Alfonsín dismiss the army's chief of staff, raise military salaries, and grant amnesty to all officers, Seineldin negotiated with his commanders and went into their custody two days later only to be released not long after that. A few weeks later Alfonsín dismissed the army chief of staff, General José Ciardi, but went no further. Seineldin, a brash right winger, was especially popular with young army officers because of his brazen nationalism and his opposition to the army leadership.

Had the military rebellions been the only problems that Alfonsin faced, he might have led the Radical party to victory in the important congressional and gubernatorial elections that were held in September 1987. Unfortunately he also had the economy to deal with, and, after an impressive success in late 1985, he ran into trouble from which he never really escaped.

An Economic Reeducation

Alfonsin's initial popularity had sustained him while he tried to figure out what to do about the unprecedented economic infirmities that he had inherited. It was an old story but even worse this time. The economy was in the fourth year of a deep recession and overwhelmed by an annual inflation rate that rose from 400 percent to more than 600 percent during his first six months. Moreover, the public-sector deficit had risen to 20 percent of the gross domestic product, unemployment was at 10 percent, and dollar reserves in the Central Bank were nearly depleted. As if that were not enough, the country also faced a record foreign debt of $46 billion whose servicing it could not pay. These were hardly the conditions under which one wanted to test the viability of democratic government.

Unfortunately, neither Alfonsín nor his closest colleagues knew what to do. Not having expected to defeat the Peronists, until polls indicated they might do so just before the election, had something to do with their lack of preparation, but the enormity of the problems they faced also overwhelmed them. Without a well-developed plan at their disposal, they approached the economy as if they believed that the president's popularity, along with some price controls and wage increases, would be enough to restore confidence in it. Such thinking is a common fault of Argentine politicians, none more so than Radicals who always seem to assume that their honesty, integrity, and good populist intentions will cause everyone to relax economically. But creative management, not overconfidence, was what the economy needed, and Alfonsín's "trust me" approach failed to excite investors—gross investment reached a five-year low before his first year was over—or impress the working class.

The government was also handicapped by the Radicals' conviction, one they shared with most members of society, that upper-class greed, along with the stupidity and treachery of the armed forces, were responsible for the economy's malaise. Had José Martínez de Hoz and the insatiable financial elite not sold the country for their own profit, went the line, the current mess would have been avoided. It would be a year before the Radicals would admit to themselves that bankers and foreign investors had not created the mess, but only taken advantage of it. Its causes were more fundamental, starting with a well-known failure to produce enough goods at competitive prices to earn the income required to sustain the standard of living to which Argentina's people have become accustomed. There was no quick fix available to cure it. Restoring confidence and promoting investment in an economy as damaged and demoralized as Argentina's were beyond anyone's capacity to deliver quickly.

Price controls, wage indexing, and personal appeals for public trust were a dismal failure, and inflation continued to rise and foreign debts to mount during 1984. Industrialists complained that a dramatic rise in labor costs was destroying their profitability, making new investment impossible as they watched the value of the peso fall rapidly after midyear when people rushed to acquire dollars to protect themselves from the effects of a hyperinflation that reached an annual rate of 800 percent in October. On top of this something had to be done about the country's foreign debt. It had risen from $12.5 billion at the end of 1978 to $46 billion when the Radicals took over, a nearly fourfold increase in five years, $31 billion of it belonging to the public sector, and two-thirds held by over 300 foreign banks. The debt's size was bad enough, but its expansion, along with deterioration in the term structure of the debt and rising interest rates abroad, led to an alarming increase in the burden of debt service, from $4.9 billion in 1979 to $20.3 billion in 1982. As a result interest payments absorbed about 60 percent of the country's export earnings in 1982.[18]

As much as he disliked doing so, Alfonsín had no choice but to seek temporary help from the International Monetary Fund, an organization that nationalistic Radicals love to hate. On September 25 Minister of Economy Bernardo Grinspun stepped to the podium at the annual IMF. meeting in Washington, D.C., and announced the dreaded agreement. In exchange for a standby loan of $1.5 billion the Argentine government agreed to everything it had refused to do previously, including a tighter monetary policy, limiting wage hikes, raising public-service tariffs, and eliminating price controls, albeit over one year.[19] Two months later Central Bank President Enrique García Vázquez announced the refinancing of $25 billion of the debt.[20] This was done despite the fact that many bankers doubted that Argentina would be able to stay within the terms of its agreement with the IMF once unions protested their wage losses. Of course, this skepticism proved justified, for by the time Alfonsín spoke to a joint session of the U.S. Congress on March 20 to plead for more toleration of debtor nations, it was apparent that Argentina could not live up to the terms of the IMF agreement.[21]

He knew that he had failed economically and admitted as much at year's end.[22] Then, while most people were seeking relief from a sweltering summer, he announced he was starting over and dismissed both Grinspun, his close friend and advisor, and Central Bank president García Vázquez, Grinspun's chief rival and critic in the economic cabinet.[23] Juan Sourrouille, who replaced Grinspun, was a Harvard-educated economist and the author of a major study of the Illia administration, but never a member of the Radical party. Where Grinspun was outspoken and argumentative, Sourrouille was the cool technocrat who spoke from behind dark glasses in a soft monotone, explaining the nation's plight like a seminar instructor intent on explaining the nation's woes.[24] He announced his own five-year recovery plan that sought to reorder priorities, starting with the promotion of agricultural exports and business investment, both of which evidenced the administration's abandonment of what remained of its populist aspirations. The plan committed the government again to making war on inflation by enforcing the unpopular austerity measures required in the September 1984 agreement with the IMF and private creditors. It also promoted the growth of export-related industries, much as Martínez de Hoz had tried to do, though without using such drastic methods to accomplish it. The plan mixed a little Milton Friedman with some John Maynard Keynes to come up with an innovative (critics would say contradictory) solution to Argentina's problem. It seemed that many of the realities that had convinced Martínez de Hoz that the country's future prosperity rested with the addition of industrial exports to its agricultural ones were inescapable: Argentina had to grow outward to grow much at all, and to accomplish that the nationalism that had sustained the Radical party throughout its history had to be moderated.

Sourrouille was very frank about how slow the nation's economic recovery would be during the next five years, making it clear that losses during the past decade could not be made up quickly. Between 1986 and 1989, if all went according to his design, the per capita national product would increase at an average rate of 2.5 percent, as would real per capita income, though both predictions were admittedly optimistic.

The key to its success was an increase in investments by 11.3 percent annually over the next five years, coupled with a 7 percent annual increase in exports. At the same time, a lid would be put on public-sector outlays, reducing them from 44.5 percent of the national product in 1985 to 41.8 percent in 1989.[25]

It did not take much knowledge of economics to appreciate that the Radicals had changed course, meeting the internationalists about half-way. That was a long distance for someone like Alfonsín to go, given his belief in social reform and the need to supervise capitalists closely. But the choice was not really his to make anymore. Like social democrats abroad, most notably President Mitterrand in France, Alfonsín had to "bite the bullet" and go to work on his unproductive economy. Europeans he respected had been telling him as much for almost a year, and he finally gave in.

If his people needed any reminding of the seriousness of his intent, Alfonsín gave it at a massive rally in the Plaza de Mayo at the end of April 1985, much as Perón had done under similar circumstances in 1952. He told the nation that it was in for very hard times, and that everyone stood to lose something before they could gain anything. In June everyone watched and waited to see if he really meant what he said, many hoping that, as before, he would "chicken out" under pressure from the CGT whose leaders staged their own rally in May to express their opposition to further austerity.

The CGT's demands were basically very simple. They wanted the government to break with the IMF and return to the "people," proving its devotion to the people by decreeing huge wage increases and seizing the wealth of the Argentines and foreigners who were profiting from the nation's travails. The trouble was, of course, that the government could not possibly do such a thing without making the situation a great deal worse for everyone, including wage earners. The CGT belief that every-thing could be solved by a simple act of will is deeply rooted in Argen-tina—the Radicals themselves were known to believe much the same thing before they came to office—and persuading them of the futility of such notions in 1985 seemed impossible.[26]

This duel between the Peronists and the president was a familiar sight to Argentines but it looked bizarre to most foreigners. Govern-ments and oppositions always try to demonstrate their power over one another, but in most democracies their efforts are confined primarily to the legislative process where votes are tallied and power measured. But Perón had added another arena to power politics in Argentina when workers stormed the Plaza de Mayo on October 17, 1945, and secured his release from prison, and ever since mass demonstrations have been a primary manifestation of power in Argentina. Until 1983 it had been taken for granted that Peronists would always win the contests held in the plazas, but then Alfonsín came along and attracted hundreds of thousands to his campaign rallies, giving the Radicals a sense of power that they had not known since Yrigoyen. After he was inaugurated and the challenge of the CGT began, journalists spent much of their time counting heads to determine which of the two political masses was the largest, giving politics the appearance of a popularity contest measured by the number of people who showed up at demonstrations. When Alfonsín spoke to an estimated 200,000 enthusiasts in the Plaza de Mayo in late April his popularity was judged to be as great as ever and his power still intact. Then the Peronists announced their intention to fill the same plaza and the lines were drawn. As one journalist noted: "If the labour unions fail dismally—and until a few days ago failure seemed certain—to get near this figure [200,000], the Radicals will be able to heave a sigh of relief and carry on as before. Should the CGT rally prove really big, however, they will be in deeper trouble than at any time since winning power."[27] Of course the Peronists did attract about the same number, and no sighs of relief were heard.

Nevertheless, Alfonsín did not retreat this time. Instead, he announced drastic measures that were intended to catch everyone by surprise and force a drastic change in their economic assumptions and expectations, the kind of thing that was needed to break from the familiar vicious circle of public doubt and economic subversion for personal gain.

In April 1985 he was informed by Sourrouille that procrastination since September 1984 had put Argentina $1 billion in arrears in the payment of its foreign debt, and the amount was continuing to rise at a rate of $150 million a month, threatening to force a downgrading of the country's credit rating internationally, which would deny it the new funds that it needed. Alfonsín's only recourse was to return to the IMF to ask for another $1.2 billion in standby loans and the U.S. government for help in arranging a $450 million bridge loan from sympathetic countries. Economist Mario Brodersohn went to Washington and a new package was signed on June 11. But before they had gone to IMF this time, the Argentines had worked out their own grand solution, one that was more drastic and comprehensive than anything the Radicals had tried before.[28]

The Austral Solution

In a national broadcast on Friday, June 14 the Argentine people learned what their government was up to. As the president made clear: "I come to you to present the battle plan so that together we will be able to definitely cancel the chapter of national decay. . . . We do not have any option, we have to reconstruct Argentina."[29] What this meant concretely was the Central Bank's ceasing to print money to pay the public debt (it was paying about 25 percent of it then), and the raising of prices for government services to make up the difference. Equally important was the announcement of a new currency, called the austral, whose value was established by dropping three zeros from the peso and making it worth US $1.28. Moreover, prices and salaries were frozen for an indefinite period, and the authorities promised to reduce the federal deficit from 10 to 5 percent of the GDP.

It was a strange sight since shock treatments had never been a Radical specialty. They had always preferred to see themselves as the party of patronage and service, having built their constituency by elevating the middle class with subsidies to small businesses, jobs in government, and education for all. Demanding sacrifices was alien to them, but now Alfonsín was announcing that they had no choice but to pay for society's past sins. Needless to say, it was quite unpopular within the Radical party, politicians fearing that it would take them down to defeat in congressional elections in November 1985.[30] But they were not running the country. Alfonsín and Sourrouille were, and they went ahead with the program whether party stalwarts wanted it or not.

Especially disturbing to Radicals was Alfonsín's reliance on technocrats who had little or no ties to Radicalism. His new advisors expounded an economics critical of populism that they had learned at Harvard, Stanford, and Minnesota where they, like Martínez de Hoz's advisors, had received their doctorates.[31] As they saw it, there were two things that had to be done to eradicate perennial inflation: first, a way had to be found to reduce government expenditures permanently yet provide society with reliable services, and second, enough revenues had to be collected on a permanent basis to finance a reasonable level of expenditures. With this in mind they recommended a swift reduction of the budget by keeping wages below the rate of inflation, making state corporations operate at a profit, and reducing subsidies and transfer payments to the private sector. They also urged creation of a new currency. Overwhelmed by the consensus of expert opinion, Alfonsín decided to do as his tutors recommended.

The public response to the plan was surprising. Simultaneously with his announcements President Alfonsín closed the banks and waited for the customary outcry. But to his surprise it never came. Instead, an uncharacteristic calm fell over the nation, followed by praise from nearly every sector for his courage and common sense. Argentines, it seemed, were relieved that the president was trying to end the economic insanity that raged throughout their nation. In a few days trading on the stock market picked up, the dollar stabilized, and, most impressive, prices rose only 3 percent in August and 2 percent in September (compared to 30 percent in June). And as prices came down Alfonsín's popularity ascended to levels it had not seen since his election eighteen months before.[32]

The *Plan Austral* (Austral Plan) continued impressively into the new year, with prices rising by only 1.7 percent in February in the midst of an induced recession that saw the domestic product decline 4 percent during 1985, most of it occurring after Austral began.[33] But it was not long before the political cost of Austral austerity began to make itself felt. Growing unemployment and depressed real wages—an estimated 20 percent loss in real wages during the last half of the year—generated a groundswell of rank and file discontent that helped the CGT mobilize widespread protest. They not only wanted incomes raised, but also hoped that by disrupting Alfonsín's recovery efforts they could shake voter confidence in him and win congressional elections in 1987. Accordingly, they began calling twenty-four-hour general strikes every five or six weeks, starting on January 24, to upset the recovery and give the impression that Alfonsín had never really gained control.[34]

April 1986 proved critical to Austral. The government, determined to prevent a two-day general strike at the end of the month, persuaded CGT leaders to sit down and discuss new wage and price rules with them and business representatives. But as so often happened during Alfonsín's presidency, the talks faltered, this time because the government suggested 7.7 percent wage increases for the quarter, business urged 8.5 percent, and the CGT demanded 15 percent. When the authorities limited wage increases to 8.5 percent, the CGT leaders called another general strike on June 13.[35] When prices began to rise again, going up 8.8 percent in August alone, Alfonsín applied controls once more, though only briefly this time, bringing the rate down to 4.7 percent in October only to see it rise again to 7.6 percent by January 1987.[36] Officials celebrated the GDP's growing by 5.5 percent, but inflation, at 82 percent for 1986, was well over the initial target of 28 percent.[37]

Worried that the Radicals might lose the congressional elections in September 1987 if the public regarded the Austral Plan as a failure, Alfonsín authorized new measures early in the year, including another wage and price freeze, this time until June. But it was clear that he was jumping back and forth between controls and softer policies with increasing speed, all the time raising doubts about whether the Austral program would succeed. While it was easy to claim that all of these "minor" revisions were inherent in the government's plan, most people had begun to wonder if anyone really knew where it was going.[38]

It did not help that grain prices on the world market continued to fall after having already dropped by 25 percent between 1981 and 1985, or that the country's creditors refused to make concessions that would reduce Argentina's payments on its huge foreign debt. But if anything undermined the plan it was Alfonsín's obvious failure to get control over the government's budget and its notorious inflation-generating fiscal deficit. He always found it hard to resist demands for more lenient treatment from nearly all economic sectors even though he was controlled by none of them. For example, with international prices for agricultural products in decline, and farmers insisting that he reduce export taxes, a major source of government revenue, Alfonsín complied; and when demands for higher wages grew among public employees, supported by friends in the Radical party, he also gave in.

Such pleas are hard to ignore, especially in a democracy where votes matter, so Alfonsín tried to have it both ways. He instructed his economists to get prices under control, then little by little he made concessions to those who complained about their adverse consequences. He even agreed to share the Labor Ministry with the dissident "15" faction of the CGT that was not loyal to CGT leader Saúl Ubaldini. In private meetings with interest-group and party leaders at the presidential residence in Olivos he also became the negotiator who traded concessions for cooperation. It was the way that Radicals like Alfonsín had always done politics, and he was not about to change now.[39]

Unfortunately for Alfonsín, none of this averted disaster for his party in the 1987 congressional and gubernatorial elections. Inviting some dissident CGT factions to join his government a few months before the election had made him and his party look weaker rather than stronger. Until election day in September Alfonsín pretended that the Radicals would retain their slight advantage over the Peronists; but instead they suffered a resounding defeat, losing twenty-three seats in the Chamber of Deputies when only half of the seats were contested; even more shocking, the Peronists took sixteen of the nation's twenty-two governorships.

Alfonsín was on the defensive after he lost his working majority in the Chamber of Deputies and his party's control in most of the largest provinces. In October he reimposed a price and wage freeze and raised

7.1   The Chamber of Deputies, 1987

	Before Sept. 6, 1987	After Sept. 6, 1987
Radicals	130	117
Peronists	103	108
UCD	3	7
PI	6	5
Others	12	17
Total	254	254

Source: La Nación, September 7, 1987, p. 1.

taxes. The CGT responded with two general strikes, one on November 3 and the other on December 8 and 9. At every turn he faced a resurrected Peronist opposition that sought to impede the government enough to guarantee Radical party unpopularity in the May 1989 presidential election. Having already impeded implementation of the Austral Plan, the Peronist leaders were confident that they could restrict Alfonsín even more during his last two years.

It was hardly an optimal time to rescue an economy when labor and industry demanded more compensation for their recent economic losses. With everyone seeking instant advantages over everyone else, bringing down inflation became nearly impossible. Alfonsín's Central Bank president summarized the government's plight perceptively when he later noted that for Argentines,

> a low inflation rate was never a "public good." Labor union leaders, some entrepreneurs, the Peronist party, the administrators of public enterprises, the governors, and at the beginning even some members of the Radical Party, did not conceive of economic stabilization as something that needed to be defended every day. In this context the stabilization was almost an impossible task for a technocratic elite occasionally (most of the time) supported by the president but whose effective influence was confined only to some segments of the central power.[40]

Argentines still debate whether the Austral Plan's failure was caused by democracy and its combative political process, or whether Alfonsín failed to use his political authority to maximum advantage. Certainly both contributed to his predicament, but he was also hampered by the fact that the Argentines really did not regard reducing inflation as a "public good," that is, something that all individuals expected to solve together. Instead, Argentines were accustomed to insisting that someone else was always responsible for problems like inflation and only such troublemakers, not themselves, should pay the price of solving them. In short, everyone had a reason for avoiding as much of the cost as they could.

Plan Primavera

On August 3, 1988, Alfonsín's economics minister, Juan Sourrouille, announced a new economic program that was labeled the *Plan Primavera* (Spring Plan).[41] It aimed at slowing inflation—prices had risen by 26 percent in July—and attracting more financing from abroad, and was launched by using agreements with industry to keep price increases under control and by freezing the wages of public employees. Alfonsín was also counting on assistance from the International Monetary Fund, the World Bank, and the U.S. government with loans totaling $2.5 billion to deal with the likely exhaustion of the country's foreign exchange reserves. He wanted to keep the dollar at around 14 australes, reduce the rate of inflation, and then keep it down until after the presidential election in May 1989.

The Spring Plan was risky because its success depended partly on the good performance of conditions the government could not really control, such as tax revenues, foreign credit, and private-sector wage agreements. The plan was designed to help the increasingly unpopular Radical party win the 1989 presidential election, but from the outset the Peronists did all they could to convince everyone that it would not work. They were aided, as the opposition always is in Argentina, by dozens of economic columnists who constantly predicted its failure.[42] Nor did it help that IMF officials and commercial creditors became skeptical about the government's ability to make the changes in its organization and finance that were required in exchange for new loans.[43]

Inflation did become less initially, descending to a low of 4.8 percent by November, and the government did launch some major reforms, most notably reductions in tariffs on imports to achieve freer trade.[44] Nevertheless, strains in the plan's execution became obvious by the year's end. Interest rates rose very high because the government borrowed heavily to pay its own bills. Worry increased when the government gave larger wage increases than anticipated to public employees to settle a strike that had occurred in November and December. The national government also transferred more money to the provinces than anticipated to help them pay their bills while tax evasion increased and lowered anticipated revenues. At the same time the Congress, then controlled by the Peronists in coalition with minor parties, refused to let Alfonsín increase the value-added tax as much as he wanted, putting additional pressure on his budget.[45]

It was becoming a bad summer in other ways too. After a good crop the year before and high prices during a major drought in the United

States in mid-1988, Argentina was hit by its own drought at the end of that year. Along with ruining much of the grain crop, the drought left local hydroelectric facilities without water and caused embarrassing shortages in electric power. Worried about where all of this disruption would lead, many people started buying dollars in January to protect themselves even though government officials tried to assure them that there would be no major changes in policy or in the value of the austral. To make its point, the Central Bank sold $900 million during the first thirty-four days of the year to meet demand for dollars at the austral's declared value.[46]

But the IMF and World Bank officials held back. They were annoyed that the Central Bank sold so much of its dollar reserves to prop up an overvalued austral, and were still unhappy with Alfonsín's failure to get his budget deficit under control and his halting interest payments on most of the foreign debt. To make their point they refused to disburse the new loans that Alfonsín had counted on.[47]

Central Bank president José Luis Machinea virtually ran out of dollars by February when some of the large Argentine corporations bought huge amounts from the Central Bank and grain exporters held on to their dollars rather than sell them to the bank because they expected they would get more australes for their dollars after the government was forced to devalue the national currency. It is an old game often played by the wealthiest Argentine institutions. Machinea finally gave up trying to sustain the fourteen-austral price on February 6 after protecting the overvalued austral as long as he could (consumer prices rose 82 percent in the previous six months while the austral was being devalued by only 17 percent); once turned loose, the dollar that cost fourteen australes on February 5 was selling for thirty just a couple of days later. And fearing that it would rise even more, the rush was on: by April 6—just two months later—the dollar's price had risen an incredible 180 percent.[48]

It was tragic and Alfonsín knew it as he watched public confidence in his government, which was already in swift decline, disappear almost entirely. His demise was not entirely his fault. The Peronists had given him little leeway after their victory in the 1987 elections, and he was not helped by a very disappointing grain crop in 1988 and the nation's creditors' refusal to reduce the country's enormous debt burden. But even his economists accepted some responsibility for their failure, blaming it on their not implementing proposals to reduce the government's deficit and restructure the overburdened public sector by selling off its most costly enterprises. The Spring Plan had been a last-minute exercise in economic acrobatics, but hindsight made it clear that far more should have been done.[49]

The Peronist opposition did all that it could to broadcast the government's failure to an electorate that would select a new president in May. Their task was an easy one since prices, which had increased by "only" 9.6 percent in February, rose by 18 percent in March 1989 and 33 percent in April. People turned angry at Alfonsín, converting their once popular president into someone whose rapid retirement they welcomed.[50]

The Constitution did not allow Alfonsín to succeed himself, so the Radical party nominated one of his rivals, Córdoba governor Eduardo Angeloz, in their national primary in mid-1988. He distanced himself from Alfonsín's record and promised to open up and modernize the nation's economy far more than Alfonsín had done, but he won little new support with his promises. That is why he insisted that the government's economic team, led since 1985 by Minister of Economy Juan Sourrouille, be dismissed, and Alfonsín reluctantly complied in March. But that only made the situation worse since there was no one who could overcome the government's loss of credibility as the election approached.[51]

Worst of all, hyperinflation seized Argentina as the dollar's price rose. Prices increased by 30 percent in the first week of April and by 70 percent during the last week. By the end of May they were rising by an incredible monthly rate of 150 percent, the worst Argentines had ever known. It was entirely self-defeating, for as consumer prices rose so did the price paid by the government for all that it purchased, increasing the budget deficit that it had been trying to reduce.

Meanwhile everyone scrambled to find a means for surviving the hyperinflation. Businesses raised their prices above cost increases in order to protect themselves from more cost increases, workers demanded to be paid weekly rather than once or twice a month, and exporters delayed sales abroad in order to trade the dollars they earned for more australes later on. Confidence in the Radical party government disappeared almost entirely.

By April 1989 all ten of the nation's polls predicted that Peronist party candidate Carlos Saúl Menem would defeat Radical Eduardo Angeloz in the May 14 presidential election. For once they were right. Menem won with 47 percent to 37 percent for Eduardo Angeloz. The electorate left no doubt about their desire to expel the Radicals on whom they had once relied for the nation's economic and political recovery.

When asked why he lost, Angeloz confessed that too many within

7.2   Gross Domestic Product and Consumer Prices, 1983–88
(annual percentage change)

	GDP	Price Increase
1983	3.0	434
1984	2.6	688
1985	−4.5	385
1986	5.5	82
1987	1.9	175
1988	−3.1	387

Source: Argentina, Banco Central

his party had never really recovered from the defeat they suffered in 1987 when the Peronists swept the congressional and gubernatorial elections. Nor did the people around Alfonsín welcome Angeloz' candidacy since he drew much of his support from factions within the party that Alfonsín had defeated in 1983 during his rise to the presidency. As the election approached, Alfonsín, the once-admired democrat, took on the demeanor of a disgruntled politician who refused to admit to himself that the electorate was quickly losing confidence in him.[52]

The same Radicals who only a couple years before had been convinced that they were building a durable new majority suddenly discovered how wrong they were. Alfonsín had led the nation's return to democracy quite skillfully, but that was never enough for his party to retain more than 35 percent of the electorate. Had Alfonsín done better with the economy, Angeloz probably would have triumphed, but Alfonsín's failure to turn his 1985 Austral Plan into a permanent conquest of inflation doomed Angeloz to defeat. The acrobatics of the Spring Plan never had a chance of making up for the Austral Plan's failure.

According to the Constitution, Alfonsín was not to turn over the presidency to Menem until December 1, more than six months after the election. To sustain himself he tried to get President-elect Menem to support another emergency stabilization program, but Menem kept his distance. On May 18 Alfonsín proclaimed a 40 percent increase in rates for public services, a 10 percent increase in taxes on farm exports, and a higher value-added tax. Nevertheless, confidence continued to plummet as did the value of the austral: a dollar, which had cost fourteen australes in early February, now cost 220. Inflation accelerated immediately after the election and the public's confidence in elected officials all but disappeared, making it impossible for Alfonsín to make any of his policies credible. Within a month of the election panic struck the business community whose members joined the general public in demanding that Alfonsín depart and give Menem a chance to make a fresh start as soon as possible.

At first Alfonsín resisted, going on television on May 23 to announce that he would stick it out, but he quickly realized that he could do nothing to prevent prices from rising 115 percent in June.[53] He soon recognized that, with the economy in disarray, Argentina faced the very real danger of a social explosion during the seven-month gap between the mid-May elections and the transfer of power to President-elect Menem. So after bickering with Menem over his date of departure he decided to leave on July 8, five months ahead of schedule.

Winners and Losers

When Raul Alfonsín launched the Austral Plan he had hoped to halt spiraling inflation enough to give his officials an opportunity to implement some real reforms in the economy. They knew the government was too costly and they proposed to privatize some of the state-owned enterprises, hold the national budget down, and modernize the banking system. But repeatedly, projects were proposed only to disappear in Congress, often with the help of the Peronist opposition, or just get bogged down in interministerial committees where Radicals found it hard to navigate. Far too often they resorted to what they knew best: party politics. They tried to govern as they had campaigned, first announcing their goals and then asking people to support them. Unfortunately, this had little to do with making a bureaucracy implement practical solutions to real problems.

Raul Alfonsín and the Radical party advanced democratic government in a nation unaccustomed to it, and that was no meager achievement. But Alfonsín's triumph in 1983, though extraordinary, now looks incredibly brief. In 1987 the Peronists bounced back, soundly triumphing in congressional and gubernatorial elections all over the country. Suddenly, the ambitious Alfonsín, who was convinced that he could combine the nation's transition to democracy with his party's burial of the Peronists, was worse off than before his presidency started. He could no longer carry the party that had relied on him so much for its return to prominence less than four years before.

Alfonsín suffered in part from a barrier to anything but superficial reform that prevails within the political culture from which he came. Argentines wanted fast solutions to the problems they faced, including inflation. When pressed by hyperinflation in 1985 the cabinet united in support of the Austral program. But the initial effectiveness of the Austral Plan reinforced perceptions within the party that after prices came down they could revert to their old ways of doing business. Instead of devoting more enthusiasm to the government's reform effort, most people in the party demanded that Alfonsín instantly restore prosperity. And Alfonsín, career politician that he was, wanted to please them as best he could, and found it easy to convince himself that nothing would be harmed if he let up just a little. But it could not work that way, and Austral came to naught.

The Peronists did all they could to assure Alfonsín's political failure. By blocking passage of his new labor law, resorting to occasional general strikes against his austerity policies after 1985, and using increasing public discontent with his unsuccessful economic program to win the 1987 election, they helped transform the once popular Alfonsín into a very weak president nearly two years before his term expired.

Without any explicit agreements between his government and the nation's most important social and economic interest groups, Alfonsín resorted to negotiating, case by case, hoping to "work it all out" in the only way he had been trained to do it. But what he gained from such tactics was not a new consensus, but postponement of real policy innovation. Interest groups did not celebrate every time Alfonsín consulted with them, but played along without really believing that he would deliver what he promised. They were always quick to flee from any agreements they made on prices, wages, and investments, frequently undermining even his best efforts when they did.

In fairness to Alfonsín, it should be recalled that his party had never been very popular with business or labor. Radical party leaders were seen by many in the corporate world as exclusionary, petit-bourgeois politicians who nurtured themselves on their sense of moral superiority, their unsophisticated beliefs about the government's ability to manipulate economic forces for everyone's advantage, and their perpetual condemnation of businessmen for what the Radicals claimed was their affection for military authoritarian regimes.

Relations improved somewhat after the government announced its Austral Plan in 1985, indicating that it was at last pushing economic reforms long advocated by businessmen, but this never became a close relationship since neither the Radicals nor the businessmen from organizations like the Unión Industrial were prepared to trust one another. As industrialists saw it, the Radicals, though more realistic in their economic programs at last, were likely to undercut them once economic conditions improved as was their habit in the past, while Alfonsín, quite aware how quickly industrialists had always castigated and undermined their government suitor when it served their individual interests to do so, was not prepared to rely entirely on their compliance no matter what they promised in exchange for more direct influence over policy.

Securing the collaboration of organized labor was bound to be even more difficult. Alfonsín knew that the CGT could make governing the nation nearly impossible as they had for Radical presidents Arturo Frondizi and Arturo Illia. It was harder for labor this time since Juan Perón was no longer alive to inspire their opposition, union membership was smaller, and the Peronists were now a minority party. But it was never just their size that mattered for the Peronists; they also had the power to upset public order by halting government services and closing major industries. Led by Saúl Ubaldini, the CGT called a series of general strikes to weaken the Austral Plan after 1985. Alfonsín tried to break the impasse by inviting the more moderate unions to join his government in 1987, but that did not prevent the Peronists' defeating the Radicals badly in congressional and gubernatorial elections that year.[54]

Alfonsín also made a critical mistake politically, though more from ambition and wishful thinking than from any malicious conspiracy. It involved something called the Tercer Movimiento Historico. With the Peronists finally in the opposition, he wanted to build a political movement that everyone would consider the historical successor of Peronism, which had called itself the Segundo Movimiento Historico. Why anyone would accept the Radicals doing them such a favor was clear only to the people around Alfonsín who had never recovered from their celebrations in 1983.

Creating *movimientos políticos* assumed that the people wanted one party to supervise the entire nation—in this case the Radical party. It also supposed that people would join the party to avoid exclusion from the nation's governance. Alfonsín knew that this concept of government was certainly part of the Argentine political culture and, therefore, not alien. Moreover, he also believed that for democracy to work and for a democratic government to deal with the nation's economic and social problems, people would have to be taught to participate in their government without destroying it, and a consensual movement offered them the best means for doing that.

It retrospect it seems obvious that the strategy was doomed from the outset. As one Radical party legislator concluded when he assessed his government in 1989,

> . . . this concept [tercer] did not take into account the high level of social and political conflict in Argentina; moreover, it was inappropriate, even rhetorically because it put Peronism in a subordinate position, making it impossible for Peronists to enroll. While the Peronists believed in such movements, they had no intention of joining one headed by a Radical like Alfonsín.[55]

It was a hard lesson to learn, and even after the Radicals had departed no one was certain that they had really mastered it. Moreover, with the Peronists taking over and the Radicals licking their wounds, it would be some time before we would be given an opportunity to find out.

Notes

1. Seats in the Chamber of Deputies were distributed among provinces in accordance with the size of their populations. Deputies were elected in each province using the D'Hont method of proportional representation, i.e., voters selected a party whose list of candidates was prepared by the party. Because senators are appointed by provincial legislatures, the deputies are regarded as far more representative and important legislatively.

2. One of the most outspoken critics of the obsession with "independence" objectives is historian Carlos Escude. See his *La Argentina: paria internacional?* (Buenos Aires: Editorial de Belgrano, 1984).

3. *Clarin,* international ed., November 19–25, 1984, p. 1.

4. *The Economist,* May 4, 1985, p. 18.

5. Leonard S. Spector, *Nuclear Proliferation Today* (New York: Vintage Books, 1984), pp. 199–209.

6. Ibid., pp. 213–224.

7. Ibid., p. 228.

8. *Buenos Aires Herald,* July 26, 1984, p. 3, and *Buenos Aires Herald,* March 10, 1985, p. 3.

9. See the Sabato Commission Report.

10. Argentine criminal trials normally involve neither adversarial procedure nor oral testimony (below, p. 212). The trial of officers from the *Proceso* juntas was a very unusual exception to this rule because of its obvious public importance. Luis G. Moreno Ocampo, "The Trials and Punishment for Massive Human Rights Violations in Argentina," unpublished paper, 1990. Moreno Ocampo was one of the prosecuting attorneys.

11. *Buenos Aires Herald,* September 23, 1984, p. 3.

12. Moreno Ocampo, "Trials and Punishment," pp. 11–13.

13. *Clarin,* international ed., April 15–21, 1985, p. 1.

14. Moreno Ocampo, "Trials and Punishment," pp. 15–17.

15. The name *carapintadas* translates as "painted faces," from the black substance that commandos put on their faces for nighttime combat.

16. Responsibility for the concession did not rest with Alfonsín alone. The final legislation for the *punto final* passed in the Senate by 25–10 and in the Chamber of Deputies by 126–16.

17. Civilians also used violence, as was demonstrated on January 23, 1989, when a couple of dozen persons invaded the Third Army Regiment base at La Tablada, just outside Buenos Aires. Well-armed, they drove onto the base in cars and trucks and fired on those who resisted them, gaining control over portions of it until they were routed the next day by armored units. Their affiliation with clandestine organizations on the extreme left was evident, but their motives are still not clear after several months of trials. According to one theory, they believed that officers like Seineldin would rise up again, this time implementing a coup against the government, so they attacked in the hope of mobilizing other civilians to join them. However, there is no evidence that a coup was contemplated, nor did the attackers do much to mobilize public opinion behind them. Another theory claims that they were tricked into doing it by the military itself in order to remind people that the armed forces were the only thing that stood between them and leftist insurrection. Yet, to date there is no convincing evidence to support this conspiracy hypothesis either.

18. An excellent survey of the country's economic condition in early 1984, and the one from which these data are taken, is World Bank, *Economic Memorandum on Argentina,* June 22, 1984.

19. *New York Times,* September 12, 1984, p. 41. (The largest American creditors were Manufacturers Hanover, Citicorp, and Chase Manhattan.)

20. *Washington Post,* October 13, 1984, p. D1.

21. *New York Times,* March 21, 1985, p. 5.

22. In a lengthy year-end interview Alfonsín pointed to his failure to get any control over inflation as his biggest disappointment, and made it clear that he knew that he would lose what respect his people had shown for him if he let this continue for another year. What he would do about it was not apparent at first, then came the announcement of a new "plan" followed by Sourrouille's appointment and finally Alfonsín's "bitter medicine" address four months later in May. *Clarin,* international ed., December 10–16, 1984, p. 3.

23. Radicals never abandon their friends entirely and a month later Alfonsín gave Grinspun Sourrouille's old job as head of the planning agency.

24. R. D. Mallon and J. V. Sourrouille, *Economic Policymaking in a Conflict Society: the Argentine Case* (Cambridge: Harvard University Press, 1975).

25. *Clarin,* international ed., January 7–13, 1985, p. 6.

26. *Buenos Aires Herald,* May 19, 1985, p. 3.

27. James Neilson is editor and writes a weekly column on politics and labor in the English-language daily *Buenos Aires Herald.* This quote is taken from the one he wrote on May 18, 1985, p. 3.

28. *New York Times,* June 12, 1985, pp. 1, 34–35.

29. Ibid., June 15, 1985, p. 1.

30. In the short term Alfonsín seemed correct. While the Radicals added only one seat in the November election of deputies, the Peronists lost seven, giving the incorrect impression that Peronism was in decline electorally. The September 1987 elections proved otherwise when the Peronists trounced the Radicals.

31. Sourrouille's principal assistants who held doctorates were: Mario Brodersohn, from Harvard, José Luis Machinea, University of Minnesota, and Adolfo Canitrot, Stanford.

32. World Bank, *Economic Memorandum on Argentina,* 1984, pp. 196–204.

33. See Economist Intelligence Unit, *Argentina: Country Report No. 2,* March 26, 1986, for more details.

34. For an informative survey of CGT, behavior during this period as well as the first years of Alfonsín's presidency, see journalist Gustavo Beliz's book *CGT, el otro poder* (Buenos Aires: Editorial Planeta, 1988).

35. Economist Intelligence Unit, *Argentina: Country Report No. 3,* July 11, 1986, p. 10.

36. In a significant move he also replaced Radical stalwart Alfredo Concepción, the Central Bank president, with José Luis Machinea, a colleague of Juan Sourrouille who had accused Concepción of permitting excessive rediscounts which pumped too much liquidity (i.e., inflation) into the monetary system.

37. Economist Intelligence Unit, *Argentina: Country Report No. 1*, January 29, 1987, pp. 1–25.

38. World Bank, *Argentina: Economic Recovery and Growth* (Report No. 6467-AR), pp. 10–13.

39. For an analysis of CGT tactics toward the Plan Austral there is no better source than Ricardo Gaudio and Andrés Thompson, *Sindicalismo Peronista. Gobierno Radical: Los años de Alfonsín* (Buenos Aires: CEDES, 1990), pp. 165–242.

40. José Luis Machinea, "Stabilization Under Alfonsín Government: A Frustrated Attempt," unpublished paper, September 1989, p. 129. He was Central Bank President from 1986 to 1989.

41. See the weekly *Somos*, July 6, 1988, and August 10, 1988, for accounts of the government's effort to secure the collaboration of big business and industry by negotiating intensely with the Argentine Industrial Union prior to the announcement of the Primavera Plan.

42. Jorge Garfunkel, *59 semanas y media que conmovieron a la argentina*. (Buenos Aires: EMECE, 1990), pp. 70–76.

43. Economist Intelligence Unit, *Argentina: Country Report No. 4*, October 10, 1988, p. 9.

44. The lowering of inflation was due in part to the fact that industries has raised their prices substantially in anticipation of the price agreement they had made with the government in August and could absorb price constraints without much difficulty for a few months.

45. World Bank, *Argentina: Reforms for Price Stability and Growth*, April 1990, pp. 18–19.

46. Ibid.

47. José Luis Machinea summarized the events as follows: "By mid-January the World Bank communicated, although informally, that it was quite difficult that the disbursement of around US $350 million scheduled for the end of February could take place, as a consequence of the macroeconomic situation and of the unfulfillment of some specific conditions of the bank loan." A day later he was told by the members of the steering committee that it was impossible to continue negotiations without an important payment and an agreement with the fund. Two days later some news agencies began to report that Argentina would not reach any agreement with the commercial banks, that the banks would discontinue negotiations unless a payment of US $300 million was made immediately, and finally that they would begin to cut the trade lines. See Machinea, "Stabilization Under Alfonsín Government." Also see: Judith Evans, "The February Crash," *Latin Finance*, May 1989, p. 47.

48. Jorge Garfunkel, *59 semanas y media*, pp. 40–70.

49. See interviews with Economic Coordination Secretary Adolfo Canitrot in *Somos*, May 24, 1989, pp. 48–52, and *Ambito Financiera*, May 28, 1989, p. 35.

50. Garfunkel, *59 semanas y media*, pp. 70–74. Some of Alfonsín's economists later confessed that they had failed to implement their own proposals to reduce the government's deficit and restructure the overburdened public sector by selling off its most costly enterprises. The Spring Plan had been a last-minute exercise in economic acrobatics, but hindsight made it clear that far more should have been done. See interviews with Alfonsín's Economic Coordination Secretary Adolfo Canitrot in *Somos*, May 24, 1989, pp. 48–52; and *Ambito Financiera*, May 28, 1989, p. 35.

51. Alfonsín replaced Sourrouille with Juan Carlos Pugliese, a noneconomist but one who had served as economics minister in the 1960s under Radical Arturo Illia. When Pugliese's efforts failed dismally, he was replaced by Jesus Rodriguez, a thirty-three-year-

old legislator who headed the Chamber of Deputies budget committee. His package, announced after a ten-day suspension of all exchange transactions and most banking activities, reintroduced a fixed exchange rate (after a month with floating rate). The rate was set at 175 to the dollar after soaring to 220.

52. *La Semana*, August 3, 1989, p. 15.

53. He was also upset by the rioting that occurred at the end of May, leaving sixteen persons dead and nearly one hundred injured. They were not so much riots as people, panicked by inflation, looting supermarkets in some working-class neighborhoods. Real purchasing power had fallen by 30 percent in April and early May. See *Latin American Regional Report*, June 29, 1989, p. 2.

54. These words are my own but in putting them together I benefited immensely from discussing these matters with Juan Carlos Torre and reading his excellent analyses of the period, e.g. his unpublished paper "Transición democrática y emergencia económica: el gobierno de la economía bajo la presidencia de Alfonsín," 1990.

55. "Para un debate necesario," Documento 2, 1989, p. 9. This is an anonymous analysis of the Radical party after its defeat in the May 1989 election written by a Radical member of the Chamber of Deputies.

8

A Peronist Surprise

It is always risky to assess an Argentine government when it has been in office for only a short time. The first edition of this book was written when President Raul Alfonsín launched his bold Austral Plan in 1985 and optimism reigned. Now we know the dismal results that followed, resulting in the Radical government's virtual collapse, and Alfonsín's early departure from the presidency. What we say about the government of Carlos Saúl Menem may quickly become ancient history in a nation so prone to sabotage the rescue operations of its own leaders. Nevertheless, the initiatives taken by President Menem during his first year were too pivotal to be ignored in this volume.

Menem's presidency also merits study because adverse circumstances compelled him to address some vital questions about democratic politics and capitalist economics. If anything was learned from Alfonsín's failures—and many things were—the most obvious was that democratic government did not guarantee the nation a more productive economy. Neither presidential decress nor congressional legislation could force people to run the economy differently. There was simply too much to reform and too little appetite to do it.

It pays to recall that many late-industrializing nations like Argentina began their economic modernization midway through this century by deliberately resorting to cooperation between the public and private sectors. They set out to achieve the most benefits from industrialization at the lowest possible cost to everyone, be they labor or industry. Juan Perón, for example, not only sought to accelerate the nation's industrialization, but also wanted to reduce risks for capitalists and improve the security of organized labor. Some of his successors tried to break from this system, but none managed the feat. In 1989 the people who had been reared on it still feared the consequences of replacing it with a far more open and competitive economic system.[1] Nevertheless, Menem decided that he had no choice but to give this a try.

All of this left Argentines with a real political dilemma. While seeking to build a viable political democracy, they also wanted a president who would do everything necessary to halt inflation and restore prosperity. As before, it was tempting for the president to do it by using his authority to decree emergency legislation rather than let partisans in Congress or private interests participate directly in the nation's governance. Yet the more he did that, the more real democrats as well as insincere ones would accuse him of destroying the political process that had made him president and legitimized his government. Menem struggled with this during his first year, trying negotiations from time to time while often resorting to decrees as soon as bargaining did not give him the response he desired. Argentines were left to wonder if that was the way they wanted their new democracy to function.

Peronist Reformation

In May 1989 the Argentine voters not only replaced an elected incumbent with a new president via free elections for the first time in several decades, but after demanding in 1983 that the Peronists retreat to the opposition and earn their right to return to power, the electorate rewarded them in 1989. An indigenous version of liberal democracy was under way.[2]

Menem did not win because of a sudden surge of popular affection for Peronism, however. As in 1983, loyal Peronists composed about 35 percent of the electorate and their Radical opponents a little less. Menem triumphed because so many people blamed Alfonsín and the Radicals for failing to remedy the nation's economic woes. He was the only candidate who could defeat Radical Eduardo Angeloz, since the Peronist party was the only one able to wage a real contest. Menem was *el mal menor* (the lesser evil), not a crowned Peronist prince who was warmly embraced by the nation.

His triumph astounded many people, especially in Buenos Aires where the middle and upper classes were uncomfortable with this provincial politician whom few of them really knew. Moreover, they were not certain what Peronism meant in 1989, or that the Peronists were any better prepared than the Radicals to govern effectively. Organized labor was still militant but union membership had fallen considerably during the previous twenty years and, more than ever before, labor shared the Peronist label with thousands of young professionals and provincial politicians who opposed the Radicals. Together the Peronists received less than half the vote nationally and were rewarded with a financially bankrupt government and a nation suffering a bout of hyperinflation that few persons believed any president could handle.

It had always been hard to imagine Menem as president. The son of

Syrians who arrived in 1912 and prospered in commerce, he grew up in the nation's northwest where many little-noticed immigrants from the Middle East had settled and flourished in business and local politics. He received a law degree from the University of Córdoba in 1955, a few months after Juan Perón had fled into exile, then returned home to La Rioja to practice law and politics in one of the nation's poorest provinces. An amateur athlete, Menem loved sports and auto-racing, and, like most of his peers, he partied often. He went to Syria to select a Muslim wife as his parents desired, but that did not prevent his converting to Catholicism early in his career. He first gained notice locally as an ambitious yet congenial politician when he sought to run for governor in 1963, but was stopped by the exiled Juan Perón who ordered party members to boycott the elections. Ten years later when free elections were held again, Menem won easily.

The military officers who evicted President Isabel Perón in 1976 jailed Governor Menem and other Peronist leaders and did not release him until five years later. He still claims that he never knew why they considered him so dangerous. He was an ambitious Peronist but never very extreme ideologically, i.e., he wanted a welfare state run by Peronists. The champion of the provincial poor, he also admired private businesses like the one his father had built in his new country. It was not capitalism that he detested, but only those who practiced it without sharing their profits with their employees or with Peronist politicians.[3]

Menem capitalized on political opportunities whenever he could, and never more effectively than during his party's presidential national primary election in mid-1988. Only a few years before, the party seemed to have little interest in Menem. In 1983 it was a disorganized, leaderless movement that hardly deserved to be labeled a political party. Then, led by Antonio Cafiero and other urban, white-collar Peronists, a faction that called itself *Renovación* sprang up and offered a social democratic platform that included proposals for the party's internal democratization and modernization. Some of the old-guard labor bosses opposed them, but in the 1985 congressional elections the *Renovación* candidates did far better than any of the others in the party. Two years later Cafiero was elected governor of the populous Buenos Aires province, which made him the party's most probable presidential candidate in 1989.

Menem was coy through all of this, one month supporting *Renovación* and the next pulling back, occasionally mentioning that he might become a candidate for president and then saying nothing. Consequently, when preparations for the national primary election began in early 1988, Cafiero's victory still seemed certain. But Menem knew that the primary served his ambitions perfectly since he stood little chance of winning the party's nomination at a convention controlled by urban party leaders. He appealed to the labor leaders who feared losing power to the *Renovación* people, but most important, he knew the public mood and campaigned against "insiders" like Cafiero at a time when Argentines were growing disenchanted with their most famous politicians, whether Radical or Peronist. To Cafiero's surprise this worked: Menem won 54 percent and the embarrassed Cafiero received only 46 percent.[4]

During the next eight months Menem campaigned all over the country's interior in his "Menemmobile" travel van, relying heavily on personal contacts at the grass roots to attract support—the same tactics that had served him so well in La Rioja where he was elected governor three times. Rather than stress specific issues, he called for "national reunification," greater productivity, and more social justice. And when that did not excite his listeners, he reminded them of what they had suffered during the past five years from astronomical inflation, substantial losses in real income, and a decline in their self-confidence as a nation.

Gradually it became clear that Menem would win no matter how much Radical candidates warned that "disaster" would follow the Peronists' return to power. He received 47 percent of the popular vote to Angeloz's 37 percent, securing majority support in only eight of twenty-three provinces, but he gathered a plurality in all but five of them, assuring his ratification by the Electoral College.[5] With half of the seats in the Chamber of Deputies up for election, he also helped the Peronists add 17 more, giving them 127 or exactly half, to go along with their plurality in the Senate. The Peronists had won in the manner the Constitution required and on July 8, in a formal ceremony, President Alfonsín passed the presidential sash to Carlos Saúl Menem five months ahead of schedule.[6]

Argentines had chosen the unconventional politician, a governor who wore his hair down to his shoulders with sideburns to match, a modern version of the nineteenth-century provincial *caudillo* in appearance if not in behavior. He was even entertaining as he revealed when, a few days after his inauguration at age fifty-nine, he played an entire *futbol* game alongside the famous star Diego Maradona in order to raise money to aid the poor. No recent Argentine president had ever dared such a feat or been in physical condition to attempt it.

From the moment he was elected Menem acted like the consummate coalition builder, not the old-fashioned Peronist partisan. He was raised within the Argentine political culture, but in a peculiar version of it where most of his friends and relatives traced their ancestry to the

Middle East. It was a one-on-one culture where quiet deals and accords were more vital than outspoken, impersonal confrontations. He suffered no embarrassment meeting with anyone, whether friends or renowned enemies of Peronism, always exhibiting a relaxed self-confidence that seemed more intuitive than contemplative. He filled his cabinet with provincial politicians loyal to him, a few renovator Peronists who were not, and persons unaffiliated with the party. As expected, Peronists like union leader Jorge Triaca and lawyer Italo Luder were given the Labor and Defense ministries, respectively, but the Foreign Ministry went to Domingo Cavallo, a free-trade economist with very recent Peronist affiliation.[7] Menem also asked free market conservative and longtime enemy of Peronism, Alvaro Alsogaray, to be his advisor on debt negotiation and assigned Alsogaray's ally and politically savy daughter to run the national phone company.

Reviving Capitalism

In the 1989 election Radical party presidential candidate Eduardo Angeloz had adopted a liberal, antistatist platform on most economic issues while Menem's *Revolución Productiva* was assumed to mean a return to populism with its reliance on statism. But it did not turn out that way. As has been noted, "During the first sixty days of the new government there existed skepticism, polemics, illusions, and surprise throughout society as people watched Menem take over, but soon it became apparent that the government was intent on making some of the most profound changes in the economy in decades."[8]

Immediately after the May 14 election everyone knew that the nation's economic situation was bad and getting worse. That is why they desperately looked for indications from Menem about what he planned to do.[9] They could not wait the required six months between the election and the inauguration to discover Menem's solutions, so nearly everyone demanded that Alfonsín leave office ahead of schedule. Businessmen as well as consumers wanted to know more about their future, and in the midst of hyperinflation they could not placidly put up with six months under a lame-duck president. Menem knew this, but he was cautious at first, recognizing that he had nothing to gain from appearing too eager to become president no matter how unpopular Alfonsín had become. If he was to govern effectively after displacing the incumbent ahead of schedule, the most powerful groups in society had first of all to demand that he take over, so he stood back and let his staff quietly negotiate the transfer of power on July 8.

Ending hyperinflation was the immediate task that Menem faced, but there were also some very familiar fundamental problems that had become too conspicuous for the provincial populist to ignore. The Argentine economy was going nowhere and its people were suffering more from this stagnation every day. While Brazil's economy grew at an annual average of 5 percent between 1970 and 1987 and Mexico's by 4 percent, Argentina's grew by less than 1 percent, and hardly grew at all after 1983. The 1980s were tough times for every indebted nation in Latin America but none became as economically immobile as Argentina.[10] The country's decline was apparent in other ways as well. For example, in 1989 the physical product of industry was nearly 15 percent less than it had been in 1973 and the number of people employed in industry was 39 percent less. Neither trend was necessarily catastrophic if other sectors of the economy made up for industry's decline, but only agriculture grew; however, when it did, grain prices fell internationally and during the 1980s the nation received less income for more production.[11]

8.1   Argentine Economic Structure

Gross Domestic Product at Market Prices
(millions of 1970 australes)

1970	1975	1980	1985	1988
8,775	10,103	11,295	10,105	10,531

Origins of GDP 1987 (percentage)

Manufacturing	23.5
Agriculture	14.7
Construction	3.7
Mining	2.5
Services	55.5

Composition of Merchandise Exports, Average 1984–88 (percentage)

Agricultural goods	49.2
Manuf. goods of Agric. origin	25.8
Manuf. goods of industrial origin	25.0

Main Destinations of Exports 1989 (percentage)

USA	11.5
Brazil	10.5
Netherlands	10.0
USSR	8.7

Main Origins of Imports 1988 (percentage)

USA	18.8
Brazil	17.3
W. Germany	10.7
Italy	6.1
Bolivia	5.9

Sources: World Bank, *Argentina: Reforms for Price Stability and Growth* (Washington, D.C., 1990), p. 215; and Economist Intelligence Unit, *Argentina: Country Report No. 2*, 1990.

Income distribution had also changed. Anyone who attended Menem's inauguration would have found it hard to believe that the nation's per capita income was really $2,300. In downtown Buenos Aires people looked affluent, their restaurants were excellent, and their stores filled with the latest fashions. But national averages said less about Argentina than they ever had before because the income disparity between the rich and the poor was greater than at any time in the past forty years. In 1970 the poorest 10 percent averaged $210 annually per capita, but in 1990 an estimated 42 percent averaged less than $200 annually. Even the middle class had changed: having been estimated to include nearly half the population in 1960, it included only one-third in 1990, nearly all of the rest having fallen into the lower class during the 1980s. Many people survived by working within an enormous "informal" or black-market economy, but it was still obvious that poverty and income disparity had increased substantially. [12]

Finally, experience during the last two decades made it clear that without a permanent reduction in inflation, Argentines would not invest in their own country, and without their investments or those of equally cautious multinational firms, the national product would continue to stagnate. The Alfonsín government had tried to get inflation under control but had failed to deal adequately with a public sector whose enormous size helped sustain it. Feeble efforts at tax collection, low prices for public services, and too many tax exemptions made it impossible for revenues to keep up with public expenditures that had risen from 25 percent of the gross domestic product in 1970 to 38 percent in 1983. The country's pathetic condition had become too obvious to deny any longer. [13]

Menem responded to all of this by making Miguel Roig his minister of economy and asking industrialists to come to the nation's rescue. Roig was a retired executive from the Argentine Bunge & Born conglomerate, once the nation's leading trader in grain, and never a friend of Peronism. [14] His consultations with big business had actually begun nearly four months before his election when Jorge Born, one of the two brothers who owned Bunge & Born, offered his firm's resources to help prepare candidate Menem's economic program. This was rather startling since no one assumed that any affection existed between Peronists and the Born brothers who had been kidnapped by terrorists in the early 1970s and forced to pay several million dollars for their release while the Peronist government did nothing to help them. But Jorge Born was a practical person, and like many of the nation's business executives, he figured that a Peronist president unprepared to handle the nation's economic disaster would welcome advice from the most powerful members of the economy. He was right.

Bunge & Born economists subscribed to the annual macroeconomic analyses of Argentina prepared by North American consultant and Nobel Prize winner Lawrence Klein, a personal friend of Jorge Born. When Klein predicted a gloomy 1989 for the Argentine economy, Born decided to share Klein's data with Menem during the campaign. Klein had forecast more inflation and an abrupt decline in consumption by mid-1989, something greatly feared by Born since his enterprises produced as much for the domestic market as they did for export. Alfonsín's people were too busy with their Spring Plan to give Born much attention when he approached them with the data, but Menem, eager for anything that might help him prepare to become president, listened.[15]

After Menem was elected and realized that he would start five months sooner than planned in the midst of an inflationary binge, he called on Born to prescribe some immediate solutions. At Born's invitation, on May 23 Menem attended a slick presentation by the firm's economists who told him how bad the nation's future looked if drastic changes were not attempted immediately.[16] Though it seemed shocking at the time to see a Peronist turn to big business for help, it was not really unusual. Juan Perón had relied heavily on businessman Miguel Miranda at the start of his first presidency, and ever since Peronist leaders have mingled comfortably with industrialists. They are populists in their labor and social welfare policies, but they were always capitalists when it came to creating wealth; that is why they made the government the nation's biggest capitalist.

Ending hyperinflation effectively would not be easy. On the contrary, after rising by 78 percent in May, retail prices rose by 114 percent in June, and then soared 197 percent in July. Minister of Economy Roig responded by persuading 300 major companies to freeze prices for ninety days and then announced a 53 percent devaluation of the austral. Most shocking to the Argentine consumer, he also raised public utility prices, some as much as 600 percent, to keep them up with other prices and replenish the national treasury.[17] But the heavy-smoking Roig died of a heart attack just one week into the new government and Menem quickly replaced him with Nestor Rapanelli, another Bunge & Born executive.

Menem also demanded and quickly received congressional passage of two vital pieces of legislation aimed at drastically reducing the size and cost of the Argentine government. Even a Peronist knew how costly the deficits of government-owned corporations had become: from $1 billion for YPF, the petroleum company, to $500 million for the railways, $430 million for Segba, the electric power company, and smaller but still impressive sums for others, totaling $5.5 billion in 1988 alone. Printing new money to pay these bills only meant higher inflation.[18]

The State Reform bill was intended to authorize the privatization of several of these corporations—something the Peronists had intensely opposed three years before when the Radicals had proposed a milder version. But now Menem argued that without such transfers of ownership there was no way in which the government could get control over its own finances. One by one, over the next three years, private corporations, including multinationals, would be invited to buy all or part of the largest government firms. The other piece of legislation, called the Emergency bill, was directed at the private sector, instructing the government to suspend its many subsidies to private business. It also authorized bolder efforts to end the common practice of tax evasion in an attempt to raise the government's tax income from 16 percent of the gross national product to 24 percent. In theory, at least, the government was pulling out, turning most of the production process over to the private sector and forcing its members to compete among themselves for profit rather than rely on the government to guarantee it.[19]

Menem admitted his lack of sophistication in economics, but he recognized that Argentina had to modernize its economic institutions and produce much more to overcome its degeneration. This required profound fiscal and monetary reforms, and the attraction of private investment to a country that had seen very little of it for more than a decade. Argentines had deposited an estimated $40 billion abroad and Menem wanted them to start bringing some of it home, hardly an easy assignment among a people as distrustful and cynical as the Argentines had become.

With a treasury that was bare, foreign reserves near zero, huge foreign debts and foreign creditors refusing to finance virtually anything Argentine, Menem had little choice but to implement unpopular solutions. In his own defense he loved to declare that it was "better that people insult me for a year and applaud me for a century, rather than the other way around."[20] Clearly, this was a different Menem from the one who as governor in La Rioja between 1983 and 1987 had more than doubled the provincial payroll, and issued worthless bonds to help pay the wages.

He also wanted to impress the IMF with an earnest effort to rein in a government budget that was out of control. The reason was clear: annual interest on the debt was $6 billion and the trade surplus only

$3.5 billion. If Argentina was to begin paying interest again, it needed the loans that had been denied Alfonsín six months before. He also believed that a better effort on Argentina's part would encourage some of the private banks to write off a few of the country's debts as they had just begun doing in Mexico under the Brady program launched by the U.S. treasury secretary.

The Roig-Rapanelli effort achieved some success in halting hyperinflation, but it came apart abruptly in December 1989, crushed by the public debt and a failure to move fast enough to reorganize the public sector to get fiscal deficits under control. Hyperinflation had been ended by August using price controls, but Menem stumbled in October when he decided not to oppose a 7 percent wage increase negotiated by big labor and big business. The press soon predicted his imminent failure and confidence in the new government's economics dwindled. A nervous public reverted to purchasing dollars once again, causing their price to rise. And when they did, so did the price of nearly everything else regardless of whether it was directly affected by dollars. Typically, Argentine merchants raised their prices in order to keep ahead of the kind of astronomical inflation that had struck the country six months before. So, after rising only 7 percent in November, prices rose by 40 percent in December.[21]

On 15 December Menem dismissed Rapanelli and replaced him as minister of the economy with the little-known Antonio Erman Gonzalez, a political ally and accountant who had worked for Menem in La Rioja before Menem had appointed him health minister in his new government. To everyone it seemed a fast retreat into the president's bunker, but they were wrong once more. Erman Gonzalez left the bunker immediately and announced his intention to accelerate efforts to restore a real free-market economy. He declared that the exchange rate would be allowed to float freely, price controls would be lifted, export and import taxes slashed back, and restrictions on foreign trade and banking eliminated. To keep australes out of the market he also disclosed that the treasury would not supply money to finance the government budget anymore. Bills would have to be paid with tax revenue or increased prices for government services.[22]

Simultaneously Menem and his advisors considered a radical plan to "dollarize" the economy, i.e., rely on dollars and not just print or circulate australes. Anticipating the announcement, Argentines rushed to trade their australes for dollars, driving the exchange rate, which was 1,000 australes to the dollar before Christmas, to 3,800 by New Year's weekend. Merchants jacked up prices accordingly. But Menem had something else in mind that was even more shocking.

Many Argentines in the middle and upper classes had grown accustomed to keeping some of their australes in interest-bearing seven-day certificates at banks. The banks, in turn, had lent the money to the Treasury to finance the national debt. But on January 3, Menem short-circuited this by decreeing that all but a million australes of each depositor's savings would be converted by law into ten-year government bonds with the interest and principal guaranteed in dollars.[23] People could sell their bonds for much less than their ten-year value, use them to pay taxes, or hold them for ten years. Essentially, this meant that every saver had less money to spend after savings were locked into new bonds by the government, and the government had fewer debts to repay to its own citizens.[24] It was a shocking decree, but everyone realized that there was nothing that they could do about it.

But Menem was not home yet. Some money still showed up in the foreign exchange market, causing hyperinflation to return, sending prices up 62 percent in February and 96 percent in March. Nevertheless Erman Gonzalez held firm. Almost every week, he issued new measures supplementing and broadening the ones already announced. Then, on the first Sunday in March, he disclosed a massive decree. He suspended payments to the private companies that regularly supplied the government with goods and said he would suspend all public employees two years ahead of their normal retirement. Together these measures were to reduce government spending by $2 billion and demonstrate that the government really was cutting back.[25]

Since there were fewer australes to pass around, the economy descended into a deep recession, bringing inflation down with it to "just" 11 percent in April. And the U.S. dollar, the thermometer to which everyone looked to measure the economy's temperature, actually fell in value from a little over 6,000 australes to 5,400. For the time being, at least, the government's tight-money policy had ended another hyperinflationary spiral.[26]

While the content of policy was important, so was building public confidence in the government as it navigated its way out of its latest hyperinflation. Erman Gonzalez did not cry, cast blame, or promise instant recovery, as many of his predecessors had done. Instead, he behaved much like the accountant that he was, methodically describing the government's condition and then reminding anyone who wanted more from the government that "there was no money to spend." While the Radicals and many others continued to insist that none of this would work, most people felt compelled after being subdued by hyperinflation to watch, wait, and hope for the best.[27]

What they witnessed was a minister of economy who continually

8.2   Average Monthly Retail Price Increases (percentage)

June 1989	114.5
July	196.6
August	37.9
September	9.4
October	5.6
November	6.5
December	40.1
January 1990	79.2
February	61.6
March	95.5
April	11.4
May	13.6
June	13.6
July	10.8
August	15.3
September	15.0

Sources: El Cronista Comercial, June 17, 1990, p. 8, and other sources.

increased his control over a defiant and chaotic public sector. In August 1990 he announced new reform measures, beginning with a takeover by himself of all public enterprises that were previously under the Defense and Public Works ministries. In effect, this meant that no one in the government could make a major decision on their budgets or on prices for their services without Erman Gonzalez deciding if it fit into his plans for government finance. The authority this gave him was immense, but he still had to use it productively to be able to claim victory. And that was going to require several more months to do.

Simultaneously officials began "privatizing" a few government enterprises. After frequent postponements, changes in terms, and sudden modifications in regulations, they auctioned ENTEL, the phone company, to two buyers, the Spanish company Telefonia de España whose purchase was financed by Citicorp, and Bell Atlantic. But nothing comes easily in Argentina. Two months later Bell Atlantic was forced to cancel its purchase since Manufacturers Hanover Corporation failed to supply Bell with the $2.2 billion in Argentine foreign debt paper that it had promised. So rather than celebrate the arrival of a Bell company, Menem turned to an Italian and French consortium whose purchase was financed by J. P. Morgan. Selling shares in Aerolineas Argentinas, the national airline, came more easily, and in July 1990, half of it was sold to the Spanish airline Iberia.[28] In October Menem announced the second phase of the privatization plan which included selling all or parts of the Buenos Aires electric power company, the government's coal and natural-gas firms, its shipping company, and the Buenos Aires subway.

As was their habit, the opposition found much to criticize in

Menem's approach to privatization, claiming he was too generous to the buyers and relied too much on swapping shares in enterprises for portions of the nation's foreign debt which the buyers had purchased on the international market and then used to pay the Argentine government for shares of the enterprises. Of course, the buyers had purchased old loans at bargain prices of less than 20 percent of their original value because Alfonsín had stopped paying interest on the debt. Initially only the unions in the privatized enterprises fought back, but that did not prevent Menem from turning the issue into a popular cause since he knew the Argentine public were willing to do almost anything to make their phones work. The real test of privatization's viability would only come later, however, after the new owners were put to the test. Meanwhile more enterprises would be sold if buyers could be found, including portions of the national railroad. Even highways were leased to private Argentine corporations and turned into toll roads in order to improve their maintenance.

After a shaky first year in which members of his cabinet resigned, several exchanged positions, and a few were fired, Menem continued to make important changes in the nation's economy. He had freed prices and wages and imposed a floating exchange rate. For a time he stabilized the price of the dollar and raised prices on government services enough to pay for their production. It might not seem like much, but coming from a Peronist in Argentina it was remarkable. But it was expensive and only partially successful. The economy was tossed into a deep recession, and inflation, though under 20 percent monthly after March 1990, remained in double digits for several months. Consequently, investors held back, causing Vice President Eduardo Duhalde to lament in September 1990: "In a nation like ours with 17 percent monthly inflation, you just cannot reactivate the economy."[29]

Cuts in the budget and the nation's recession also had terrible social costs. Government services rapidly declined, the incomes of government employees fell by nearly half, and unemployment grew, hurting the poorest members of society the most, as always, but making life tougher on the middle class as well. Increasingly government facilities fell into disrepair and people who had relied on emergency food and medicine from the Alfonsín government received less and less from Menem.

People warned that this would provoke social protests that might undermine the entire effort, but during his first fourteen months Menem insisted that everyone pay for the nation's economic reconstruction. It became his habit to announce: "We have begun a program that will extract blood and sweat, but we do it because there is no other way to save the nation."[30] Peronist Menem ignored the social discontent that was brewing for some time, and only began to promise some remedial measures after his second year began.

A New Politics?

Carlos Menem preferred the vague and the general to the precise, and agreements negotiated behind closed doors to public confrontations. He was comfortable talking to almost everyone and did not hesitate to hire any person he thought useful regardless of past affiliations. Buenos Aires mayor and fellow Peronist Carlos Grosso attributed this to Menem's having a "mysterious oriental mentality," but much more was involved.[31] Menem had been a successful politician because he knew how to deal amicably with some of his potential enemies and uncharitably with those who refused to comply. He also knew that people in business had always felt more comfortable dealing quietly with Peronists than with Radicals since Peronist politicians were always willing to talk and trade while the Radicals clung to one another against everyone else. Menem saw no need to change his way of doing politics after he became president.

Most important, Menem also knew Argentines well enough to know how crucial it was to stay firm in his commitments to reforming the economy. It was not so much the details of the policy that mattered, but his running the gauntlet of a people who were accustomed to undermining their national leaders in order to preserve what was theirs. Alfonsín had run the gauntlet less than a year after he had achieved some success with his Austral Plan, and once it became clear that he was going to let up, he could not regain the leadership that he enjoyed at the start. As Menem saw it, he had to deal with opponents across the board without appearing to back away from his efforts to force basic changes on the economy. It would not be easy, and he confessed occasional blunders, but that did not prevent him from pushing harder and faster toward opening the economy than had his predecessors.

After Menem had abandoned his populist campaign promises, many Peronists found it hard to regard him as one of their own. But it was a Peronist that he claimed to be. Espousing an economic and political "pragmatism" that he said came closer to the way Juan Perón had practiced politics than the way his successors wanted it done, he demonstrated once more just how little any ideology constrained Peronists in anything they did. He frequently claimed that Felipe Gonzalez, the Socialist prime minister in Spain, was his model, not because he was a socialist, but because he did not let his party's rhetoric obstruct his liberalizing and modernizing Spain's capitalist economy. With the government broke and nothing new in the national pie to distribute, a welfare state was impossible in Argentina, even for a Peronist, Menem declared.[32]

He also knew that he was dealing with a Peronist movement whose membership was more diverse than ever before, with leaders ranging from old-line labor bosses like Lorenzo Miguel to sophisticated free-market economists with Harvard University credentials like Foreign Minister Domingo Cavallo, two people who almost never spoke to one another. Its members, old and new, blue-collar and white, have always believed that they had more to gain from governing than from being in the opposition regardless of who led them. Like Menem, they were opportunists, who knew who distributed the resources they desired. In 1990 it was Carlos Menem, so it was to him they looked for the spoils.

Meanwhile, the Peronist party suffered rampant factionalism. Each little bloc expressed occasional discontent with Menem but they seldom broke very far from him. In the Chamber of Deputies at least six different Peronist factions were formed when the new government began, each claiming to represent Peronism more faithfully than the others, yet none daring to do anything more than assault the president with words whenever the press had space to fill.[33]

The secretary general of the General Confederation of Labor (CGT), Saúl Ubaldini, who had thrived during the Alfonsín presidency on leading union protests against economic adversity, knew such dissent was unwelcome in the new government. Still, Menem wanted Ubaldini replaced but was afraid to take him on directly since much of Ubaldini's support came from the powerful Metal Workers Union headed by Lorenzo Miguel, who had backed Menem against Cafiero. Menem knew that he could not afford to alienate labor leaders as Isabel Perón had done a decade before, so he chose to work indirectly through various CGT factions that shared his desire to evict Ubaldini. His dilemma was obvious: a united movement that supported him would make him politically invulnerable, but one that opposed him could ruin his economic rescue operation. Similarly, a divided CGT might weaken opposition to him, but it risked radicalizing opposing factions that might feel compelled to prove their militancy to the rank and file. That is why he chose to be careful with his interventions into the CGT's leadership struggles, at first doing little more than privately making his preference for Ubaldini's replacement well known.[34]

Menem's initial solution was to encourage a division between Ubaldini's CGT-Azopardo and another faction headed by Guerino Andreoni that called itself the CGT–San Martin. For a year he let the two factions dance around one another, never attacking Ubaldini directly but making his preference for Andreoni very clear. Ubaldini frequently criticized Menem's economic policy but was usually careful not to mobilize any massive confrontations with the government, while allowing individual unions to strike whenever they wished. But after waiting one year Menem finally gave official recognition to Andreoni and his San Martin faction as the CGT's only official representative with the government. Ubaldini immediately promised not to respect his decision since he knew that to some degree it was more theatrics than a real showdown: while it meant including only delegates from San Martin on government committees dealing with labor, informally conversations continued as before. Menem knew as well as anyone that he could not afford to alienate many labor leaders, so he continued to avoid direct confrontation as much as possible.[35]

But he also knew how much strikes could hamper his economic recovery efforts; after all, he was a Peronist who had encouraged strikes by labor that weakened Alfonsín when he was president. In a bold move Menem announced in April 1990 that he intended to limit the right to strike by all unions involved in essential public services. A Peronist president, not someone in the armed forces or the political opposition, was telling labor leaders that the nation's economic recovery could not tolerate their calling strikes whenever they wished. Since 1955 different governments had tried to devise new regulations to limit the right to strike, but they either backed off or resorted to military repression. Menem knew that Argentina's strike-ridden past could not be repeated if he were to win confidence among the investors he wanted back in the country, especially when there were constant disruptions of services like electricity, transportation, communications, and banking. Naturally Ubaldini and other labor leaders objected, but when they did Menem only insisted that since Juan Perón had limited strikes during his presidency so could he. Initially he wanted to use a presidential decree to seize the authority he needed, but when Peronists in Congress noisily objected he backed off, agreeing to seek congressional approval if it completed its work within sixty days.[36] But the Congress did nothing but debate the issue, so a frustrated Menem prohibited strikes in essential services by decree in October.

The first real test of Menem's stand against CGT opponents of his tough policies came in September 1990. FOETRA–Buenos Aires, the phone company union branch in the national capital had negotiated a pay increase with ENTEL management, but Erman Gonzalez, with his recently acquired authority over all public corporations, refused to approve it, declaring once again that the government could not afford it.

The union immediately called a strike, hoping to force the government to back down. Menem refused, and instead he dismissed several of the striking employees and persuaded the national phone workers union to oppose the strike by its own members. A couple of weeks later the striking workers gave in, and Menem declared a major victory for himself and government in general. He was a Peronist, but he was also a president who knew the consequences of his yielding to organized labor at a time when he was trying to end the notion that in Argentina any organization could protest and destroy any policy that it did not like. By defeating a union in this test of strength, he won a very important victory against everyone who opposed his policies. It was hard for his opponents in the Peronist party and even outside of it to swallow, but politically the rules were changing. For most Argentines this was truly a novel experience.[37]

Menem also benefited from the Radical party's unpopularity. Though Alfonsín was still active and occasionally blunt when he criticized Menem, his base of support had dwindled to almost nothing. Even within his party he was forced to share leadership with Eduardo Angeloz who disagreed with him on many issues. Theirs was a party so discredited by Alfonsín's presidency that few people paid any attention to it. There were many Radicals who knew that a reassessment of the party's organization and operations was essential to its recovery, but they were slow to exhibit any ability actually to do it. Menem was quite aware of this, so he paid only minimal attention to the Radical opposition when it denounced him for being too cruel and arbitrary in his economic effort.

Many people were unhappy with the sacrifices that Menem asked them to make during the 1990 recession, but there was little that they could do about it at first. After three bouts of hyperinflation they recognized that something drastic had to be done to avert its repetition. Moreover, very few of those who disagreed with his program had a reasonable one of their own to offer the nation. And channels for expressing displeasure continued weak. Virtually no one wanted the military to return and most Peronists were reluctant to undermine their own president just yet. Congress was noisy but disorganized and the CGT deeply divided. Menem also understood the game that labor leaders played in order to retain their positions, so he knew that even if they objected to his stabilization efforts or disliked him personally, they had more to gain by preserving his authority than by destroying it.[38]

Yet in spite of Menem's strength many voters were frustrated not so much with his economic measures as with the way the new democracy operated. They complained that it had become elitist, with too much power concentrated in the hands of the Peronist and Radical parties. The discontented voters came not just from the left and right but also from the center of national politics. They expressed themselves first by electing candidates from smaller parties in several provinces, then in mid-1990 they rejected what they regarded as an outright conspiracy between the two parties. This was especially frightening to Peronist politicians who had failed to mobilize the support they needed to accomplish what seemed a routine task.

The conspiracy came with the drafting of a new constitution for the province of Buenos Aires by leaders of the two parties working privately rather than at a constitutional convention. Much of what they proposed was needed, such as more authority to local governments to raise taxes and expropriate property for public use, and abolishing the one-term limit on governors as had been done in most other provinces. The problem was that the proposed constitution gave incumbent governor Antonio Cafiero, who helped write it, the right to run for another term. It just seemed too self-serving for the Buenos Aires electorate, as they made clear on August 5, 1990, when 67 percent of them rejected the new constitution. They came from all social classes and both parties. When asked their reasons for voting no, 54 percent said it was because of the methods used by party leaders to draft the constitution, 38 percent mentioned their growing antipathy to politicians, and 34 percent said it was also because they disagreed with various provisions of the constitution. What made this so shocking was that people had been urged to vote yes by leaders of the Peronist and Radical parties, the CGT leaders, and fifty-nine of seventy deputies of the Buenos Aires Chamber. The Argentine electorate had been given a chance to express their frustration with what they regarded as elitism within the ruling parties, and many of them did so.[39]

But they were not rejecting constitutional democracy as they had done before. Quite the contrary. What they demanded was more control over their elected officials. For example, in 1990 it became popular to criticize the way the people were represented. Members of the national Chamber of Deputies are chosen using the D'Hont system of proportional representation, something that has traditionally been regarded as very representative because it distributes seats in proportion to the votes received by each party. But some people demanded that it be replaced with a single-member district system much like that used by the House of Representatives in the United States. They complained that proportional representation allowed party leaders to distribute the seats among themselves, leaving voters with a choice of parties rather than persons. They wanted to know and influence the candidates and believed that a single-member district system with party primary elections would give party members and the general electorate a better chance to select whom they wished. For the moment they did not care to worry about the adverse effects of such a system on minor parties and its tendency to favor incumbents over challengers. They were more concerned about breaking up the control exercised by party elites. Increasingly, the issue became a way for expressing demands for what people hoped would be more democracy rather than less.

People were also disgusted with the nation's judicial system and its repeated failure to prosecute the people responsible for big-time financial crime. Bank fraud had cost Argentina's federal government at least $4.5 billion during the previous ten years. More than 250 bankers had been indicted but no convictions had been achieved. And banking was only one example. Government efforts to promote industry became a dinning hall for the corrupt. When credit lines were given to firms to promote their exports, many of them illegally diverted millions of dollars into speculative investments. And when tax-exempt zones were created in marginal regions to promote industrial activity, "ghost" factories that did not even consume electricity flourished. Subsidized firms even exported scrap metal and called it steel to get the maximum from the government. Many cases were brought before the courts, but no one was sentenced. No matter how much free-marketeers talked about the blessings of the market economy, people who lived in this corrupted atmosphere continued to believe that the biggest profit came from fraud rather than competition. But little was being done to change it in a society whose justice system is dominated by judges who, even when honest, are reluctant to change anything.

This stems from the very nature of the Argentine judicial system that was set up in 1889 in imitation of the Spanish system, which was itself drastically revised only a few years later. The Argentines, however, have done almost nothing to reform theirs. Essentially, it differs from the Anglo-American system in several fundamentals. First of all, there are no jury trials. Instead, judges decide guilt or innocence. But judges also supervise all investigations. Prosecutors can present them with information but the judges rely on their aides to take testimony from witnesses whom they choose to interview. Nor are there oral trials with debate between the prosecutors and the defense attorneys before the judge. Instead they present their arguments in writing and the judges make their decisions on guilt or innocence whenever they wish. Many young attorneys now argue that this system no longer works because it is too secretive and too bureaucratic to handle most complex modern cases. It also impedes public access through prosecutors and gives advantages to those who wish to block prosecution, as seems evident from the lack of convictions in important and complex economic cases. Nevertheless, the lawyers who advocated an efficient judiciary received little support from most members of their profession or from the major parties.[40]

President Menem's first effort to reform the judicial system was not directed at basic reforms in procedures but at increasing the size of the Supreme Court. He rushed through Congress a bill that added four new positions to the five-member court, and then in one day appointed all four of them. After the resignation of two others, the president suddenly had the majority he wanted on the court. Whether it would become a "Peronist court," and what that would mean in the nation's new democracy, no one really knew.

Political reform commanded much attention during Menem's second year, but never enough to eclipse the economic insecurities that most Argentines suffered when 1991 began. The Argentine currency had been unusually stable during the previous seven months at the cost of becoming grossly overvalued. At year's end the dollars that Argentines had used to store their savings bought them only half as much as they had a year before. Then, suddenly, the austral tumbled from 5,500 to 9,000 per dollar in just one week. Argentines knew that their overvalued currency would have to adjust sooner or later, but they were shocked when it lost so much value so fast. Aware that he needed to send a message that this was intolerable, Menem immediately dismissed Minister of Economy Erman Gonzalez and Central Bank director Javier Gonzalez, both of whom had seemed quite secure just a few weeks before. Foreign Minister Domingo Cavallo replaced Erman Gonzalez and promised to continue with the economic strategy that he had helped Menem design a year before. A Harvard-trained, free-market economist, Cavallo started by tightening the national budget even more, giving the Central Bank more freedom to operate on its own to keep the currency in line, and promising to collect the income taxes that most Argentines had never paid. Whether or not it would work, no one knew; what Argentines did know was how difficult it was becoming for Menem to hold his cabinet together. After having just fired some ministers who had been accused of corruption in the press, he was also forced to appoint his fourth economy minister after fewer than eighteen months in office.

A Reprieve for the Armed Forces

Menem neither feared nor loathed the armed forces as Alfonsín did. He knew that he could not allow officers to claim any more authority than Alfonsín had allowed them, but he also believed that direct assaults on the military had to stop. Nor was it his style to confront them directly or overtly to take revenge for the five years they had kept him under guard less than a decade before. Rather, he wanted quietly to weaken them a little more institutionally while allowing them to survive professionally.

He handled this in two ways. The first was money. When he cut the government expenditures at the end of 1989, the military were not excluded despite officers insisting that their services were far more important to the country's welfare than most others. This forced them to cut the annual draft, reducing the army to less than 30,000. Where once the three branches of the armed forces had totaled nearly 200,000 in military personnel, they had fallen to around 100,000 by 1990. To the embarrassment and disgust of army officers, they had to turn many jobs once done by draftees over to noncommissioned career personnel and some to junior officers. Meanwhile, because of their reduced budgets even air force pilots had to limit their flying time to only six hours a month, hardly enough for them to train. Menem also included Fabricaciones Militares, the enormous conglomerate of industries that the armed forces had collected over the years, in his privatization scheme, requiring that all but the armaments factories be sold as soon as possible. When officers protested publicly Menem ignored them, though he was sensitive enough to their hostility to raise their salaries periodically, sail with the navy, and dedicate monuments to those who had died in the Malvinas War.

The military initially made it easier for him by refusing to offer their own plans for reorganizing the three services. One might have expected the armed forces to come up with a plan to build a more modern force as many junior officers were demanding, but senior commanders resisted making any changes, characteristically fearful that their institutions would be weakened or destroyed by concessions. Nothing was more important to them than preserving the military institution in which they had lived since adolescence. But their professionally reactionary response to modernization, along with lower salaries and budgets, increasingly caused junior officers to retire very early and return to civilian life.

Menem also had to decide whether to pardon officers who had been convicted after 1983. At first he refused to rush to judgment. Many different crimes were involved, from the killing of several thousand civilians during the *Proceso* (between 1976 and 1983), to fighting an ill-conceived war against the British over the Malvinas islands, and, more recently, rebellions against military and civilian authorities. Moreover, some officers like Videla made it clear that they would not accept pardons since they did not believe that they had committed any crimes.

Initially two schools of thought within the presidency surfaced on the pardon issue. One argued that pacification of the military was vital to restore order to the nation and attract foreign investors back since none of them was eager to participate in a country plagued by rebellious armed forces. In contrast, others argued that, apart from the obvious morally repugnant aspects of legal absolution for kidnapping, torture, and murder, meddling with the justice system would be frowned on by the liberal democratic governments on which Argentina depended for political and economic support. Peronists were joined by Radicals on both sides of the issue: Angeloz favored pardons while Alfonsín intensely opposed them.[41]

In October Menem began to resolve the matter by announcing pardons for 280 persons. About forty of them were retired military officers who had been involved in the *Proceso;* others were participants in the Malvinas War or had participated in recent army rebellions. Menem also extended pardons to about sixty civilians, many still in exile, who were charged with subversion. None of the people who took part in the recent attack at La Tablada were on the list, however. Moreover, eight others, including military presidents Jorge Videla and Roberto Viola, and Montonero leader Mario Firmenich, were also excluded, but promised that their cases would be reconsidered later in the year. Menem insisted that the pardons were essential to building respect for constitutional government within the armed forces; nevertheless, some people protested against what they considered to be an immoral presidential decision, especially as it applied to those who had exterminated several thousand civilians between 1976 and 1980.[42] Nevertheless Menem went a step further just as 1990 drew to a close when he pardoned everyone whom he had turned down during the first round, including Videla and Firmenich, despite the opposition of over 60 percent of the population surveyed in opinion polls.

Menem was not spared military protests, however. Just before sunrise on December 3, 1990, uniformed disciples of Colonel Mohammed Ali Seineldin, the leader of the *carapintada* movement that had rebelled against Alfonsín a couple of years before, seized control of army headquarters in Buenos Aires and four other small installations within or near the city. They demanded that army chief of staff, Lieutenant General Martin Bonnet, be replaced by Seineldin and that the military budget be increased, all the time denying that they sought Menem's eviction. But they made two mistakes: Their movement was composed primarily of noncommissioned officers not lieutenants and majors, causing fear among most high-ranking officers, and they started their rebellion by killing two base commanders who tried to block their entrance. Menem seized on the opportunity and ordered the army's leaders to put down their disloyal subordinates immediately. A few hours later they sent the tanks in and did just that. Menem celebrated his triumph the next day when President George Bush arrived for a brief visit, but that could not hide the fact that discontent continued to rage among the nation's lowly paid rank and file within the armed forces. Pardons had relieved retired officers from punishment, but those on active duty still wanted higher salaries, better equipment, and more draftees to command.

"Pragmatism" Abroad

When he visited Chile in September 1990, Menem announced: "We want to emerge once and for all from that provincial enclosure that made us think a few years ago that we could develop in privileged solitude."[43] He spoke for most Argentines when he cast away the illusion of "privileged solitude" to which they had clung for a half century.

He made it seem effortless to abandon the nationalist vanity that had circumscribed his predecessors, acting as if it had been inevitable. And once he began, everything that followed drew less and less criticism, starting with the ending of the country's trade embargo against Great Britain and the restoration of relations between the two countries less than a year later. His motives were quite practical: Argentina needed better relations with Europe in order to increase its trade there.

Foreign Minister Domingo Cavallo called this approach "pragmatic." More production and trade required more capital, as did the effort to modernize the nation's industry and make it more competitive. Using the Association for Latin American Integration (ALADI), he also sought to create a new free-trade system among the Latin American nations. He was even more ambitious within the Southern Cone where he spoke about creating a real common market involving Brazil, Uruguay, and Chile.

Most unusual was Menem's apparent enthusiasm for building a closer relationship with the United States, starting with proposals for mutual tariff reductions and pleas for debt relief for Argentina, either through the so-called Brady Plan or some other means. Foreign Minister Cavallo acknowledged that several factors had prevented good relations between the two countries in the past, including Argentina's internal political instability, its conflict with Great Britain, its nuclear policy, and mutual accusations of unfair trade. But he hoped to make progress on these issues either unilaterally or through careful negotiations. It helped that the Argentine public had changed its attitudes toward the United States, recent polls indicating that 50 percent approved closer relations while only one-third opposed this.

Cavallo argued that Argentina would only gain from closer ties to the United States and to Europe (Eastern and Western), especially through trade. If this required that it accept U.S. government demands, such as for Argentina to cease building the Condor II missile, then it would do so in order to discover if the United States would reciprocate with positive responses to Argentina's demands. In other words, uncharacteristically, Argentina was deciding to pursue its objectives by making concessions first and seeking responses later rather than the reverse.

No one outside Argentina celebrated its "getting in line" at first. It was a line that it had been compelled to join and to which it remained unaccustomed. Moreover, if doing so did not generate the economic benefits promised by its advocates at home and abroad, their frustration would probably lead to renewed defiance of other nations since that was how Argentines traditionally announced their displeasure. Moreover, there were some difficult issues that even "pragmatism" could not solve, such as the Malvinas/Falklands conflict. Menem still claimed sovereignty over the islands but could only hope that if the Conservatives in Great Britain were defeated by Labor in the next elections, the new government would be more willing to recognize Argentina's sovereignty over the islands.

The President's Predicament

A Peronist president devoted to opening the Argentine economy to competition and selling off government enterprises astonished many people. Yet in the early 1950s when the first Peronist economic boom was abruptly interrupted by economic problems at home and abroad, Juan Perón did not hesitate to impose austerity on the nation and invite foreign enterprises to return. That is why it was not entirely "unPeronistic" for Menem to attempt to revitalize Argentine capitalism using unpopulist measures. The Peronists had relied on populism to build their welfare state, but when it became impossible to finance it without inducing more hyperinflation, they knew that they had to slow everything down.

Conventional wisdom contends that Peronism is uncouth because its leaders are demagogic and dishonest. Such habits seldom disappear quickly, but Peronists certainly had no monopoly on them; the Radicals, after all, did nothing to stop the executives who pillaged the banks the

Radical government ran or enriched themselves from its industrial promotion schemes.

Whatever their reputation, the Peronists actually enjoyed some practical political advantages over the Radicals. Alfonsín had been forced to work within a political party that was managed by local and provincial activists who were devoted to campaigning for their candidates and preparing for future elections. The Peronists, in contrast, have little authentic party organization. They practice politics by trying to accommodate one another when they are in government, and fighting against incumbents when in the opposition. Alfonsín had to live within his party once elected, often to his annoyance. But the Peronists have always allowed their president substantial leeway unless he or she ignored them entirely, as Isabel Perón did during her last year. They expected leadership from their president and were cautious about impairing the president publicly. Menem capitalized on the license they gave him in ways that were unpopular with the rank and file yet necessary, as he saw it, to enforce economic reforms.

Argentina's condition in 1991, as always, was described differently by different people. Some praised Menem for so boldly attempting to dismantle the populist state, and were cautiously optimistic about the future of Argentine capitalism. As they told it, Argentina, like Poland and Hungary, faced an unusual opportunity to ignite private enterprise and build free markets, and Menem understood this. They hoped the government could coax shell-shocked enterprises into buying and selling efficiently and that soon they would be able to make contracts to deliver supplies at prices set months in advance. They stressed the need to borrow at nonextortionate rates in order to operate normally, and to supply consumers with the cash they needed to consume. Menem was slow to help with the latter because of his fight against inflation, but they hoped that soon confidence would build and production increase.

But there were others who were very saddened by what they saw. Their Argentina was becoming an impoverished, crime-ridden society. Where once the Argentine people had as much work and food as they needed and committed few crimes against anyone but the bureaucrats who pretended to govern them, they were now becoming divided into a wealthy upper class that could handle high inflation and austerity, and the rest who had been losing wealth continuously for over a decade. There was more poverty among the lower class and more fear and fatigue among a once-prosperous middle class that now also worried about thieves in their midst. It was a novel scene for them, and promises of bounty after the free market was restored offered little consolation.

Actually both observers accurately described the country. And therein rested the dilemmas that plagued Menem in his attempt to reignite the nation's dormant economy. Populism had to be cut back and entrepreneurs and laborers had to compete at home and abroad in order to stimulate them to produce and export more goods. But as they charted this new course, public health care, education, and the justice system suffered from near-starvation. It was a high price to pay, and people began to wonder if it was really worth it.

Few people in Argentina admired Menem as a person or as president, though his "realism" about the nation's woes was welcomed by many. He always seemed to be doing more behind doors than in front of them, and seldom displayed a complete intellectual grasp of his task. Nor did the people closest to him help his reputation a great deal with their continuous exchanges of cabinet positions and the appearance of occasional illegal activities for personal gain. This, along with inflation, caused public approval of Menem to vary between 15 and 60 percent at least twice during his first sixteen months.[44]

By trying to propel the country into free-market capitalism Menem also raised many new issues for a nation unfamiliar with democratic government. None was more challenging than his transforming the nation's state-dominated economy into a more open, competitive one with the limited authority at his disposal. Though many theorists insist that a free economy promotes democratic politics, they have said little about how a democratic president can amass enough power to make his people yield their old economic habits without damaging the democratic process, especially in a nation like Argentina where citizens are so hard to lead. They continually asked themselves if they were turning Menem into an authoritarian by demanding that he relieve them of inflation and stagnation rapidly.

In addition, they had no textbook that specified exactly how to organize a free-market economy. What seemed so clear to Adam Smith has never been so obvious in the real world of modern capitalism. No markets are completely free and most are regulated in one way or another by political authorities. As has been noted: "It is no simple or easy task to manage a market-oriented economy in such a way as to maximize its advantages, which are great, and to minimize its disadvantages, which are also great."[45] It was tempting to leap into the market economy hoping that everything that was previously so badly managed by the state would automatically be handled perfectly by private enterprise. But it would never be so easy.

Menem's predicament was obvious at the end of his first year. The cost of reform was politically very high for anyone who demanded an end to living off a heavily protected economy and subsidies for industry and consumption. He was asking people to change the ways they had been doing business for half a century. Moreover, he was causing a middle class that had been shrinking in size throughout the 1980s to become even smaller while a few million Argentines of great wealth continued to prosper. Even people who welcomed his attempt to make them live by the same economic rules as the Europeans worried that the entire effort would be exploited by a few people among them who were already rich.

Menem was gambling that the nation would be rescued by people who had done little to salvage it during the past quarter-century. He was counting on corporate executives not only for advice but also for the investments that were essential to make the nation's economy grow again. Peronists like Menem had no qualms about profit-taking, but he wanted profits to come from the production of goods and not just financial speculation. Unfortunately, Argentine entrepreneurs were notoriously cautious about following their government's pleas for long-term investment. Long before they had become creatures of very narrow, short-term interests, and were seldom among the first to take chances.

Ironically, a Peronist president was also relying on the willingness of most Argentines to live a more meager existence for some time to come. He wanted them to understand that they could no longer pay taxes as low as those in Uganda while trying to live as if they were in Paris. Life in Argentina was once comfortable for nearly everyone, but a national product that had kept 20 million people living satisfactorily could not do the same for 30 million. The national product had to grow, debt burdens had to end, and the new bounty had to be distributed throughout a society accustomed to giving everyone a few pieces of the national pie. If not, Menem knew he would become as unwelcome as his predecessor.

That is why he watched anxiously when the public voted in the first midterm elections of his presidency on September 8, 1991. He could not help but fear Peronist losses after his new economy minister, Domingo Cavallo, had cut social services and government pensions while increasing taxes. Nor did new accusations of widespread corruption among his bribe-seeking subordinates help him much. His only hope for support came from an impressive drop in the monthly inflation rate to only 1.5 percent in July and 1.3 percent in August.

Cavallo had used a controversial "dollarization" scheme to halt inflation, exactly like the one that Menem had spurned more than a year before when Cavallo first recommended it. Essentially, it tied the money supply to the country's dollar reserves and allowed unrestricted conversion of australes into dollars. Consequently, the government could no longer just print new australes in order to pay its bills. Its domestic money supply depended on how many dollars its government held since Cavallo was convinced that Argentines could not discipline themselves without such a constraint being imposed on them. To his delight most of the public initially approved the measures when asked in almost every newspaper poll, though they also voiced doubts about the government's ability to operate for very long under such tough limitations.

When the votes were counted on September 8, Menem's fears proved unwarranted. Instead of punishing the Peronists, the electorate gave them ten additional seats in the Chamber of Deputies, most of the new members coming from pro-Menem factions in the working-class Buenos Aires province. Simultaneously the voters took four seats from the Radicals by giving them only 30 percent of the total vote, their lowest total since democracy was restored in 1983. What was the message in all of this? Clearly the reduction in inflation had helped the government just as the Austral Plan had helped the Radicals in Alfonsín's first midterm elections in 1985. But instead of disclosing a new fondness for the Peronists the Argentine electorate seemed to be saying that it could find no preferable alternative to the incumbents despite their obvious ethical and organizational faults. Perhaps they also had decided that for the time being they had little choice but to rely on Menem's bizarre leadership and painful economics in order to preserve their infant democracy.

Notes

1. Such collusion was not unique to Peron or even Latin America as I have argued in "Opening Late-industrializing Economies: Lessons from Argentina and Australia," *Policy Sciences,* no. 23 (Summer 1990), pp. 185–204.

2. Polls conducted in Argentina in the late 1980s indicated that while people were very unhappy with Alfonsín and government in general, most of them still preferred democracy to any other form of government. They were not certain that it would continue to work, but they believed that it was the best alternative available to them. See Edgardo Catterberg, *Los argentinos frente a la política: cultura política y opinión pública en la transición argentina a la democracia* (Buenos Aires: Editorial Planeta, 1989).

3. For more on Menem's biography see the book by journalists Alfredo Leuco and José Antonio Diaz, *El heredor de Perón* (Buenos Aires: Planeta, 1989).

4. Cafiero did win in the city of Buenos Aires but he lost in the Buenos Aires province where he was governor and where Peronists have their largest concentration of voters. See Ricardo Gaudio and Andrés Thompson, *Sindicalismo Peronista/Gobierno Radical: Los años de Alfonsín* (Buenos Aires: CEDES, 1990), pp. 226–227.

5. There are actually twenty-one provinces plus the national capital of Buenos Aires and the district of Tierra del Fuego; hence the reference to twenty-three provinces in the elections.

6. Menem received 3 percent more votes than Peronist deputies did. When compared with the 1983 presidential election, the Peronists received 7 percent more in 1989 and the Radicals 15.2 percent less.

7. Domingo Cavallo's ideas about how to rescue the Argentine economy are evident in his book: *Economía en tiempos de crisis* (Buenos Aires: Sudamericana, 1989). Though foreign minister, he was also consulted frequently about the nation's economic reforms in 1989 and 1990.

8. Jorge Garfunkel, *59 semanas y media que conmovieron a la argentina* (Buenos Aires: EMECE, 1990), p. 225.

9. For a survey of the mood see the weekly *El Economista*, May 5, 1989 and May 19, 1989.

10. Guillermo Vitelli, "Algunos rasgos de la economía," *Conferencias* (Fundación Arturo Illia), February 1990, pp. 12–19. Between 1983 and 1987 the Latin American economies together grew at an annual average of 2.6 percent and Argentina 0.3 percent.

11. *El Economista,* June 15, 1990, p. 15. For a survey of the inflation problem since World War II, see: Guillermo Vitelli, *Cuarenta años de inflación en la Argentina* (Buenos Aires: Editorial Legasa, 1986).

12. *Noticias,* May 27, 1990, p. 24.

13. World Bank, *Argentina: Reforms for Price Stability and Growth* (Washington, D.C., 1990), pp. xi–xii. See also Rudiger Dornbusch and Juan Carlos de Pablo, *Deuda Externa y inestabilidad macroeconomica en la Argentina* (Buenos Aires: Editorial Sudamericana, 1988), chs. 4 and 5.

14. Raúl Green and Catherine Laurent, *El poder de Bunge & Born* (Buenos Aires: Editorial Legasa, 1989).

15. For an interview with Lawrence Klein on these matters see *Somos,* May 31, 1989, pp. 40–42.

16. For a detailed account of this unusual new relationship between big business and Peronism see *La Nación,* section 3a, July 23, 1989, p. 1.

17. Gasoline, for example, went from about 40 cents a gallon to over US $1.50 in one day.

18. *New York Times,* September 11, 1989, p. 30.

19. Ibid., September 15, 1989, p. 6.

20. *Washington Post National Weekly Edition,* July 17–23, 1989, p. 15.

21. Luis Galeno del Puerto wrote very familiar words as December began: ". . . in our judgement the government program suffers from great instability and is condemned to fail . . ." *El Economista,* December 1, 1989, p. 8.

22. Ibid., December 22, 1989, p. 1.

23. To understand how this came about, one must recognize that for several months the government had paid its bills by going on a binge, borrowing money from its middle class by selling them short-term bonds at very high rates of interest. By mid-December it found itself with huge interest payments and did not want to print up all the money to pay it, so it transformed all of these bonds into Bonex '89, or new bonds that started at 20–30 percent of the original bonds' value on the market, promising to pay their entire value with interest in ten years. Meanwhile people could sell them at the reduced rate if they wished. It really hurt seniors and people trying to make money from interest fast.

24. *El Economista,* January 5, 1990, pp. 1–7. For an excellent summary of the decisions made in December and January, see also Peter Passell, *New York Times,* January 30, 1990, p. C1. Passell also points out that "the freeze relieved the government of a chronic burden on the budget. While the internal national debt is relatively small, the government had often paid as much as 200 percent a month in interest—far more than the inflation rate. Now most of the money supply is locked in long-term bonds indexed to dollars, with interest payable at the international lending rate of about 8 percent a year."

25. *Buenos Aires Herald,* March 5, 1990, p. 1.

26. Luis García Martínez, "Dinero, precios, confianza," *La Nación,* May 5, 1990, p. 14.

27. Atilio Cadorín, "En el borde," ibid., March 6, 1990, p. 6.

28. The phone company was divided into ENTEL Sur, sold to the Telefonica-Citicorp group and ENTEL Norte which ended up with the consortium composed of the Italian STET SPA state company and the French Telecom state company. In essence the phone company was sold to three foreign government-owned companies that were financed by North American banks that swapped pieces of the Argentine foreign debt to pay for their shares. In the Aerolineas sale the Argentine government retained 49 percent of the airline. The total sale was expected to wipe out $5 billion of Argentina's $40 billion debt with commercial banks. *New York Times,* October 6, 1990, p. 19.

29. *La Nación,* international ed., September 10, 1990, p. 5. During Menem's first year inflation was 5,600 percent. While some of it began before he took over, much came from his inability to get it under control after Gonzalez ended hyperinflation in March 1990.

30. Ibid.

31. James Neilson, *Noticias,* April 22, 1990, p. 39. In issuing decrees he was no different from all of his predecessors, including Raul Alfonsín, who found it easier to order changes in policies to deal with economic emergencies than to wait on the legislature to debate and amend them.

32. He described his intentions in his usual blunt fashion in a lengthy interview in *Noticias,* April 8, 1990, pp. 22–25.

33. They were the Alianza menemista-renovadores (47 members), chaired by Chamber president José Luis Manzano, the Grupo Parlamentario Federal (24 members), Saadismo (10 members), the antimanzanistas no alineados (13 members), the Independientes (11 members), and Los "8" (8 members), who called themselves the Peronist left and were the most critical of the president's new, free-market economics. *Clarin,* 3 June 1990, p. 6.

34. *Buenos Aires Herald,* August 13, 1989, p. 3.

35. *La Nación,* international ed., August 27, 1990.

36. Eduardo L. Bonelli, *La Nación,* section 3, April 22, 1990, p. 2.

37. *Clarin,* international ed., September 10–16, 1990, p. 1. Some of Menem's fans referred to his victory as equal to Margaret Thatcher's triumph over Arthur Scargill's coal miners in Great Britain and Ronald Reagan's defeat of the air traffic controllers in the United States. It was truly an unusual time when people placed a Peronist president in the same class as two of the most conservative leaders in the industrial world.

38. Alberto Dearriba, "Cuando el gato no esta," *Pagina/12,* June 2, 1990, p. 2.

39. See *La Nación,* August 12, 1990; and *Buenos Aires Herald,* August 5, 1990.

40. I want to thank Prosecutor Luis Moreno Ocampo and his colleagues in the Poder Ciudadano for this information.

41. *Buenos Aires Herald,* August 27, 1989, p. 12.

42. *New York Times,* October 10, 1989, p. 3.

43. Ibid., September 4, 1990, p. C3.

44. *Somos,* May 2, 1990, p. 12; In another survey there was a sharp difference between opinion of Menem the president and opinion of the government in general. The latter was always at least twenty points lower than the president, ranging from a low of 15 percent approval to a high of 42 percent during the first six months of 1990. *La Nación,* June 10, 1990, p. 10.

45. Robert Dahl, "Social Reality and 'Free Markets,'" *Dissent* (Spring 1990), p. 228.

9

Prospects

There are no political institutions or political leaders who are recognized by society as legitimate mediators of conflicts between diverse groups; neither is there any real agreement over legitimate methods for resolving these conflicts.[1] (June 1990)

The strongest impression I leave with is that Argentina is a country of the living dead, where an event can incense the mass media for a week, only to then disappear, without being resolved, forever.[2] (August 1990)

Argentina suffers from a syndrome of grave isolationism. . . . Changing our mentality is very difficult because changes in cultures are always slow. We have made some progress, but not much. Yet gradually Argentines are discovering that the world offers them real opportunities. . . .[3] (Fall 1989)

Argentines disagree about why it is so hard for them to prosper economically or collaborate politically. They once claimed that it was due to their unfortunate victimization, insisting that they were exploited by foreigners who were always economically more powerful than themselves. The people who ran the world economy, they said, controlled the nation's governments.

This interpretation of the country's plight is appealing because of its simplicity and surface plausibility, and also because it leaves most Argentines blameless for the nation's decline. The oligarchy's taking control of the government by force in 1930 followed a world recession that caused them to beg for trade; more recently, their debts to multinational banks have forced renewed conformity with foreign rules whether or not they liked them. Yet, as appealing as this argument is, it relies too much on a single cause to account for the way Argentines practice politics. Moreover, it ignores the fact that countries facing similar economic woes do not always share Argentina's political vices. To explain Argentine behavior something else is required.

Another possibility is the nation's Hispanic heritage and the authoritarian political culture that some Argentines claim it created. Habitually their governments have been run by persons who preferred to rule over their citizens rather than through them. That is why democracy has been such a charade most of the time. The arrival of Spanish and Italian immigrants at the turn of this century did little to change any of this. Or so the argument goes.

While this explanation should not be dismissed casually, it, too, is incomplete. A political tradition does not simply perpetuate itself. People must sustain it from one generation to another, adapting it to their particular needs. In Argentina people have created authoritarian governments not just because they were Spanish or Italian but also because they sought to preserve their economic advantages. And when they did, they forced their opponents to respond in kind, making it ever harder to achieve political cooperation within the nation. Everyone became educated in the advantages of monopolistic politics, and each, from Peron in the 1950s to the armed forces in the 1970s, thought he could prevail indefinitely.

Subsequent attempts to govern the country in authoritarian and democratic ways produced a "revolving door politics." It was as if each political force in society, be it rural or urban, upper class or working class, believed that its triumph over its rivals was vital to its survival; coexistence, in contrast, was synonymous with defeat. Groups stood up against one another and individuals focused almost entirely on averting subjugation by the authorities whom they opposed. The military fought to defend itself while claiming to defend the nation; labor unions demanded membership in the government or sought to undermine it when they were excluded; and business leaders distrusted and disobeyed the authorities whenever they wanted. Argentina was not a nation of wayward fascists, as sensationalists contend, but one in which authoritarian government became the most familiar solution to its problems. That is how it was in 1966, and again in 1976, when most citizens not only failed to protest military intervention but frequently justified it as necessary to overcome the country's economic and political afflictions.

This is what makes it so easy to portray Argentines as nothing more than selfish, rigid, and self-destructive authoritarians. But that does them a disservice because it ignores additional motives for their behavior in recent times. Like everyone else, Argentines learn early in their lives how to satisfy their needs and wants, and they quickly acquire ideas about the purpose of politics and how to practice it.

Juan Perón seized the government from a greedy and decadent upper class and set out to generate vast amounts of new wealth and distribute it widely, but after a short binge the entire economy went into decline. At a time when most other export economies were booming, Argentina's languished, never exploiting its natural advantages efficiently enough to sustain its modernization and growth.

Argentines soon discovered that the nation was left in an economic hole from which there was no easy escape. What Perón's successors offered them was not swift prosperity but demands that they compensate for past government errors and misfortunes. Austerity, more than growth, became the principal objective of government in a nation that was perpetually plagued by high inflation and balance-of-payments' deficits. That is how it was with Perón in 1952, Frondizi in 1959, Onganía in 1966, Perón again in 1973, Videla in 1976, Alfonsin in 1985, and Menem in 1990. Unfortunately, Argentines do not enjoy making sacrifices any more than anyone else does. Even worse, they discovered how little they gained individually from complying since some among them always refused to do so.

They became quite clever and manipulative, always studying daily indicators of prices, wages, exchange rates, and deficits and anticipating how the authorities would respond to them. They made their calculations about the next round of austerity measures and defended themselves against them, often undermining them as they did. Defiance became their way of life and eventually seemed the natural way to behave. Who cared if they relied on black markets or did not pay their taxes; that was the Argentine way of doing things.

Will any of this change during the 1990s? No one knows, of course, but it does seem that Argentines realize they must do things differently. They know that they have become notorious "underachievers" with a decaying economy that is plagued by enormous debts, frequent inflation, and little investment. Their predicament has been described in page after page of this volume because it has continued in one form or another year after year, undermining public confidence in nearly every government since the early 1950s. A president's policy options are always few in number under these conditions. How else can one explain why Raul Alfonsín and Carlos Menem, two populist politicians, behaved like antipopulist, free-market economists once in office. Both of them wanted to make everyone happy using the power and wealth of the state to guarantee the public's security and serenity, but neither of them had enough wealth at his disposal even to try.

Instead, they inherited governments that had mortgaged too much over the years to accumulate the surplus that populist presidents needed to sustain existing social welfare. So they quickly became desperate leaders who were forced to devise new ways to generate wealth that would eventually produce enough of it to allow them to restore populist politics. They did so more in desperation than from any conviction that free markets would guarantee prosperity.

Under these conditions, the president's predicament was obvious. Liberal, competitive economics was politically very risky because it threatened people who relied on government employment and industries that depended on tariff protection and subsidization. Menem was asking them to change the ways they had been doing business for over a half century. Moreover, in the short term he was also causing a middle class to shrink while a few hundred thousand wealthy Argentines prospered more than ever.

In the midst of this came new efforts to build something called "constitutional democracy" to replace reliance on authoritarian politics. Democrats were asking everyone to adjust their conduct considerably.

Today they insist that the nation's wealthiest citizens admit the futility of looking to the armed forces for protection against the politicians and labor leaders whom they have come to regard as parasites and intruders. They should know that such behavior is not only unpopular but also risks provoking the kind of distrust and rancor that have cost the nation dearly.

Foreigners who do business in Argentina are also being told not to look for armed authoritarians to defend them anymore. Argentines prefer to determine their own fates without foreign encroachment whenever possible; most are too proud to abdicate control over themselves, even when it benefits them materially to do so. Of course, no economy as vulnerable as Argentina's will operate of its own volition or without foreign capital; economic adversity and insecurity will remain a way of life as long as the European Common Market and North American governments exclude so many Argentine products from their markets and the nation's foreign creditors refuse to accept the losses produced by their own mistakes.

This generation of democrats also wants their armed forces to understand that public wrath, not respect, will be their reward for treating civilians as if they were juveniles who had to be kept in check until they had learned to respect and obey uniformed patriots who erroneously believed that they were ordained with unique political wisdom. If they want to preserve military institutions, officers must learn to behave more like politicians than tank commanders, accepting constitutional authorities as legitimate and then exercising limited influence over them. If they do not discover how to distinguish democratic rules from authoritarian ones, democracy's chances of surviving in Argentina will not improve.

In the 1980s soldiers were forced to live with civilian authorities, but they privately refused to surrender to them entirely. Today some civilians are trying to discover exactly what they must do to redefine the military's role in a democratic society, realizing that the burden of reform falls as much on them as it does on people in uniform. Bridging the gap of distrust and disrespect will not be easy.

Political parties are being asked to forsake their partisan exclusiveness. Citizens want better communication and representation with their elected officials. They insist that the legislators they send to Buenos Aires and provincial capitals listen to all of them rather than just the privileged few. Party leaders hear this, but, as in most democracies, they do not want to be the first to yield. That is why voters have begun to reject the old guard in local and provincial elections, hoping to send a message using the only means that civilian politicians ultimately understand.

Last but not least is organized labor. What makes Argentina different from other countries with free labor movements is the persistent waging of symbolic and substantive wars between labor and government that cannot be easily regulated. Not only do labor leaders believe their combat is popular among the rank and file, but they are addicted to achieving individual fame and fortune by pounding on public institutions regardless of how destructive their conduct can be.

When a Peronist returned to the presidency, this began to change if only because the incumbent understood the game and how it was played. Whether dividing the largest labor movement and manipulating its leadership using the power of the presidency will lead to permanent reform no one knows. Still, now more than ever sincere democrats realize that unless relations between government and labor are pacified and opened to public scrutiny, the society will be divided perpetually.

With all of this said, it pays to note that military officers and labor leaders are not the only people who habitually defy civilian authorities in Argentina. In one way or another everyone does, many of them quite routinely. There is little sense of "obligation" to obey the government and its rules and regulations. This is why the transition to democracy is so difficult, and democratic institutions are still quite superficial. Liberal democratic government requires that citizens obey the law out of a sense of obligation derived from their voluntary acceptance of the democratic process and the disciplined conduct that it requires. People must agree about what is right and comply accordingly.

The government can use force to punish a few transgressors, but it cannot survive if everyone defies it routinely. A democratic government is what citizens make it, not something that is sustained by a few hundred elected officials. The president and the Congress can reorganize some institutions, change laws, and enforce them more effectively, but it is still up to individuals and organizations to obey them.

Argentines were acutely aware of this as they entered the 1990s, and while some continued to feel sorry for themselves, others demanded that all people undertake major revisions in their private and public conduct. As a people they can be incredibly rhetorical, sentimental, and contentious, especially in their politics, but they can also be as earnest, industrious, and prudent as circumstances require, much as their Spanish and Italian ancestors are today. While none of this guarantees that they will figure out how to live by the same rules, it does mean that they at least know that the choice is theirs to make.

Notes

1. Enrique Zuleta Puceiro, *El Economista,* June 8, 1990, pp. 4–5.

2. This comes from the reprint of an article by *Financial Times* correspondent Gary Mead on his departure after spending two years in Argentina: *Buenos Aires Herald,* August 19, 1990, p. 12.

3. Natalio Botana, "Reportaje," *Noticias de la Fundación Arturo Illia* Cuatro Trimestre de 1989, no. 8.

Index

The letter _t_ following a page number indicates a table.

DATE DUE